AF254323

Thomas K. Burch

Model-Based Demography

Essays on Integrating Data, Technique and Theory

Thomas K. Burch
Department of Sociology
   and Population Research Group
University of Victoria
Victoria, BC, Canada

DOI 10.1007/978-3-319-65433-1

Preface

The papers in this collection – most of them previously published – are the fruits of an intellectual odyssey over the last decades of my career as a sociologist/demographer. Beginning in the late 1980s, longstanding questions about the status of demography as a science came to the surface, and I began to pursue them actively. Looking back, I realize that at some point I became less a demographer and more a demography critic – cf. art critic or music critic – and an amateur philosopher of science.

My central concern has been with the role and status of theory in demography. For some, it was enough that demography did rigorous analysis of data using standard demographic and statistical techniques, notably emerging methods of multivariate analysis as applied to micro-data files. Theoretical explanations and models of behavioral processes often were left to other disciplines. Becker and the microeconomists had become the leading theorists of demographic behavior, while social demographers made relatively little *systematic* use of the large fund of relevant theory from sociology, social psychology, and cultural anthropology.

Microeconomic theory enjoyed widespread acceptance, if not consensus, among economists. And it was stated in clear, unambiguous form, often mathematically. Social-behavioral theory, by contrast, was formulated with less rigor, in loose verbal form, and commanded nothing approaching consensus.

As a graduate student in sociology and demography in the late 1950s, I had taken several excellent courses on social theory and cultural anthropology (Wilbert Moore; Marion J. Levy, Jr.; and Melvin Tumin) and trained in demography and statistics with leaders in the field – Frank Notestein, Ansley Coale, and Frederick Stephan. But there was little integration. My dissertation was a largely technical work on measurement of internal migration, with virtually no behavioral content and no theory. Some of my sociology professors were dismayed. My demography and statistics professors were satisfied if not ecstatic. As I pursued my career, I lived this schizoid life as an empirical demographer with an interest in theory – a small example of the split between theory and empirical research famously described by Robert Merton (1957). With a primary commitment to demography, my relationship to theory, like that of the discipline, was characterized by ambivalence and malaise.

In reviewing the development of my thinking on these matters, I can single out three works as crucial. Robert Hanneman's *Computer-Assisted Theory Building: Modeling Dynamic Social Systems* (1988) provided a detailed introduction to dynamic systems modeling as a potential theoretical tool for demographers and other empirical social scientists. It promised rigor in the statement and manipulation of theoretical models – including complex dynamic models with feedbacks and delays – and reoriented thinking away from comparative statics and equilibrium toward process and change. To this day, I remain puzzled why social scientists, including demographers, have made so little use of this powerful analytic tool.

An earlier work – discovered much later and by accident – was *Explanation in Social Science: A System Paradigm* by Eugene Meehan, a political scientist (1968). Meehan provided a convincing critique of logical positivism as a dead-end approach to social science and set forth a practical alternative involving 'systems' – roughly equivalent to theoretical models. He also insisted on the importance of purpose or aim, as well as logical consistency with data, in evaluating models. A model well-suited to one purpose may not be adequate for another.

Ronald Giere's *Science Without Laws* (1999) appeared to me to support Meehan's general approach, while placing it in the context of late twentieth-century philosophy of science. Accessible to the nonprofessional philosopher, this work argues that the model, not the law, is the central element in science. Models are not 'true' in any strong sense of that word. They simply fit some portion of the real world closely enough in certain respects to make them useful for certain purposes. At best, they embody 'realism without truth.'

Taken together, these works convinced me that demography had more and better theory than generally recognized and pointed the way toward fruitful systematization and codification. Demography could be a full-fledged discipline, with its ample foundation of empirical data and technique balanced by a rich body of theory.

From time to time, I have wondered whether I had touched bottom with respect to the philosophical and methodological issues involved in demography as a science. Eventually, I realized there probably is no bottom. Professional students of science – philosophers, sociologists of science, and cognitive psychologists – disagree on many points. It is not likely that I would be able beat them at their own game and come up with a definitive view on science. I agree with Paul Teller (2001), who has warned against 'the perfect model model' of science, and with Samir Okasha who writes: 'Like most philosophical questions, these questions do not admit of final answers, but in grappling with them we learn much about the nature and limits of scientific knowledge' (2002, p. 39).

In any case, I am convinced that the model-based view of science as developed by Giere and others has much to offer demography as a liberating view of demographic theory. Its acceptance and routine application to our work could lead to a rich collection – a toolkit – of useful theoretical models, general, middle range, and "low range." As noted above, we can achieve a better balance among data, technique, and theory and become a complete science of human population.[1]

Even after a career of nearly 60 years in demography, however, I may be presumptuous to sit in judgment on the discipline and to suggest directions for its future development. But I have been encouraged by many other demographers who, over the years, have expressed their concern for the character and status of the field, their lingering feeling that something was missing. It seems to me that the model-based approach to science will encourage and enable us to provide what has been missing, notably a carefully crafted body of theory.

But just as there is no perfect model *in* science, there is no perfect model *of* science. And I am not a philosopher of science nor familiar with the practice and accomplishments of all the sciences, social, behavioral, biological, and physical. I can do no better than to close with a quote from E.O. Wilson. In the Preface to *On Human Nature*, in which he argues for the usefulness of evolutionary biology for understanding human behavior, he comments: "I might easily be wrong" (p. x). But it will be enough if this work promotes a lively discussion of what demography is and might become.

As lightly edited versions of papers written at different times and in different contexts, many of the following chapters repeat central ideas, for example, the contrasts between logical empiricism and the model-based approach to science, or the idea that much of 'technical' demography can be viewed as theory. Sometimes, this repetition may seem unnecessary. But it has the advantage that chapters are freestanding, so that the reader can read later chapters without having read all that preceded.

Victoria, BC   Thomas K. Burch
Canada

References

Giere, R. N. (1999). *Science without laws*. Chicago: University of Chicago Press.

Hanneman, R. (1988). *Computer-Assisted theory building: Modeling dynamics social systems*. Newbury Park: Sage Publications.

Meehan, E. (1968). *Explanation in social science: A system paradigm*. Homewood: The Dorsey Press.

Okasha, S. (2002). *Philosophy of science: A very short introduction*. Oxford: Oxford University Press.

Teller, P. (2001). Twilight of the perfect model model. *Erkenntnis, 55*, 393–415.

Wilson, E. O. (1978). *On human nature*. Cambridge MA: Harvard University Press.

---

[1] Adoption of a model-based view of science has the added advantage of encouraging cooperation and synthesis across disciplines. I develop this thought in: "The model-based view of science: an encouragement to interdisciplinary work." *21st Century Society* 1 (June 2006) 39–58. I was unable to obtain permission to republish in this open-source collection.

Acknowledgments

I begin by acknowledging the support of Jim Vaupel, Founding Director of the Max Planck Institute for Demographic Research, without whom this book would not be. Many years ago, he expressed interest in my work and urged me to bring it together as a book or monograph. In a casual conversation at the Rostocker Ring, in September 2015, I voiced regret that I had never followed through on his suggestion. His reply: 'It's not too late.' Thus ended my retirement for a while.

Frans Willekens, also at Max Planck, worked out the contractual arrangements with the institute and regularly reassured me of the value of the project to the discipline. Given my age, I had some doubts about taking on a substantial editorial/writing project. But it was clear to me that if Jim Vaupel and Frans Willekens thought it worthwhile, it was worth the time and effort.

Upon Frans Willekens' retirement from Max Planck, Andre Schmandke took up the administrative tasks and helped negotiate a contract with Springer-Verlag. Further negotiations with Springer-Verlag went smoothly thanks to the prompt, clear, and helpful communications from Evelien Bakker and Bernadette Deelen. Carol Hamill (Victoria, BC) constructed the index; her work reminded me why it's generally a good idea to go to a professional.

In 1993, in the early stages of this project, I had the privilege of spending a stimulating sabbatical term in the Department of Demography, University of Rome (La Sapienza), at the invitation of Antonella Pinelli. Graziella Caselli, of the same department, would later encourage my work on the model-based approach to teaching demography by invitations to present at two International Union for the Scientific Study of Population (IUSSP) meetings on the subject, with papers later published in *Genus* under her editorship (see Chaps. 11 and 12).

During her tenure as Director of the Center for Studies in Demography and Ecology, University of Washington, Martina Morris invited me to become a Regional Affiliate of the center and encouraged my participation in a year-long series of seminar on computer modeling and simulation. It was during visits to the CSDE that I first became aware of Adrian Raftery's papers on the "two cultures of quantitative analysis," a distinction that helps explain much about contemporary demography and its approach to computer modeling. Chapter 5 in this volume is based on a presentation to this seminar in February 2004. The presentation was repeated in June 2007 at the Universities of Rome and Padua and published in *Canadian Studies in Population*, at the invitation of Frank Trovato, Editor.

I am grateful to Francesco Billari, for his favorable response to my early work on marriage models (which led to an ongoing correspondence), but mostly for his pioneering work in bringing agent-based modeling into demography.

John J. Macisco, my oldest friend and demographic colleague, has been a steady source of encouragement over the years, reminding me from time to time that I had a right – but also an obligation – to tell it the way I saw it regarding the scientific status of demography.

Discussions with David Swanson regarding applied demography have provided a constant reminder of the importance of purpose or aim in the evaluation of any scientific analysis, an idea central to the model-based view of science.

Frank Trovato has provided regular encouragement of my work, and was directly instrumental in the writing and/or publication of at least three of the chapters below. The methodological work of Bill Wunsch and Ron Lesthaege have instructed me over the years, but, just as important, have reinforced my confidence in the importance of such work as applied to demography.

My interest in the status of sociology as a discipline has been kept alive over the last 16 years by regular 'sociology seminars' at local pubs with my friend Alan Hedley. David Johnston, friend and counsellor, helped me find strengths I didn't know I had.

Most recently, I have had the good fortune to be in regular correspondence with Daniel Courgeau, Robert Franck, and Eric Silverman, who together and separately are making great strides in advancing the cause of demographic modeling. Chapter 3 derives from a working conference organized by Robert Franck and his edited volume of conference papers, *The Explanatory Power of Models*. Chapter 4 was first presented in a session on epistemology in demography, organized by Courgeau at the 2005 meetings of the IUSSP in Tours, France. Over the years, he has been generous in sharing his deep insights into the social science enterprise and honest in cautioning me if he saw me moving in a wrong direction. It was also he who introduced me to the 'popular' writings on scientific method by the French mathematician Henri Poincaré, whose 1908 book *Science and Method* in many ways anticipated the central ideas of late twentieth-century philosophy of science.

Lastly, I must acknowledge my congenial and supportive colleagues at the University of Western Ontario (now Western University) over the period 1975–2000 and at the University of Victoria (UVic), from 2001 to the present. I am especially grateful to Zheng Wu, who facilitated my appointment as Adjunct Professor at UVic, providing space, library privileges, and other support for my post-retirement activities.

Much of the research for this work was supported by the Social Sciences and Humanities Research Council, Ottawa, Canada.

My apologies in advance to anyone I may have neglected to mention in these acknowledgments. Writing them has reminded me of how much the work of any individual depends on the help and support of others.

Contents

Part I
A Model-Based View of Demography

Chapter 1
Demography in a New Key: A Theory of Population Theory

1.1 Introduction

The status of theory in demography has been problematic ever since I can remember. Sixty-five years ago, Rupert Vance, in his Population Association of American presidential address, asked 'Is theory for demographers?' (1952). There is ample evidence that many demographers – then and now – would answer 'Of course, but it's not a high priority.' But if demography is a true science – as opposed to a body of techniques or a branch of applied statistics – it must have theory, recognize that it has theory, codify its theory, and seriously teach theory to its students.[1]

In his presidential Address to the Population Association of America, Nathan Keyfitz (1971) adopted what he termed a 'liberal view of models.' In this chapter, I sketch a liberal view of scientific theory, and discuss some of its implications for the way we think about demography and the way we present it to others.

This view of theory is known in philosophy of science circles as the 'semantic' view, or more recently and descriptively, the 'model-based' view of science. In describing this approach, I draw heavily on the work of Ronald Giere, an American philosopher of science (1988, 1999), but also on some methodological writings of Nathan Keyfitz (1971, 1975). Keyfitz introduced these ideas to demography years ago, although they never became mainstream.[2]

Based on a presentation to a Symposium on Theory in Demography, part of celebration of the new building of the Max Planck Institute for Demographic Research, 31 March–1 April, 2003, Rostock, Germany; originally published in *Demographic Research* 9(2003):263–284.

[1]For a while, the cover of *Demography* (official journal of the Population Association of America) defined the field as 'the statistical study of human populations,' seeming to imply that demography is a branch of statistics, not a science in its own right.

[2]I also have benefited greatly from the following: Meehan (1968), Newton (1997), and Cartwright (1983, 1999). For a summary and assessment of the semantic school, see Teller (2001). I am grateful to John Wilmoth for reminding me that Keyfitz had written several papers on the role of models in demography.

T.K. Burch, *Model-Based Demography*, Demographic Research Monographs,
DOI 10.1007/978-3-319-65433-1_1

In the model-based view, models, not empirical laws, are the central element of scientific knowledge. A model is any abstract representation of some portion of the real world. A model may contain basic principles generally regarded as 'laws.' In this case, the laws 'function as true statements, but not as statements about the world. They are then truths only of an abstract model.[3] In this context, such statements are true in the way that explicit definitions are true' (Giere 1999, p. 6). A model contains generalizations, but they are formal generalizations, not empirical ones. Empirical assessment of theory, therefore, relates not to whether a theoretical model is empirically true or false – strictly speaking all theories and models are false because they are incomplete and simplified representations of reality – but 'how well the resulting model fits the intended aspects of the real world' (Giere 1999, p. 6). This view stands opposed to many familiar teachings of logical empiricism, by which theory is based on empirical laws, and judged true or false solely by its agreement with data. The model-based view is equally concerned with empirical data, but these are used to judge whether a model fits some portion of the world closely enough for a given purpose, not whether the model is true or false in any absolute sense.

The model-based approach has two general implications for our view of demography

1. Much of formal demography (techniques, methods) can be viewed also as theory, that is, as a collection of substantive models about how populations and cohorts behave;
2. Many theories in behavioral demography which have been rejected because of empirical exceptions or on the grounds they are too simplistic can be viewed as perfectly good theory, especially if they were to be stated more rigorously.

Indeed, at the theoretical level, the classic distinction between formal/technical and substantive/behavioral demography loses much of its force. In both sub-areas of demography, theoretical models have essentially the same epistemological standing, even if they may differ on other dimensions such as scope and complexity, and even if different kinds of day-to-day work may be involved in their development and use.

The word *theory* is ambiguous in the non-pejorative sense of 'having two or more meanings.' It means different things to different people, both in everyday speech and in scientific discourse. It is futile to try to establish the 'correct' definition or the 'true meaning' of theory. But it is possible to suggest a new – though not entirely new – approach to theory that might prove more fruitful than older ideas to which we are accustomed. In the next section, I summarize the main elements of the model-based view, noting some ways in which it differs from, but also agrees with, logical empiricism. A key part of this exposition is a partial re-definition of such terms as *model* and *theory*. But terminology is not crucial,

---

[3]Cartwright refers to theoretical models as 'nomological machines,' that is, models generate laws, not the other way around. See (1999, p. 4).

and some may want to define these words differently, and to preserve a sharp distinction between *theory* and *model*. The central ideas I wish to convey are an emphasis on formal demography as substantive knowledge, and a plea that empirical exceptions to otherwise useful behavioral theories should not lead to their discard.

In the logical empiricist view of science, theory comes from data through a process of induction and generalization. Theoretical knowledge and empirical knowledge occupy different but parallel planes, layered upward into ever more general and abstract propositions. In the model-based view, theory and empirical studies occupy non-parallel planes. The planes must intersect, of course, since we are discussing empirical science. But the origin and character of the two kinds of knowledge are qualitatively different. In the model-based view of science, as the name suggests, models, not laws, are the central element of scientific knowledge. The prototype of scientific knowledge is not the empirical or theoretical law, but a model plus a list of real-world systems to which it applies. To quote Giere:

> In this picture of science, the primary representational relationship is between individual models and particular real systems, e.g., between a Newtonian model of a two-body gravitational system and the Earth-Moon system…Here we have not a universal law, but the restricted generalization that various pairs of objects in the solar system may be represented by a Newtonian two-body gravitational model of a specified type. (Giere 1999, p. 93)

A model is any abstract representation of part of the real world, constructed to understand, explain, predict, or control. Giere distinguishes three types of models:

1. Physical models (for example, an automobile in a wind tunnel);
2. Visual models (for example, maps showing plate tectonics, or a diagram of the demographic transition);
3. Theoretical models (for example, Newton's Law of falling bodies, or the theory of evolution).

Physical models have little relevance to demography and other social sciences. Visual models have great potential, but are not as widely used as they might be, with the bulk of graphics in demography limited to the representation of data frequency distributions, time series, and age-structures rather than processes or systems.

Theoretical models can be expressed in ordinary language, formal logical systems, mathematics, computer code or diagrams.[4]

In the model-based view, no sharp distinction is made between model and theory. A collection of small models relating to the same realm can be called *theory* (for example, the theory of harmonic oscillators, or the theory of population aging).

---

[4]The idea that theory consists of purely verbal statements seems peculiar to social science. In the physical sciences, many of the most important theories are in mathematical form – Newton's law of gravity, Relativity, etc. For a recent indication of this way of thinking, see, for example, Baylis (1994). His book on *Theoretical Methods in the Physical Sciences* is an introduction to the use of a computer mathematics program, Maple V, to solve substantive problems in elementary physics.

These models typically contain a small number of variables, and are constructed to represent very limited portions of the real world. Or, *theory* can refer to a system of very general ideas (for example, the theory of relativity, or transition theory) attempting to represent larger, more complex real world systems. The difference is not qualitative, but relates to differences in scope, complexity, and other quantitative dimensions.[5] There may be advantages to preserving fine distinctions among the words *theory, model,* and *theoretical model* in some contexts. In this chapter, they are used interchangeably.

Giere draws a useful analogy between scientific models and maps, viewed as simplified representations of our physical surroundings (1999, pp. 25–26; 81–82; 214–215), Like theoretical models, maps vary in purpose and scope. Some maps give a broad overview of nations or of whole states or provinces, and more detailed maps, often as insets, of smaller areas such as cities or metropolitan areas. Some maps are extremely simple. An example is the straight-line map found on metro trains or subways, which show only the stops and transfer points, which is all the rider needs to know. A topological map is useful for backpacking but no substitute for a road map. Maps differ in scope and detail, but all are abstract representations of reality.

A theory or theoretical model is a formal system: a set of propositions involving objects, variables, and relations among them. It must be clear and logically consistent. A model is constructed to represent or explain some empirical reality. But it need not be derived from empirical generalizations. And it does not have to be – indeed it cannot be – empirically true. In Giere's words, models are true 'in the way explicit definitions are true' (1999, p. 6). They can never be absolutely and literally true because they are always partial and approximate representations of an infinitely complex real world. Scientific theories, he notes elsewhere (1988, p. xvi) can be viewed 'not as empirical statements but as definitions of models variously related to the real world.' And so, 'Science does not deliver to us universal truths underlying all natural phenomena; but it does provide models of reality possessing various degrees of scope and accuracy' (1999, p. 6). One can have, says Giere, 'realism without truth.'

Keyfitz, discussing models of the demographic effects of eliminating deaths from heart diseases, comments similarly that his conclusions '...are conditional statements, and as such they are true beyond debate, given their assumptions that death rates by age from all other causes and birth rates by age of mother will remain as they are' (1971, p. 574). Conclusions drawn from a model follow inexorably from assumptions and model structure. Later, he contrasts the firmness of these conclusions with those established by 'direct observation, which tend to provide enigmatic and inconsistent reports' (1975, p. 267).

---

[5]Some authors distinguish theory and model, assigning the latter a role as intermediary between theory and empirical data. See for example, Gould and Tobochnik (1996) and Skvoretz (1998). Their distinction is on a general/specific axis and is not fundamental.

How then does one evaluate a model or theory? A model is a good model – Giere would not say a 'true' model – if it fits some portion of the real world (1) closely enough, (2) in certain respects, (3) for a specific purpose. All models are approximations. The question is whether the approximation is good enough for the purpose at hand. All models have a limited number of variables; none can mirror the numberless qualities of the real world. And finally, any model is to be evaluated with reference to the purpose for which it was designed or constructed.

The map analogy cited earlier helps clarify the last point. A highway map and a topographic map can both represent the same area. But the highway map is relatively useless for back-country hiking. It is not an incorrect or false representation, just the wrong one for the purpose. Similarly, a metro map correctly tells a rider where to get on and off the train, but is practically useless when one emerges above ground. A map of city streets is needed.

Over time in any science, some models receive widespread acceptance because they seem to embody central principles, or because they are widely applicable. In physics, classical mechanics provides an example. These models are taught in every introductory physics course. It is well understood that such models do not work as well at the sub-atomic level, or on the scale of the universe. But they are not therefore abandoned, since they serve many purposes in our everyday world.

The fit of a model to the real world is a matter for empirical examination. It is this empirical research that links model and data. But the conclusion that a model does not fit a particular case – perhaps not even closely – is only a conclusion that the model does not fit, not that the model is inherently false or invalid. It may well fit other cases. Decisions about whether or how well models fit the real world are based on scientific judgement, not on purely logical criteria. Giere again: 'judging the fit of a model to the world is matter of decision, not logical inference' (1999, p. 7).

The model-based view of theory has developed in opposition to logical empiricism, the dominant philosophy of empirical social science during the second half of the twentieth century. It differs from logical positivism in that the elements of a model do not have to be or be derived from or be logically consistent with broad – some would say universal – empirical generalizations or 'laws.' Such generalizations as exist may be incorporated into a model, but they are not essential. Many proponents of the model-based approach conclude that the logical empiricist program has been self- defeating precisely because empirical generalizations in social science are relatively rare.[6] The model-based view agrees with logical empiricism in its emphasis on the importance of empirical observation. It is the

---

[6]Critics of social science often take the absence of universal empirical generalizations as evidence that the social sciences are not really science. See, for example, *The Economist* (8 May, 1999, p. 84): '...unlike physics, economics yields no natural laws or universal constants. That is what makes decisive falsification in economics so difficult. And that is why...economics is not and never can be a proper science.' This statement reflects a common misunderstanding of physics. The constant in Newton's law of gravity is only 'relatively constant.' Depending as it does on mass, it is much different on the moon, and even differs across earth, at different altitudes and locations.

real world, insofar as it can be observed, that one is trying to understand and explain, not some imaginary world, a pure construct. The imagination is at play in theorizing and model building. But it begins with some empirical observation to be accounted for, and it returns to empirical observation to see if the account is a good or useful one. Otherwise, there is endless speculation.

The model-based view differs from a common view of economic theory, in which theory is derived from a limited set of axioms such as 'impersonal markets,' 'maximizing behavior,' and 'well-ordered preferences.' In the model-based view, the canonical axioms of economics may be incorporated into a model, but they need not be. Model construction is less constrained than in logical empiricism or mainstream economics. It is a creative leap from some empirical phenomenon that needs to be understood or explained, to the construction of a model that seems to do the job. Whether or how well it does so, as noted above, is a matter for empirical examination and scientific judgement.

The model-based view agrees with economics in an emphasis on the need for rigor in the statement of theories. The empirical assessment or use of models depends on their capacity to yield definite implications or predictions, and to support truly logical explanations.

In the model-based view, however, theory is not deductive in the sense of being inferred from a limited set of axioms. But explanation using a model is deductive, in the sense that the event or outcome to be explained must follow logically from the model, must be deducible from it. Nor is theory inductive in the sense of being derived from an examination of many cases to arrive at broad empirical generalizations. It is inductive in the broader sense that it starts with empirical observation and arrives at an abstract, and therefore general, model. But the process involves a creative leap of the imagination, not just generalization of the facts.[7]

A model or theory need not deal with general classes of phenomena. Otherwise, there could be no theory of the evolution of the human species or of the origins of the universe, both unique events. It is one of the strengths of the model-based view of science that it directs us to use abstract models to study unique events, unlike logical empiricism which requires empirical generalizations about classes of events. In the latter system, to the extent an event is truly unique, it cannot be subsumed under a class or a class-based generalization, and therefore resists explanation. The model-based approach to unique events enables us to pursue theoretical explanations, rather than falling back on the pure descriptions of ethnography or narrative history.

In this liberal view of theory, there are many different kinds. There are simple theories or theoretical models, and complex ones; cross-sectional and longitudinal or dynamic; and, as noted above, theories which apply to classes of phenomena, and those which apply to unique events. Clearly the latter kind of theory cannot be based on empirical generalizations based on the study of many cases; there is only one case. The generality lies in the model itself, not in data. In Meehan's words, '...

---

[7]See Franck (2002), especially his introductory and concluding remarks, on 'classical induction.'

timeless or general propositions are assumed to belong to the logical rather than the empirical world' (1968, p. 32).

To apply to a concrete phenomenon, of course, a theoretical model must be given greater specification. But even with such specification, it remains a theoretical model. The term *theoretical model,* for Giere, refers 'either to a general model or to one of its specific versions obtained by specifying unique values for all parameters and initial conditions' (1999, p. 177).

In physics, a distinction is sometimes made between *phenomenological* and *fundamental* theories (see Cartwright 1983). The former is essentially a description of what happens and how, without too much concern for why. A classic example is Newton's principle of gravity, which tells us that bodies released from a height will fall, and approximately how fast they will accelerate, but does not tell us what gravity is (Ekeland 1988). Fundamental theory delves more deeply into causes and mechanisms.

Meehan (1968) makes a similar distinction between models which can only predict a phenomenon, and those that can also explain why it will occur, by explicating processes or mechanisms. He views the latter as more difficult to construct, but also as more powerful, insofar as they make it possible to control events – at least in principle – not just adjust to them.

Other things equal, fundamental or explanatory models are of greater scientific value, because they involve deeper knowledge and understanding, and have more varied applications. But model assessment is related to purpose. And for some purposes, a phenomenological model may be just as effective and, often as not, easier to use.

1.2 Some Demographic Models Revisited

The model-based approach to science leads to a new perspective on demography; demographic knowledge, old and new, is seen from a different angle. Or, to use a musical metaphor, the same old demographic songs can be sung in a new key and reharmonized. This approach, I believe, greatly enhances demography's status as a science, notably its status as an autonomous discipline with its own large body of good theory. A few examples will illustrate the point.

The Exponential Growth Model No one would question the validity or 'truth' of the expression $P[t] = P[0]e^{rt}$. It is a standard mathematical function. In demography, the empirical question cannot be whether it is true, but only whether it applies to concrete human populations. And this depends on purpose. It is a good theoretical model to describe the basic character of the growth of the human and many other biological species, namely, that growth is proportional to population size. It is a good model to calculate an annual average rate of growth over some historical period, although like many averages the resulting figure may be misleading. The exponential model, however, is not a good model to describe the actual growth trajectory of many, perhaps most, real-world populations; consider the many examples of supra-exponential growth during the last three centuries. But we do not therefore say that the exponential model has been falsified, only that it doesn't fit the cases at hand.

Is the exponential model demographic theory? Perhaps some would prefer to call it a theoretical model or just a model. But when taken together with several others – the logistic, a supra-exponential model, the stable model, the cohort-component projection model – one can legitimately speak of the resulting collection as a 'theory of population growth.'

The Life Table The life table usually is presented as a complex measurement device, primarily a measure of current mortality. But it is basically a model of cohort survival. The algorithm for calculating a life table from assumed death rates or probabilities is true, depending as it does on the straightforward application of basic arithmetical operations. And, a life-table based on observed rates is a true summary of those rates. Again, the relevant question is not whether a specific life table is true or false, but whether it fits a real-world population closely enough for the purpose at hand. To summarize current age-specific death rates and re-work the information they contain into a more useful form (for example, for calculating e_0 or survival ratios), the life table works quite well. Whether the input rates somehow misrepresent some true, underlying mortality level is another issue, as is the question of whether a current life table can be used to forecast future mortality. The very best life table for contemporary humans would do a poor job of characterising the survival patterns of early humanoids or of other species, say insects.[8] But we can only say that it does not apply in these cases, not that it is invalid or false. Incidentally, I would describe the life table and other objects from formal demography as being *behavioral*, in the sense they characterize the survival behavior of a cohort – aggregate behavior to be sure, but behavior nonetheless.

The Coale-McNeil Marriage Model The Coale-McNeil model of first marriage (Coale and McNeil 1972; Coale 1977) began life as an exercise in mathematical curve fitting. Only later was it interpreted in terms of waiting times for entry into various stages of the marriage process. I once criticized the model compared to that of Hernes (see Burch 1993, and Chap. 6 below) because it was lacking in behavioral theory; I characterized the waiting-times interpretation as 'semi-behavioral.' This earlier assessment reflected my logical empiricist training and heritage, and acceptance of the conventional distinction between formal and behavioral demography. I would now say that to find a parametric model that closely fits a large collection of age patterns of first marriage is a considerable theoretical achievement – in the category of phenomenological theory. It is behavioral in the sense mentioned above – it captures important features of cohort behavior. It is not, of course, the only good model of marriage. There are several others, some of which may be better for

---

[8]The consideration of survival curves for other species or of unrealistic curves for humans (e.g., calculating a life table with a typical age pattern of q's reversed) helps put human survival and its implications for age structure and social structure in better perspective. See Carey (2002).

certain purposes. And there is both need and opportunity to develop rigorous models of marriage that are more complex and more richly behavioral. Some recent agent-based models of marriage (Todd and Billari 2003; Billari and Prskawetz 2003; Billari *et al.* 2003) represent one promising direction for these efforts.

Coale and Trussell's later (1996) discussion of the character of parametric models is instructive:

> The models are descriptive and were never intended to be anything else. No deep theory, or even shallow theory, underlies the search for empirical regularities. (p. 483)

The quality of a model, in their view, 'depends on how usefully it can be exploited for empirical research' (p. 469). Three uses are highlighted: testing data; building blocks for estimates; forecasting. The value of models is closely tied to working with 'inaccurate and incomplete data' (p. 484). Later they lament 'the virtual absence of the development and steep decline in the use of demographic models during the past decade,' related in part to increasing availability of good survey data (p. 484). But if the value of demographic models is tied primarily to the absence of good data, then there is some logic in a decline in their use as data improve. If they are viewed instead as substantive models of demographic behavior, then they have permanent value and application. This is recognized implicitly when they note that models 'can be used to make broad inferences about behavior...'; but the emphasis is elsewhere, since they continue: '...or, more commonly, to build techniques for estimating basic demographic indices for populations with limited or defective data' (p. 484).

Two Kinds of Transition Theory   One of the problems with the theory of demographic transition is that we have never quite agreed on precisely what it is (McNicoll 1992). In keeping with what has gone before, I would suggest that there are two kinds of transition theory. The phenomenological version simply states that a large, sustained decline in mortality will be followed, after a time lag, by a sustained decline in fertility, resulting in an intervening period of rapid population growth. A more fundamental version would include the determinants of mortality and fertility decline – modernisation, economic growth, secularisation, individualism, technological developments in medicine and fertility control, and so forth.

Either version of transition theory can be stated as an abstract model. In the former case, the model would assume a population in dynamic equilibrium, with constant mortality and fertility (and no migration). An assumed pattern of mortality decline is followed, after a delay, by fertility decline. There is rapid growth in the intervening period, and slower growth when a new equilibrium is established. Such a model is true by construction, 'true in the way that a definition is true.' Empirically it can be used to characterize the modern demographic history of many –

though certainly not all – human populations. For others, for example France or Hungary, a different model is needed.[9]

A more behavioral version of transition theory can also be stated as an abstract model. Mortality decline is defined as a function of development, with subsequent fertility decline a function both of mortality decline and of development. The approach would be similar to population biology's definition of the logistic model, in which mortality and fertility are functions of population density. The key difference is that in a transition model, mortality declines with development and population growth, whereas in the logistic model it rises (in both, fertility declines). The link between mortality decline and fertility decline might be explained in terms of pressure at the individual, family, or community level, because of larger numbers of surviving children. Again, such a transition model would provide an approximate but accurate description of the demographic history of many nations, along with a behavioral explanation for that history. With closer specification and real data inputs, it could provide a better approximation of the history of a particular nation. Probably no one specification could provide a close fit to the history of all nations, since this history did not occur 'in a vacuum' or in controlled experimental conditions. It was this historical fact that led Coale to conclude that the only generalization to emerge from the vast historical studies of European fertility decline was that fertility would decline when a population was, to borrow Lesthaeghe's paraphrase, 'ready, willing, and able' (Lesthaeghe and Vanderhoeft 1997). The postulated mechanism linking mortality and fertility decline, of course, does not flow from an empirical generalization, which is precisely why it is a theoretical explanation.

It would be easy to multiply examples, drawn from the demographic literature both old and new. But these suffice to show that, whether in the realm of formal demography or of behavioral demography – as traditionally conceived – we can view our models as formal models, models that are true in the way that definitions are true. In either sub-field, our models are abstract representations of the real world, inspired by empirical observation; epistemologically, they are of one piece. The models of formal demography are not just measurement techniques. They have a theoretical character.[10] The models of behavioral demography need not be rejected because they do not fit all the facts, so long as they fit some relevant

---

[9]The literature contains a few examples of formalization of transition theory (see, for example, Keyfitz 1985, pp. 23ff). But none has become standard or widely used or cited.

[10]The idea that some demographic measurement techniques are models is not novel. Newell (1988) for example has a chapter entitled 'Introduction to Demographic Models.' He distinguishes normative and descriptive models, and mentions the total fertility rate and the life table as examples of the former. He comments: 'These normative models so dominate formal demography that it is not often they are actually thought of as models; yet it should always be remembered that a move from ASFR's to a TFR, or from ASDR's to a life table, is a move from reality to a model' (p. 118). Newell does not take the further step, advocated here, of viewing such a model or a collection of related models as theory.

cases well enough to be useful for one or another purpose. In short, demography has more good theory than commonly recognized.

1.3   Demography Reconsidered

The model-based view of demography has many further implications for the way we think of the field, and the way we present it to others, notably our students. I highlight five, some of them recapitulated from above.

1. We need to become more comfortable with the idea of several different models for the same phenomenon. Logical empiricism pushed toward the view that in empirical tests, one model would emerge as a winner, with the others being falsified and rejected. I have always suspected that this idea reflects a deep, even subconscious, monotheistic belief. Early scientific thinking often was explicitly theological (note recent publicity about Newton's theological speculations). God created the universe, implanting in it certain laws. Science's job was to find them. And since there is only one God, laws of nature will be unique. This led to what Teller (2001) has called 'the perfect model model' of science.

   The model-based view prefers to think of a pantheon, or to change the metaphor, a toolkit of related models, with different characteristics and serving different purposes. With respect to population growth, for example, one can point to: the exponential model; the logistic model; transition theory; the stable model; the standard projection model. Which is the true model of population growth? The question makes no sense. With respect to fertility, similarly, one can point to: Becker's microeconomic model; the Easterlin-Crimmins socio-economic model; Friedman et al. (1994) uncertainty model; the social capillarity model; Davis's multiphasic model; Coale's model of the three preconditions; transition theory; Lesthaeghe on secular individualism; the newer models on 'social influence' and diffusion. Which is the true model of fertility? If we retain the notion of truth at all, then surely the most that can be said is that each model incorporates some element of truth. None is complete nonsense, such as the idea that fertility decline has been imposed on us by Martians to prevent our depletion of the world's resources before they can get to them.

   This toolkit approach to scientific theories does not imply that all models are equal. Some models be better approximations of a wider variety of cases, or useful for a wider variety of purposes. Such models will naturally tend to be used more often. But the lesser models also will be used on occasion. It is not prudent to discard them.

2. As noted earlier, at the theoretical level the sharp traditional distinction between formal and behavioral demography is discarded. All theories or theoretical models become formal in the sense outlined above. In Lotka's phrase, all theory is 'analytic theory' (1939). The body of work we generally regard as

demographic techniques or methods can still be thought of as techniques. But much of it also can be thought of as theoretical models of population dynamics – substantive models of how populations or cohorts behave, often under idealized conditions. Past practice in this regard is inconsistent. The stable model is commonly referred to as 'stable theory.' But the cohort-component projection model is classified as a technique, and many demographers would object to its classification as theory. Yet both models represent the development of population size and structure in the face of assumed inputs. It is hard to see why one is theory and one is not – unless one can argue for a valid distinction based on the level of mathematics involved.

Reinterpreted models from formal demography are behavioral in a limited sense of dealing with the behavior of aggregates, without explicit reference to motivation, values, norms, and decision making (see McNicoll's 1992 reference to 'the limitless depths' of human behavior). But they are behavioral nonetheless, in the same sense that Newton's law speaks to the behavior of falling bodies.

But surely, it may be objected, the classic distinction between necessary and contingent relationships (see Lotka's distinction between 'analytic' and 'statistical' demography) is valid. I reply with a distinction. There is contingency in our empirical observations. But we construct theoretical models in a way that contingency is left behind. The statement 'natural increase equals births minus deaths' states a necessary relationship; the empirical statement 'high rates of female labour-force participation are associated with very low fertility' is contingent, and not universally true. But the assumption that it is true can be incorporated in a model. It is then true by construction, true 'in the way that a definition is true.' This is essentially the message of Keyfitz's (1975) paper on 'How do we know the facts of demography?'

In the teaching of demography, I have come to see the formal-behavioral distinction as arbitrary. Consider a lecture on the determinants of population growth, based on a series of models. Successively we show that growth depends on numbers of births, deaths, and migrants (in and out). We then show that the number of births depends on a rate or set of rates interacting with population size and age-structure. A student asks: 'But what determines the rates?' The conventional answer might be: 'This course only deals with formal demography and techniques. To consider that question you must take another course.'[11] A model-based approach would simply move on to the next set of theoretical models, those dealing with the determinants of fertility, for example, Easterlin-Crimmins or Coale. I have never encountered a physics or chemistry text that made such a sharp distinction between formal and behavioral physics or chemistry, or between substance and method.

---

[11]Another manifestation of this distinction is seen in the common practice in introductory textbooks of relegating technical demography to appendices, and in demographic methods texts of omitting all but cursory discussions of behavioral models and theory.

3. Many computer simulations in demography may be viewed as theory or as tools
   for theoretical analysis. For many social and behavioral theorists, manipulation
   of a numerical model with a computer is 'number crunching,' not theory. For
   many empiricists, it is theory in the bad sense of armchair speculation, yielding
   numbers that are made up. The model-based view would say rather that a
   simulation is an abstract model of a real demographic system, and can be
   manipulated to yield insight into how that system works, or applied to real
   world systems to explain or predict. There is no inherent difference between
   this use of a simulation model and the classic uses of stable population theory to
   clarity dynamic interrelations among fertility, mortality, population growth, and
   age structure. An interesting question is why demographers have generally been
   more receptive to stable analyses than computer simulations.

This view of simulation is not unknown in demography. It has been expounded
and illustrated over the years by researchers such as Hammel and Wachter, to give
but one example. In fact, a computer model is just another kind of model, written in
a new kind of language. And the model-based view of science does not differ
greatly from the mainstream tradition of mathematical modelling, in which a model
is constructed for a specific purpose and its performance judged explicitly with
regard to that purpose. Mathematical modellers have generally not viewed their
work as *theory,* however, although in many contexts, it can be so viewed.

In his 'liberal view of models,' Keyfitz noted, '...they may be algebraic, arithmetical, computer simulation, or verbal' (1971, p. 575). His example of a verbal
model is 'demographic transition' theory. And as his later paper (1975) strongly
suggests, there is no essential difference between a model and a theory.

4. To qualify as theoretical models of the kind I am advocating, many of our
   'behavioral' models must be defined more clearly and rigorously (Burch
   1996). This is necessary for discovering logical implications of the models. It
   is not enough to work with highly discursive models which 'give us a feel for
   what's going on.' Such models, as is well known, can be used to explain or
   predict almost anything, and therefore explain or predict nothing.

The need to derive definite implications, incidentally, is why the 'probabilistic
finesse' – the reliance on probable generalizations rather than universal ones – is not
able to save the logical empiricist approach to theory. A chain or other combination
of several probabilistic empirical statements yields implications of at best low
probability (by the multiplicative rule). In the model-based approach, within the
model itself the inferences are certain, allowing only for some stochastic elements.
Uncertainty comes when the inferences are applied to the real world, since the fit is
never perfect. But this is a matter of scientific judgement, not just logic. To quote
Giere, 'It is enough that the premises confer some appropriate degree of 'probability' or 'rational warrant' to the conclusion' (1988, p. 11).

5. The model-based view is comfortable in dealing with unique phenomena. In the logical empiricist model of science, theory is based on generalization across many cases of a phenomenon considered as a class, e.g., national fertility transitions. Explanation of a particular case is achieved by 'subsuming' it under some general theoretical propositions about the class.

There are at least two problems with this approach. First, there may be no class. Some phenomena are unique in the literal sense of the word – there is only one case. The origin of the universe and the evolution of the human species are examples. Secondly, even if there appears to be a class, often it will have been defined for extra-scientific purposes (e.g., national and provincial political boundaries). Theoretical considerations do not guide the definition. But in this case, there is no reason to assume that the classes are homogeneous with respect to characteristics of interest. To try to find a general model of such a class may involve trying to represent systems that differ in ways that are centrally important.

The model-based view of science, by contrast, has no problem with constructing models to deal with unique events. It offers an alternative to giving up on theory in the face of the tremendous variability of real-world phenomena, which seems – perhaps rightly – to defy generalization. To some, especially historians and anthropologists, this variability means that one can only resort to detailed or 'thick' description. But as has been seen above, we can have theory without generalization.

1.4   Conclusion

But what difference does it make? Why should we take the trouble to change our way of looking at our discipline, and the way we present it to students, policy makers, and the public. Why bother to revamp our textbooks and our courses, as might be necessary were the model-based view to be taken seriously?

My first answer is that the model-based view should be taken seriously because it makes more sense than the views to which we are accustomed. It accords with an emerging mainstream in philosophy of science, and with what scientists in some of the most successful fields think about their work and teach their students. Without being inconsistent, of course, I cannot argue that this is *the true* approach to science, only that it is a liberating and fruitful one.

A second answer is that this liberal view of theory and of models enhances the stature of demography as a science, an autonomous, well-balanced scientific discipline, with a large body of good theory, as well as of techniques, data, and empirical findings.

Thirdly, other than some mental effort, there is little downside risk in doing demography in a new key. There need be no wholesale abandonment of what we currently think and do. We can still think of the life table as a measurement tool, while beginning to think of it also as a theoretical model of cohort survival. We still will spend a great deal of time and effort on the statistical analysis of census, vital statistics, and survey data, providing descriptive studies of demographic trends. Techniques will be refined, and descriptive studies will continue apace, both detailed descriptions of individual cases and attempts to generalize where possible.

Collectively, more time and effort will be spent on the construction of new models and on the rigorous statement and systematisation of those we already have (theoretical synthesis). Not everyone is likely to become a theorist or model builder. But, one hopes, empirical research will be better informed by explicitly and rigorously crafted models, used to design the research, not just heuristically in the introductory sections of papers, or for ad hoc interpretation in the concluding sections.

The danger of an uncontrolled profusion of models seems unlikely in a discipline so closely wedded to empirical data. But the model-based approach itself guards against this danger, with its great emphasis on purpose: every model is built for some clear purpose, and is judged accordingly. One doesn't model for the sake of modelling. If a model doesn't yield insights into basic principles or fit some important empirical case – some of the data – then it may be abandoned, or better, reworked or refined.

What is at issue is a balance between empirical observation and theory, in a complete science. Demography has been exceptionally strong at empirical observation, and has one of the largest bodies of reliable data of any of the human sciences. But what does it mean? How can it be organized and presented to others? That is the role of theory and theoretical models.

Nancy Cartwright writes of theory: 'Explanations [at least the high-level explanations of theoretical science...] organize, briefly and efficiently, the unwieldy, and perhaps unlearnable, mass of highly detailed knowledge that we have of phenomena' (1983, p. 87). A large dose of the right kind of theoretical thinking could help us all digest the vast body of demographic information. Teller (2001) speaks of 'humanly accessible understanding.'

Cartwright continues in the above quote: 'But organizing power has nothing to do with the truth.' Truth, if only of a relative sort, lies in our facts (The largest national population in the world is that of China), and in our empirical generalizations such as they are (Low fertility in the modern world tends to be associated with high levels of socio-economic development).

With a better appreciation of demography's large fund of theoretical models, we can have the best of both worlds: truth in our empirical observations, and, in Giere's words, 'realism without truth' in our models. But models don't have to be true to be useful. Sufficient realism for the purpose at hand supports understanding, explanation, prediction, and policy guidance. And, to give Keyfitz the last word – 'no models, no understanding' (1975, p. 275).

References

Baylis, W. E. (1994). *Theoretical methods in the physical sciences: An introduction to problem solving using maple V*. Boston: Birkhauser.

Billari, F. C., & Prskawetz, A. (Eds.). (2003). *Agent-based computational demography: Using simulation to improve our understanding of demographic behavior*. Heidelberg: Physica-Verlag.

Billari, F.C., Prskawetz, A., Fürnkranz, J. (2003). On the cultural evolution of age-at-marriage norms. In Billari & Prskawetz (pp. 139–158).

Burch, T. K. (1993). Theory, computers, and the parameterisation of demographic behavior. *IUSSP International Population Conference, Montreal*. Liege: International Union for the Scientific Study of Population., *3*, 377–388.

Burch, T. K. (1996). Icons, strawmen and precision: reflections on demographic theories of fertility decline. *The Sociological Quarterly, 37*, 59–81.

Carey, J. R. (2002). The importance of including biodemography in the demography curriculum. *Genus*. [Special Issue: *Teaching Demography in the Early 21st Century*, edited by G. Caselli], *58*, 189–199.

Cartwright, N. (1983). *How the laws of physics lie*. Oxford: Clarendon Press.

Cartwright, N. (1999). *The dappled world: A study of the boundaries of science*. New York: Cambridge University Press.

Coale, A. J. (1977). The development of new models of nuptiality and fertility. *Population* [numero special], *32*, 131–152.

Coale, A. J., & McNeil, D. J. (1972). The distribution by age of the frequency of first marriage in a female cohort. *Journal of the American Statistical Association, 67*, 743–749.

Coale, A. J., & Trussell, J. (1996). The use of demographic models. *Population Studies, 50*, 469–484.

Ekeland, I. (1988). *Mathematics and the unexpected*. Chicago: University of Chicago Press.

Franck, R. (Ed.). (2002). *The explanatory power of models: Bridging the gap between empirical and theoretical research in the social sciences*. Boston: Kluwer Academic Publications.

Friedman, D., Hechter, M., & Kanmazawa, S. (1994). A theory of the value of children. *Demography, 31*, 375–402.

Giere, R. N. (1988). *Explaining science: A cognitive approach*. Chicago: University of Chicago Press.

Giere, R. N. (1999). *Science without laws*. Chicago: University of Chicago Press.

Gould, H., & Tobochnik, J. (1996). *An introduction to computer simulation methods: Applications to physical systems*. Reading: Addison-Wesley Publishing.

Keyfitz, N. (1971). Models. *Demography, 8*, 571–580.

Keyfitz, N. (1975). How do we know the facts of demography? *Population and Development Review, 1*, 267–288.

Keyfitz, N. (1985). *Applied mathematical demography* (2nd ed.). New York: Spring-Verlag.

Lesthaeghe, R., & Vanderhoeft, C. (1997). *Ready, willing and able: A conceptualization of transitions to new behavioral forms* (IPD Working Paper #8). Brussel: Vrije Universiteit.

Lotka, A. J. (1939). *Theorie Analytique des Associations Biologiques, Deuxieme Partie*. Paris: Hermann & Cie.

McNicoll, G. (1992). The agenda of population studies: A commentary and complaint. *Population and Development Review, 18*, 399–420.

Meehan, E. J. (1968). *Explanation in social science: A system paradigm*. Homewood: The Dorsey Press.

Newell, C. (1988). *Methods and models in demography*. New York: The Guilford Press.

Newton, R. (1997). *The truth of science: Physical theories and reality*. Cambridge, MA: Harvard University Press.

Skvoretz, J. (1998). Theoretical models: Sociology's missing links. In A. Sica (Ed.), *What is social theory: The philosophical debates* (pp. 238–252). Oxford: Blackwell Publishers Ltd.

Teller, P. (2001). Twilight of the perfect model model. *Erkenntnis, 55*, 393–415.

Todd, P.M., & Billari, F.C. (2003). Population-wide marriage patterns produced by individual mate-search heuristics. In Billari, & Prskawetz (pp. 117–138).

Vance, R. B. (1952). Is theory for demographers? *Social Forces, 31*, 9–13.

Chapter 2
Data, Models, Theory and Reality: The Structure of Demographic Knowledge

2.1 Introduction

The development of demography as a science has been hampered by inadequate attention to theory and to methodology (broad issues of scientific procedure, as distinct from specific techniques or methods). Demography has been preoccupied with the analysis of empirical data, to the neglect of the systematic theory formulation. In turn, theory development has been hampered by the widespread acceptance, if only implicit, of the methodological ideas of logical empiricism. This is the philosophy of science of such mid-twentieth century writers as Nagel, Hempel, Popper, and Reichenbach. But there also is an older intellectual tradition deriving from nineteenth century scientists such as Karl Pearson and Ernst Mach. It is a tradition that finds expression in other social and behavioral science disciplines, of which Skinnerian behaviorism in psychology is a prime example.

The key ideas of logical empiricism are: (a) that empirical science should focus on observable phenomena, and avoid discussion of unobservable entities or processes; and (b) that scientific theory, if possible at all, must be based on empirical generalizations, preferably universal empirical generalizations or laws.[1]

With respect to abstract analytic theory and abstract models, demography has been schizoid. Few demographers would deny the validity of the stable population model or its fruitfulness in generating substantive conclusions, even though few

---

Based on a presentation to a workshop on 'Agent-Based Computational Demography,' at the Max Planck Institute for Demographic Research, Rostock, Germany, 21–23 February 2001; originally published in F.C. Billari and A. Prskawetz [eds.] 2003. *Agent-Based Computational Demography.* Heidelberg: Physica-Verlag, pp. 19–40.

[1] Another important influence on the scientific character of demography, not further discussed here, has been its heavy involvement in largely descriptive work, due to its close association with government statistical bureaus. The central mandate of these agencies is accurate data collection and description, not the overall advancement of demographic science as such. This close association clearly has had great advantages for demography, but also costs.

T.K. Burch, *Model-Based Demography*, Demographic Research Monographs,
DOI 10.1007/978-3-319-65433-1_2

real-world populations closely fit the stable model. By contrast, abstract behavioral theories such as transition theory or the microeconomic theory of demographic behavior are often dismissed because they admit of empirical exceptions or are 'unrealistic.' The tendency has been to draw a sharp line between formal demography, built on necessary relationships, and behavioral demography, built on empirical generalizations regarding contingent relationships.

Insight into these methodological issues can be garnered from a consideration of two leading North American demographers of the late twentieth century, Ansley J. Coale and Nathan Keyfitz. To the best of my knowledge, Coale never wrote systematically on the methodology of demography, so one must seek methodological remarks, often made in passing, in his other writings. For Keyfitz, we have two papers (Keyfitz 1971, 1975), in which he argues that much of our best demographic knowledge has been produced by use of abstract models, not by means of data analysis.

Interestingly, Coale relied heavily on abstract models in much of his earlier work on formal topics such as the demography of population aging, but also on behavioral topics such as the impact of high fertility and rapid population growth on economic development in low-income countries. In his later work on historical fertility transitions, Coale appears to favor a logical empiricist approach, pruning theoretical conclusions to fit the data, and ending with a restatement of transition theory reminiscent of Notestein's writings 40 years earlier. It is arguable that the *theoretical* returns to the heavy investment of time, money and personnel into the European fertility project were not as large as they might have been. Hobcraft (2000) has made the same argument with respect to the World Fertility Survey and its successors (notably the Demographic and Health Surveys).

Keyfitz's assessment of the relative fruitfulness of abstract modeling is neither new nor unique. Descartes favored thought over observation as the way to knowledge. The 'new scientists' such as Francis Bacon favored observation (data). John Locke attempted a synthesis that comes close to a balanced view of empirical science: experience and reflection on experience, or, observation and theory. More recently, Karl Pearson and Ronald Fisher are reputed to have parted ways over the issue of correlational studies of large samples (data) versus experiments on smaller samples to test ideas about mechanisms (theory).

John Platt, in a classic paper on scientific methodology (Platt 1964), recalls a 1958 conference on molecular biology, at which theoretical modelers were criticized by experimentalists. Leo Szilard is quoted as commenting about protein synthesis or enzyme formation that 'If you do stupid experiments, and finish one a year, it can take 50 years. But if you stop doing experiments for a little while and *think* how proteins can possibly be synthesized, there are only about 5 different ways, not 50! And it will take only a few experiments to distinguish these' (p. 348). An experimental researcher is reported to have replied 'You know there are scientists; and there are people in science who are just working with these oversimplified model systems – DNA chains and in vitro systems – who are not doing science at all' (p. 346). The subsequent history of molecular biology suggests who was on the right track.

Keyfitz's view is echoed and supported by a wide variety of writings on scientific methodology, all seeking an alternative approach to logical empiricism, seen as leading to dead ends and theoretical frustration. As examples, I cite and briefly discuss an early statement by political scientist Eugene Meehan (1968), some representative authors of the 'semantic' school in the philosophy of science (Cartwright 1999; Giere 1999), and a call for a return to abstract analytic theory and the search for social mechanisms by sociologists (notably, Hedström and Swedberg 1998).

The critique of logical empiricism common to all these writers suggests the need for greater respect for and attention to abstract models in demography. It also suggests dropping the sharp distinction between formal and behavioral demography, since all good scientific theories or models are in fact formal. The qualitative distinction between theory and models is minimized; at best, the difference is one of scope. And the pervasive but false characterizations of theory as verbal speculation, of modeling or simulation as quantitative speculation, and of empirical research as quantitative bedrock may seem less cogent.

Finally, given the complexity of the real world and the ability of the computer-aided scientist to handle larger amounts of complexity, in the future much of our fruitful theoretical work will consist of computer modeling (Burch 2002, and Chap. 3 below). The genre of *agent-based modeling* will likely occupy a central place in this work. It provides a feasible approach to study interrelations between the macro- and micro-levels in demography – exploring links between individual decisions and aggregate demographic patterns, a realm that up until now has resisted analysis (but see Courgeau 2004). It also can introduce rule-based behavior into complex demographic models that formerly relied on purely stochastic assumptions (e.g., Monte Carlo simulations). Microeconomic decision-making models (as well as decision models from sociology and social psychology) can be used in more than a 'heuristic' manner (see McNicoll 1992).

2.2   The Methodology of Ansley J. Coale

By all accounts, Ansley Coale was one of the most versatile, creative, and influential demographers of our era. His contributions range widely across the field – extensions of stable population models; stunning clarifications of the relative roles of fertility and mortality change on age composition; parametric modeling of demographic behavior (fertility, marriage, mortality); pioneering work on the impact of fertility and population growth on economic development; historical studies of fertility decline in Europe; the demography of China; powerful evaluations of the completeness of census enumeration – a complete list would be still longer. His work characteristically has a sure-footed and direct quality often lacking in social science: problems are stated with great clarity, and solutions provided; there is a sense of closure. His technical innovations are geared toward important substantive issues, and typically have proven useful in further empirical research by others. Although mathematically astute, he seldom if ever did mathematics for the sake of mathematics.

But like most demographers, he seems not to have been self-conscious and explicit about the methodology of demography (logic and epistemology) as opposed to technique.[2] Implicitly, his work might be taken to suggest ambivalence regarding the proper roles of data, models, and theory, or at least some changing emphases over time.

A leitmotiv of his career is formal mathematical modeling of demographic dynamics, popularizing and extending the work of Lotka and other early pioneers. This work relies on mathematically necessary relationships in highly abstract population models, with the stable model as central. Generalizations emerge from the models rather than from extensive empirical research. A prime example is his work on the demographic determinants of age structure (see, for example, Coale 1956). Using the stable model and the standard projection model, he concludes that fertility change generally has more impact on age structure than mortality change, and that the effects of mortality change are heavily dependent on the age-pattern of change, with the possibility that some patterns of change can make a population younger, not older. Coale uses data to calculate the models, of course, but his generalizations depend on the manipulation of relatively simple abstract models, not on the systematic analysis of empirical data. Plausible but constructed data could have served as well.

His monograph with Hoover (Coale and Hoover 1958) also involves abstract modeling rather than broad empirical research, but on issues generally viewed as behavioral rather than formal, and involving a considerably more complex model. The core of this work is a linking of a standard population projection model with a standard economic growth model. The model is fit to the Indian case at length, and to the Mexican case more briefly. There is some discussion – but no systematic empirical research – of the wider applicability of the analysis. It was what today is known as large-scale simulation. The researchers were no doubt hampered by the absence of computer tools we take for granted, although they did engage in what would now be called sensitivity analysis.

Coale was more deeply involved in the demographic parts of the work, Hoover in the economic. But they stress that there was co-operation of both in all parts. Sometimes they are clear about the abstract character of their analysis: 'Our calculations entail a "model" of the Indian economy, designed to take into account as realistically as an extremely simplified model can the main relevant features of that economy...' (p. 259). But the conclusions are set forth as general, applying to India, Mexico, and to most other low-income nations in the developing world.

---

[2]As has been pointed out many times, excessive self-consciousness of methodological issues can hamper scientific progress. The development of demography has probably benefited from the efforts of investigators who simply got on with the job with the tools at hand. It also is true that theorizing without an adequate empirical base often is sterile. My methodological critique is aimed more at present and future work than at the past.

They seem at times to overlook an element of circularity that is characteristic of all simulation, namely that the conclusions follow from the assumptions. For example, they conclude: '... through this whole gamut of projections, despite the wide variation in rates of progress that they imply, the differential associated with reduced fertility is remarkably persistent and stable' (p. 281).[3] But earlier they have told us that the model does not contain all important growth determinants, but only 'the growth determinants most clearly affected by the difference between our alternative rates of population growth' (p. 260). Since alternative rates of population growth in their scenarios depend mainly on alternative fertility assumptions, in hindsight the conclusion quoted just above is inevitable. And it is completely possible that the model is not relevant to concrete cases in which the omitted growth determinants are crucial.

Several passages in the book suggest that the abstract and speculative character of their work was partially obscured by the fact that the analysis was quantitative, that it dealt with concrete cases, and that it dealt with a very specific question – what difference would different fertility patterns make to economic development? In his preface to the work, Frank Notestein, who generally disliked abstract theory, seems to have been misled, describing it as a '...highly original demonstration of the way careful *factual analysis* can illuminate the vital interrelationships of economic and population change' (pp. v–vi, emphasis added). But clearly it is factual only if one accepts as facts theoretical and modeling assumptions as well as quantitative empirical data. And perhaps it is factual by contrast with pure theoretical speculation, not grounded in the details of a concrete case. But it certainly is not empirical work in the ordinary sense of that term. Of course, this is easier to see this in hindsight, given many decades of experience with computer modeling.

The important point is that general propositions emerging from the project were based on the model not just on empirical data. Indeed, critics of Coale-Hoover (e.g., Kuznets, Easterlin) criticized it precisely because comparative empirical research showed no strong or regular relationship between population growth rates and economic development. But this in no way diminishes the importance of their work. Like all good models, their simulation of population growth and development provided crucial insights into mechanism at work and a systematic framework for discussion and further research. In addition, their analysis almost certainly provides a relevant explanation as to why some nations with rapid population growth – then and now – have shown so little economic progress.

When Coale turned his attention to fertility transitions, the orientation became more empirical. In one of his earliest papers on the European fertility project (Coale 1965), he presents his indirectly standardized ratios and a few early results at the national level. The paper does not explicitly deal with classic transition theory, but implicitly calls it into question. Methodological comments made in passing suggest

---

[3]This language is almost identical to that would be used by the *Limits to Growth* researchers, some years later. But it did not deter harsh criticism of this study by many demographers and economists. See Bardi, 2011.

a radical logical empiricism. Speaking of the decline of marital fertility, he comments 'There are few, if any, universally valid generalizations about the circumstances under which neo-Malthusian fertility reduction occurs' (p. 5). After a list of frequently hypothesized causal factors, he notes that 'Examples can be found illustrating the presumed influence of each of these factors, but counter-examples or exceptions are nearly as prevalent' (p. 6). He concludes: 'Fertility reduction seems to be a nearly universal feature of the development of modern, secular societies, but its introduction and spread cannot yet be explained by any simple, universally valid model or generalized description' (p. 7). Looking to the future he expresses the hope that further empirical research 'tracing the decline of fertility more systematically, and by geographic units smaller than nations, will certainly establish a fuller record of fertility reduction, and will perhaps make possible generalizations about the causes of the decline' (p. 7).

Eight years later Coale (1973) deals with what would usually be called theoretical issues, in a paper on the demographic transition. But the emphasis is still on the search for universal empirical propositions. Interestingly, he never uses the word *theory,* either with reference to Notestein's work or his own (the word does not appear anywhere in the paper). He speaks instead of the 'idea' of demographic transition. It is difficult to know just what was intended by his studious avoidance of the word *theory,* which would have seemed quite natural in the context.

In fact, the paper eventually produces very broad statements that most social scientists would view as theory. Coale posits 'the existence of more than one precondition for a decline.' 'Three general prerequisites for a major fall in marital fertility can be listed': (1) it must be within the calculus of conscious choice; (2) reduced fertility must be advantageous; (3) effective fertility control techniques must be available (p. 65). The language is borrowed from mathematics; the three preconditions or prerequisites are in fact 'necessary conditions' for fertility decline (p. 69). A weakness of 'the idea [sic] of the transition is that it tells us that a high degree of modernization is *sufficient* to cause a fall of fertility, but does not tell us what degree (if any) of modernization is necessary to produce a fall' (p. 69). He notes that one or more of the three preconditions can exist in the absence of modernization.

Coale acknowledges many good points about 'the idea of the transition' (Notestein's transition theory] but faults it on its inability to make more than qualitative statements about the course of demographic and fertility transitions. He notes, for example, that with respect to developing countries, transition theory was 'accurate in direction but inaccurate in detail, with respect to mortality' (p. 68). Transition theory was qualitatively correct regarding the past of developed countries and qualitatively correct in its predictions for less developed countries. But, 'In neither instance does it specify in terms that can be translated into quantitative measures, the circumstances under which the decline of fertility began' (p. 68).

But Coale's three preconditions clearly are subject to the same criticism, especially since they are not presented as quantitative variables. He speaks of 'the degree of change that must occur before the preconditions are introduced,' but does not always discuss the preconditions themselves as matters of degree, using words that suggest a 0–1 variable – whether the preconditions are 'present' or 'absent' (p. 66). There is little attention to the issue of how they might be quantified and operationalized.[4]

Coale's last major statement on fertility transitions is in his introductory chapter for the multi-authored summary volume on the project (Coale and Watkins 1986). The spirit of this essay is different from that of the 1973 paper, with a return to reliance on abstract models to gain insight into population dynamics. There is, for instance, considerable discussion of what might be called a cyclic logistic model to describe pre-modern or even pre-historical population dynamics. Population growth leads to rising mortality; populations react by reducing marriage and/or fertility or otherwise reducing population growth; mortality declines to former levels; and the cycle starts over. Interestingly, the model is purely qualitative, and, of course, there is little empirical evidence to support it, at least for the earlier, pre-modern periods. On transition theory, Coale seems to have given up the hopes expressed in earlier papers that the project would arrive at 'universal empirical generalizations.' The three preconditions are not mentioned. One long paragraph (p. 24) summarizes the causes of transitional mortality decline in broad terms that would not have passed muster by the standards of his 1973 paper. Ultimately, he writes of the fertility transition in language not so different from that of Notestein 40 years earlier, speaking of 'typical' patterns of transition and some exceptions (pp. 28–29). There is no attempt to quantify the 'idea of transition' beyond the presentation of empirical measurements of fertility and nuptiality, and their time trends and intercorrelations with a limited number of independent variables. It is as though the sheer mass of data has led to an abandonment of attempts to develop new and better theoretical ideas or models, including a revised and more rigorous statement of transition theory.

This is a long story, but it makes an important point: a massive 20-year project with substantial resources and collaboration by many first-rate demographers did not result in a major improvement in theory, nor in consensus on transition theory. This is not to deny the immense scientific value of the work as an empirical, descriptive study. And, in Coale's mind, description may well have been its central aim. Recall the quote cited earlier: 'tracing the decline of fertility more systematically... will *certainly* establish a fuller record of fertility reduction, and will *perhaps* make possible generalizations about the causes of the decline' (11, p. 7, emphasis added). But theory did not flow from the data; the methodological stance was such that theory would flow from universal empirical generalizations, and these were not forthcoming.

John Hobcraft has recently commented in a similar vein on the small theoretical returns to the large number of comparative fertility surveys under the aegis of the World Fertility Survey and its successors such as Demographic and Health Surveys. Entitled 'Moving beyond elaborate description: towards understanding choice about parenthood' (Hobcraft 2000), the paper argues that 'the results [of these

---

[4]But see Lesthaeghe and Vanderhoeft (1997).

surveys] did not live up to my own or to others' highest expectations; comparative analysis projects today are much less common; the Demographic and Health Surveys, the daughter of the WFS, have never had a serious comparative analysis capacity (beyond the mainly descriptive Comparative Studies)' (p. l). He speaks of 'meagre returns,' and of 'meagre progress to date in moving forward our real understanding of fertility behavior through cross-national comparative surveys' (p. 11). He adds that 'a profound shift of emphasis is required in order to make real progress' (p. l), that is, progress towards understanding. Hobcraft's diagnosis:

> ...the main problem for comparative analysis, over and above the sheer scale of data manipulation, has always been the rather limited number of explanatory variables which are sufficiently standardized and accorded enough credibility to be collected in every country. In part, this problem arises from a lack of a commonly accepted theoretical framework for understanding fertility behavior, but it is also arguable that we shall never remedy the problem without better agreement and testing of comparable information [p. 2].

He seems to agree with Griffith Feeney, who earlier (Feeney 1994) noted that the surveys in question contained a lot of data but not necessarily the right data for testing or developing explanations and theory. Hobcraft comments, with respect to the comparative fertility surveys, that there has generally been 'a lack of conceptual and theoretical clarity about what elements should receive priority,' and that 'an explicit theoretical orientation has been lacking' (p. 4), noting that the surveys were done for policy or even political purposes, not primarily to advance science. Hobcraft's remedy would be to collect more and better data, with variables to be selected based on the best theoretical thinking about the determinants of fertility. The emphasis would be on variables that are comparable cross-culturally, and especially on variables relating to the fertility decision-making process (defined broadly to emphasize the decision to become a parent), and on community-level variables. Analysis of such data would aim at 'global models,' models involving 'not just the same range of regressors but also the same parameters'(p. 3):

> A deeper understanding would involve a closer specification, whereby the strength of the relationship was the same everywhere net of the correct range of other controls, or, the development of models which incorporate the factors which bring about variations in the strength of the relationship as a step towards the fuller model' [p. 4].

Hobcraft thinks 'progress toward such models is essential for good theory' (pp. 3–4), but not that theory will flow from the data. Rather, the appropriate data-collection and analysis will necessarily be informed and guided by theory. Of comparative description and 'detailed society-specific accounts,' he concludes that 'Neither holds out great hope for reaching general theoretical understanding' (p. 5). In the final analysis, however, Hobcraft's faith in future progress tilts towards better data and more sophisticated data analysis. And the goal of 'global models' suggests an assumption that widespread, if not universal, empirical generalizations are there, if only we can find them. The logical empiricist approach maintains some hold.

2.3 Nathan Keyfitz on the Fruitfulness of Abstract Modelling

A very different approach is found in the work of Nathan Keyfitz, one of a relatively few leading demographers who wrote specifically on scientific methodology (as opposed to technique) (Keyfitz 1971, 1975). In answer to the title question 'How do we know the facts of demography?' Keyfitz comments 'Many readers will be surprised to learn that in a science thought of as empirical, often criticized for its lack of theory, the most important relations cannot be established by direct observation, which tends to provide enigmatic and inconsistent reports' (Keyfitz 1975, p. 267). Citing E.O. Wilson, he speaks of 'the resistance of data to generalization' (p. 286).

To illustrate his point, he first looks at the issues of the interrelations among growth and proportion of elderly, and of the relative impact of fertility and mortality on age structure, both of which are best answered using population models. In another section, entitled 'No model, no understanding,' he notes that statistical observations of differential incidence of breast cancer remain largely unexplained, and comments 'Here is just one more question that is unlikely to be solved by any volume of statistics by themselves' (p. 276).

He then considers the issues of the effect of marriage delay on completed fertility, of promotion in organizations, and the relationships between development and population growth – all questions involving behavioral models, on which there is less consensus than on the stable model.

The important point is that Keyfitz attributes our accepted answers to these issues to work with theory or models. In addition, he does not make a sharp distinction between formal models (e.g., the stable model) and behavioral models (e.g., transition theory). The logical procedures involved in the statement and use of the two sorts of models are seen to be much the same. In a final section entitled 'The psychology of research,' he comments:

> The model is much more than a mnemonic device, however; it is a machine with causal linkages. Insofar as it reflects the real world, it suggests how levers can be moved to alter direction in accord with policy requirements. The question is always how closely this constructed machine resembles the one operated by nature. As the investigator concentrates on its degree of realism, he more and more persuades himself that his model is a theory of how the world operates' [p. 285].[5]

Keyfitz's thought and language anticipates that of leading proponents of the semantic or model-based school of the philosophy of science, such as Giere and Cartwright.

---

[5]Note the equation of model and theory in the closing sentence.

2.4   A Model-Based View of Science

The logical empiricist view of science has dominated social science, including demography, in the latter half of the twentieth century. By this view, theory – a summary of what is known in a field – is made up of statements derived by further generalization and abstraction from universal empirical generalizations or laws. Explanation, in this perspective, consists of subsuming some fact under a broader general proposition, which in turn is subsumed under a still broader generalization, and so forth – the so-called 'covering law'approach to explanation. Laws are subject to empirical test, to be 'proven,' or, in keeping with the widespread Popperian view, to survive efforts at falsification.

Not all social scientists have adhered to the dominant view, as Keyfitz's essays attest. As a discipline, economics has departed from literal logical empiricism at least to a degree sufficient to allow and encourage abstract analytic theory and models, even if they seemed to some 'unrealistic.' Milton Friedman's essay on 'The Methodology of Positive Economics' (Friedman 1953) is representative. Theories and models are viewed as analytic tools that may or may not be useful for analyzing specific empirical phenomena, with their usefulness judged by their ability to yield understanding, and to predict phenomena not previously observed. Friedman acknowledges the formal or logical character of models, but still speaks of 'falsifying' or 'validating' them in terms of their ability to predict with regard to whole classes of empirical phenomena. The notion of the search for universal laws, so characteristic of logical empiricism, lurks just below the surface of the essay.

Many sociological theorists have attacked logical empiricism, but the attack often has been aimed at positivism or empiricism as such, especially in its quantitative forms, not just at the approach advocated by Nagel and Hempel. The resulting schism between theory and empirical research in sociology remains strong.

A frontal attack on logical empiricism that rejects neither empiricism nor formalization is to be found in an extraordinary but neglected work by the political scientist Eugene Meehan, *Explanation in Social Science: A System Paradigm* (Meehan 1968). Meehan argues that the search for universal empirical generalizations is largely doomed to failure in social science, since such generalizations are, and are likely to remain, few and far between. He proposes instead explanation by 'systems' (contemporary terminology would call them 'models' or 'theory'), formal structures which entail or logically imply the phenomena to be explained. The systems are true only in the sense of being logically coherent. The relevant empirical question is not whether they are empirically true or false, but whether, when 'loaded' with specific empirical information, they sufficiently resemble some portion of the real world (in his words, whether the system is sufficiently 'isomorphic' with reality) to enable the analyst to accomplish his or her purpose.[6] The

---

[6]In mathematics, the word isomorphism refers to a one-to-one correspondence between two systems. In chemistry and biology, the word refers only to some similarity between systems. Meehan clearly has in mind the latter meaning, which admits of degrees of isomorphism.

purpose can be prediction, which enables human beings to adjust to the world, or, even better, explanation, which provides insight into process and mechanisms such that one could at least in principle control the real-world system in question.

Meehan is wary of trying to explain large classes of events for the same reason that he is pessimistic about discovering universal empirical generalizations – classes of social events are often defined independently of attempts at scientific explanation, and typically are not particularly homogeneous.[7] The focus is on specific concrete events, but the key tool is abstract analytical reasoning.

A more recent, but similar, approach to explanation in social science is *Social Mechanisms: An Analytical Approach to Social Theory* (Hedström and Swedberg 1998), a collection of essays calling for a return to so-called 'middle-range theory,' and generally rejecting the logical empiricist emphasis on empirical generalizations.

In their introductory essay, the editors call for 'an analytic approach that systematically seeks to explicate the social mechanisms that generate and explain observed associations between events' (p. 1). They contrast a mechanism approach to science with pure description, with theory as labelling or classification, and with the search for 'laws'. They quote Francis Crick, co-discoverer of the structure of DNA, to the effect that contemporary biologists prefer to think in terms of mechanisms not laws, commenting that 'The reason for this is that the notion of "laws" is generally reserved for physics, which is the only science that can produce explanations based upon powerful and often counterintuitive laws with no significant exceptions' (p. 3).[8] Mertonian middle-range theory, in their view now out of favor, is seen as an appropriate middle ground between pure description and the search for social laws.

The search for mechanisms, or underlying processes, is contrasted with statistical analyses of interrelationships among variables: 'The search for mechanisms means that we are not satisfied with merely establishing systematic covariation between variables or events: a satisfactory explanation requires that we are also able to specify the social "cogs and wheels" that have brought the relationship into existence' (p. 7). This comment is taken to apply, not just to simple regression models, but also to path models and other structural equations models. Another way to put it is that reasoning in terms of mechanisms tries to figure out what is happening in the black box between a measured input I (including multiple inputs, as in a regression model) and a measured output O. A mechanism is a systematic set of statements that provide a plausible account of how I and O are linked to one another (compare Meehan's 'system').

---

[7] Chemical compounds may behave the same everywhere because they are the same everywhere. But demographic categories like *marriage* or *fertility transition* pertain to very heterogeneous classes of events. See Burch and Belanger (1999).

[8] For a different view of the status of laws in physics, however, see Giere (1999) and Cartwright (1983, 1999).

The approach is explicitly contrasted with the covering-law model of explanation advocated by Hempel, Nagel and their followers. In this latter approach, if the covering law is only a statistical association, which is the norm in social science according to Hempel, then 'the specific explanation will offer no more insights than the law itself, and will usually only suggest *that* a relationship is likely to exist, but it will give no clue as to why this is likely to be the case' (p. 8). Finally, there is no attempt to prove that a model is true in the sense of empirically valid:

> The choice between the infinitely many analytical models that can be used for describing and analyzing a given social situation can never be guided by their truth value, because all models by their very nature distort the reality they are intended to describe. The choice must instead be guided by how useful the various analytic models are likely to be for the purposes at hand [Hedström and Swedberg p.15].

Keyfitz, Meehan, and Hedström, and Swedberg gain considerable support from recent work in the philosophy of science by members of the semantic' school. These philosophers challenge the classic logical empiricist view, arguing that it is neither an accurate description of what scientists actually do, nor a good guide to what they should do for their work to be fruitful. In this newer view, scientific laws are seldom, if ever, true representations of reality, but at best idealizations of certain features of an indefinitely complex real world. Nor are they so much discovered in nature as constructed by the human mind. Cartwright (Cartwright 1983, 1999) speaks of *nomological machines:* models created by the scientist generate laws rather than vice-versa (recall Keyfitz's use of the machine analogy).

Giere (1999) notes that most scientific laws are not universal, and that they are in fact not even true: 'Understood as general claims about the world, most purported laws of nature are in fact false. So we need a portrait of science that captures our everyday understanding of success without invoking laws of nature understood as true, universal generalizations' (p. 24). The reason is that any law of nature contains 'only a few physical quantities, whereas nature contains many quantities which often interact one with another, and there are few if any isolated systems. So there cannot be many systems in the real world that exactly satisfy any purported law of nature' (p. 24).[9]

For Giere, the primary representational device in science is not the law but the *model,* of which there are three main types: physical models; visual models; and theoretical models (Giere prefers the term 'model-based view' of science to the older philosophical term 'the semantic view'of science). Models are inherently abstract constructions that attempt to represent only certain features of the real world. They are true only in the sense that definitions are true. The question of whether they are empirically true is irrelevant, since they cannot be. The relevant question is whether they correspond to some part of the real world in (a) some respects (b) to a sufficient degree of accuracy for (c) certain well-defined purposes

---

[9]Giere, with considerable training in physics, draws many of his examples from that field. If his conclusions apply to physics, they would seem to apply with even more force to other scientific disciplines, for example biology or the social and behavioral sciences.

(compare point b to Keyfitz's phrase 'degree of realism' or Meehan's notion of sufficient isopmorphism). Giere gives the example of the model for the earth-moon system, which is adequate to describe and account for the moon's orbit and perhaps for putting a rocket on the moon, but is inadequate to describe the Venus-earth system. The prototype of scientific knowledge is not the empirical law, but a model plus a list of real-world systems to which it applies.

A model explains some real-world phenomenon if (a) the model is appropriate to the real-world system in the three respects noted above, and (b) if the model logically implies the phenomenon, in other words, if the phenomenon follows logically from the model as specified to fit part of the real world. It would never occur to most physical scientists to add the second condition. But in social science, including demography, we are so accustomed to loose inference that its explicit statement is necessary.[10]

Note that in this account of science, all models *are formally* true (assuming, of course, no logical errors or internal contradictions), that is, true in the way that explicit definitions are true. The empirical question then becomes one not of empirical truth or validity, but whether a valid model applies to a specific empirical observation.

Of course, some models are more widely applicable than others, and, other things equal, science will prefer the model with the widest applicability. In demography, for example, the fundamental demographic equation is true by definition, and applicable to every well-defined real population (neglecting error in data). The exponential growth formula is true by definition, and, for calculating the average annual growth rate over a period is also applicable to every real-world population. For describing a population's actual growth trajectory, however, the exponential growth formula applies to some populations, but not others.

A behavioral model such as the theory of demographic transition can be stated in such a way that it is formally true. Its status has been a matter of debate for over 50 years. But it is worth noting, in terms of Giere's criteria of applicability, that it correctly represents many actual cases of mortality/fertility decline, at least in qualitative terms.[11]

In my reading of these various accounts of science, they come close to what has long been the standard approach in the literature on mathematical modelling, and more recently of computer modelling. A model is an abstract construct that may or may not be useful for some well-defined purpose. In science, that purpose often will be explanation or prediction as opposed to practice. And in some schools of

---

[10]As noted above, the notion of explanation as logical inference from a model is central to Meehan's *Explanation in Social Science* (1968). The need for rigorous logic is emphasized by Platt (1964).

[11]An interesting point about transition theory is that there has been a tendency to dismiss it as not fitting all cases or as not providing details of timing, pace, etc. There seems to have been relatively little effort to accept it as a valid model and work towards a more precise specification by defining functional forms for fertility or mortality decline as functions of development, and parameters representing size of time lags, slopes, etc.

computer modelling, the emphasis is on less abstract models, trying to capture more of the complexity of the real world. But the central ideas are the same.

The model-based approach to science described above prefers not to make a sharp distinction between a model and a theory. Some authors distinguish the two on a general/specific axis; but then differences are in degree only not in kind. Giere speaks of 'theoretical models,' and sometimes describes a 'theory' as a collection of such models.

Note that this position has nothing to do with the view that science is totally a social construction. A good model is good precisely because it captures some important aspects of the real world. In Giere's words, there is 'realism without truth.'

2.5   Elements of Science

In thinking about some of the above issues involving the description and evaluation of scientific knowledge, it is useful to think in terms of four distinct but interrelated sets of elements:

1. Reality: the real-world as it exists independently of human knowledge;
2. Theory: coherent sets of ideas about how some portion of reality works;
3. Data: observations and measurements on some real-world system;
4. Models: abstract, but rigorous and specific, representations of reality, based on theory or data or both.[12]

In some sciences, but not in sociology or demography, there is another important element, namely, the controlled laboratory experiment. This is reality in the sense that it exists independently of the human mind, but it often is artificial reality since it does not occur in the natural world without human intervention.

Some further comments on these elements:

The first element implies a belief in the existence of objective reality, an assumption that will be taken for granted and not further discussed here.

The second element implies that it is possible to have theories that are not mere fantasy, but express important insights into the real world, insights that can provide a basis for explanation, prediction, and, sometimes, control. If one believes that such theory is not possible with respect to human behavior, whether because of complexity, free will, ideological bias, or some other reason, then there is no discussion.

---

[12]As noted earlier, the distinction between a theoretical model and a theory is not fundamental; differences are on a general/specific axis. There are, however, big differences between theoretical models and purely mathematical or statistical models.

The word *data* refers to a limited set of measurements on some portion of the real world. Note that virtually all non-trivial data sets involve error and various kinds of abstraction.

The word *model* is troubling in its ambiguity, but the ambiguity reflects actual usage of the word in different contexts.[13] A richer set of terms would help. In the meantime, several distinctions are necessary. The emphasis here is on the distinction between models that represent, usually in more specific form, a set of theoretical ideas about some real-world system, and models that represent a set of data or a structure contained therein – *theoretical models and empirical/statistical models.* But these two categories are not mutually exclusive; there are many hybrid or intermediate types. The distinction between theory and model is appropriate in this context, but as noted earlier, not in all contexts.

There are many modeling exercises in which the data have the upper hand, as it were, with little input from theory. An extreme case is that of *approximating functions,* where a functional form is found that best represents a data set (two or three-dimensional), without any regard to the substantive meaning of the function or its parameters. This typically will be done for purposes of smoothing, interpolation, or extrapolation. The TableCurve software provides a good explanation of this approach to modeling (Jandel Scientific 1996). It contrasts the use of approximating functions with what it terms *parametric functions,* in which the parameters can be given meaning. Parametric functions in turn can be theory based, with the functional form and its parameters mirroring some relevant theory. 'A parametric model with an underlying physical foundation relates dependent variable Y to the independent variable X via a postulated physical relationship between them' (pp. 3–19). Or, in the absence of an underlying theoretical model, the parameters may simply characterize the data set. 'Here features of the data are known to have a direct relationship with the underlying ... factors, but there is no quantitative underlying theoretical model' (pp. 3–19) – the system producing the data is treated as a black box. Parameters may describe such features of the data as maxima and minima, transition points, and slopes.

Multivariate statistical modeling often resembles atheoretical parametric modeling as described above. The parameters have substantive meaning (often as slopes), but the mechanism or underlying process leading from inputs to outputs is not represented by the model. The selection of variables may be based on theoretical considerations, but just as often is based on common sense, availability of data, or previously observed empirical correlations. The statistical model is a representation of the structure, typically linear structure, of a data set. It is an abstract representation of an abstract data set using abstract concepts for measurement. But a statistical model is not purely empirical, fully determined by data. There must be

---

[13]The English language does not help in that there is only one verb form in current use, that is, *to model.* French distinguishes *modeler,* as in the acts of a sculptor, and *modeliser,* as in the fitting of a statistical model. The *Oxford English Dictionary* lists *modelize* as an obsolete English word, but the meanings of it and *model* do not seem to parallel the French distinction. Insofar as theory construction is a creative act of imagination, the French *modeler* seems the more apt word for it.

a priori assumptions about what variables to include and about functional form. Such a model may be best fitting, but only from a very limited set of all possible models. A single-equation multivariate statistical model is not, or at least should not claim to be, a representation of the real-world system on which the data were measured.[14] Structural equations models such as path analysis, introducing such concepts as direct and indirect paths of influence or of mutual causation, are a move toward a more faithful representation of the actual real-world system.

A good example of a theory-based model is provided by Hernes' (1972) study of first marriage. Hernes starts with behavioral assumptions: a cohort has an underlying 'marriageability' or eligibility for marriage; for the individual, this marriageability tends to decline with age; pressures to marry increase as the proportion already married rises, but only up to the point where the scarcity of potential partners begins to take effect. These theoretical ideas are then expressed by means of a mathematical function, an asymmetric logistic, with the asymmetry due to an exponential decline in marriageability with age. Finally, the parameters are estimated from census or survey data on proportions ever-married by age. The parameters are estimated from data, and they take their meaning from a theory. In a sense, the equation models both the theory and the data. This analysis can be contrasted with a blind, mechanical fit of some mathematical function to a given data set on first marriage by age (an approximating function), or with a statistical model of event-history data on first marriage in relation to a set of co-variates, as in a hazards model, based only loosely on theory.

These distinctions are far from definitive. But the central distinction between modeling theoretical ideas and modeling a specific data set is paramount. ModelMaker, systems modeling software, makes a distinction between *empirical models* and *simulation or mechanistic models* (Walker 1997). Empirical models describe variation in 'some observed data for a phenomenon which shows how it varies in relation to other factors' (p. 7). 'Simulation models try to describe a number of sub-processes which can be combined to represent the behavior of a larger more complex system' (p. 9). The description of 'empirical models' – models of data – by Edwards and Hamson (1989) is worth quoting in full:

> An empirical model is one which is derived from and based entirely on data. In such a
> model, relationships between variables are derived by looking at the available data on the
> variables and selecting a mathematical form which is a compromise between accuracy of fit
> and simplicity of mathematics. . . .. The important distinction is that empirical models are *not*
> derived from assumptions concerning the relationships between variables, and they are *not*
> based on physical laws or principles. Quite often, empirical models are used as
> 'submodels,' or parts of a more complicated model. When we have no principles to guide

---

[14]See the important distinction by Abbott (1988) of the *representational* versus the *entailment* interpretations or uses of the general linear model. The entailment use of the general linear model reasons: given a theory about the social world, a certain linear structure should be observed in relevant data. The representational use involves the fallacy, in Abbott's view, of mistaking the linear model for a representation of the real-world system – the fallacy of reification or misplaced concreteness.

us and no obvious assumptions suggest themselves, we may [with justification] turn to data
to find how some of our variables are related [p. 102].

Both previous citations raise the issue of complexity, which cuts across the
theory/data distinction. Hernes uses a relatively simple theory and model to account
for a relatively simple data set, describing a relatively simple observation – proportions first married by age. Hernes does not attempt to model the complete
marriage system, which would have to deal with issues such as endogamy/exog-
amy, spouse selection (by couple or by parents), premarital conception, betrothal,
and post-marital residence – all factors bearing on age at first marriage.

And so, we must keep in mind at least three kinds of modeling: modeling a
limited set of theoretical ideas; modeling a limited set of data; and modeling a
relatively complex portion of the real world, coming closer to providing a replica –
generally known as *large-scale simulation*. The last will of necessity require many
theoretical ideas and much data, if it is to be at all successful, but success, as always,
must be defined in terms of purposes.[15]

2.6 Assessing Scientific Knowledge

The aim of empirical science is to understand some portion of the real world. How
well we do in this regard can be seen in terms of the closeness of fit among theory,
data, various kinds of models, and the real world. Empirical social scientists are
used to thinking in terms of goodness of fit between a statistical model and data. We
are less used to thinking in terms of the other relationships, shown schematically in
Fig. 2.1.[16]

The broken lines and question marks between each pair of elements are inserted
to emphasize that the closeness of one element to another is an open question. The
distance of each of the above links may vary, and no one of them is necessarily or
consistently shorter than another. It is important to include reality in a diagram such
as this, since, insofar as we can know it, reality is the ultimate reference point of all
empirical scientific work. But it often does not appear in schematic diagrams of the
scientific process.

In an older version of positivism, associated with Karl Pearson, theory and
theoretical models drop out of the diagram. The most one can expect is to find
stable correlations among data (Turner 1987). In the newer logical empiricism of
Nagel and Hempel, theory is possible, but it must be based on empirical generalizations arrived at by statistical analysis of data. In either case, it is assumed that
data and empirical models are closest to reality. In the latter case, data and empirical

---

[15]This approach favored in Casti's *Would-be Worlds* (1997), although he is clear that there are
many kinds of modeling, suitable to different purposes.

[16]Note: this diagram is a modified version of that in the original publication.

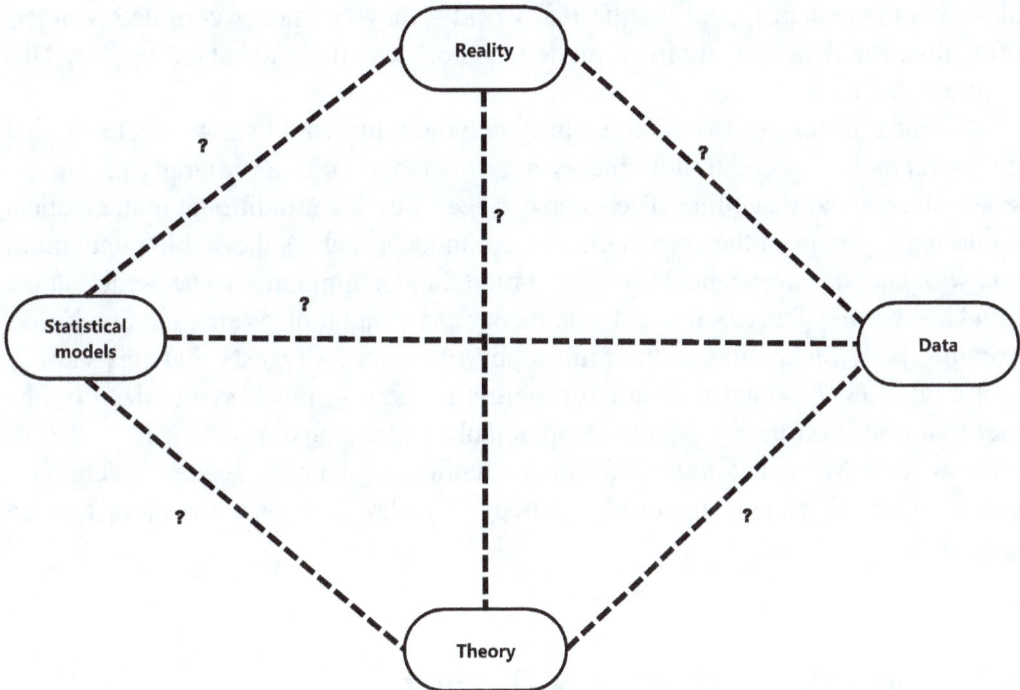

Fig. 2.1 Relations among data (observation), statistical models, theory, and reality *Theory* includes general theory and smaller theoretical models. Broken lines and question marks suggest that, in any concrete instance, the distance between any two elements is an open question; it cannot be specified *a priori*

models are the explicit foundation for theory, and a gatekeeper with respect to theoretical ideas.

But this assumption is gratuitous; it needs to be demonstrated in each case and in general. A good theory or a theoretical model can come closer to reality than data and statistical models. If nothing else, theoretical models can include variables which we know almost certainly are important, but which have not been measured or cannot easily be measured. This point is seldom recognized in the demographic literature. An exception is an eloquent statement by Bracher *et al.* (1993), in their state-of-the-art analysis of Australian divorce, using unusually rich event-history data. They comment in the concluding section:

> However detailed and comprehensive the 'explanatory' factors we have had at our disposal, they are, after all, only dim reflections of the possibly un-measurable factors that keep marriages together or drive them apart; and it would be unfortunate if the apparent sophistication of the measures were to obscure this fact [p. 423].

Theoretical models also can more easily incorporate non-linear functional forms and feedbacks, and deal with process and mechanisms. They can paint a plausible picture of how a real-world system works, in a way that no data-bound statistical model ever can. Whether that picture fits that real-world system closely enough to serve some purpose remains an empirical and practical question. And so, empirical data are necessary to describe selected features of real-world systems and observable phenomena to be explained. And, they may be necessary to help establish how closely a theoretical model fits the real world – they can never completely determine this. But data and empirical models do not close the understanding gap. This requires theory.

A critical history of twentieth century demography would show, I believe, that demography has tended to hold theory at arm's length, only grudgingly giving it a small place in our discipline. The same has been true with traditional mathematical modeling [apart from the core mathematical models such as the stable population] and with later developments in computer modeling or simulation. The demographic mind has viewed data as solid and real, theory and simulation as airy and fanciful. A growing body of opinion in the philosophy of science suggests that this view is faulty, as does the scant theoretical progress in the discipline, symbolized by the fact that transition theory is not in appreciably better shape now that it was 40 or 50 years ago. More, and more informed, attention to theory is needed if demography is to be a science as opposed to a body of techniques, or a branch of applied statistics.

2.7   Coda: On the Dangers of Dichotomies

Demography, along with other social science disciplines, has been plagued by the tendency to think, act, and institutionalize in terms of strict dichotomies: theory vs. empirical research; quantitative vs. qualitative; model vs. theory; scientific law vs. hypothesis; formal vs. behavioral demography, to mention a few of the mere obvious. Different kinds of work and different approaches to science tend to be seen as discrete, polar opposites. Often, they are seen as opposed, in the sense of being hostile to one another.

But some of these dichotomies are false; others get in the way of the harmonious working together of the many parts of the scientific endeavor. The distinction, for example, between quantitative and qualitative overlooks the historical fact that that most quantitative tool of science – differential equations – often deals only with qualitative solutions. In the more contemporary realm of computer simulation also, it is often the qualitative results that are of most importance. The precise quantitative results, after all, are essentially arbitrary.[17] In the burgeoning field of 'qualitative methods,' on the other hand, it is ironic – but a healthy development – to see the relevant software beginning to include utilities for the formation of frequency distributions.

---

[17]In a recent book review, two immunologists have commented that in biology the real contribution of mathematics is not that it introduces quantification, but that it provides '... a precise qualitative framework of reasoning. As biological knowledge becomes ever more complex and detailed, so natural language becomes more inadequate for certain types of biological questions. Mathematics provides an efficient, precise, and rigorous alternative; as the authors note, "mathematics is no more, but no less, than a way of thinking clearly"...' (Bangham and Aquith 2001).

Giere's and Cartwright's model-based views of science, by dethroning the concept of scientific law – in physics of all disciplines, the one considered most lawlike – have underlined the abstract, unreal character of all scientific theory and theoretical models. In a sense, all scientific theory is hypothetical. But the hypothesis is not whether it will eventually be proved true or valid, but whether it fits a particular part of the real world well enough to accomplish a particular human purpose. The application of this thinking to demography appears to me to abolish the sharp distinction between formal and behavioral demography, as traditionally defined. The propositions of a behavioral theory or model must be formally true, true in the sense that definitions are true. Otherwise, the model cannot serve as what Cartwright terms a *nomological machine*; it cannot generate implications or predictions that follow in strict logic from the model assumptions and structure. The idea of necessary relationships in our mathematical models in demography and contingent relationships in our theoretical models needs re-examination.

A final distinction that is breaking down is that between theory and modeling. Older texts on mathematical modeling and on social theory (as always, economics is an exception) have tended to occupy different worlds. Mathematical modeling books seldom have much to say about theory, and vice-versa.[18] The model-based view of science, on the other hand, sees the model as the primary representational device in science, encapsulating its theoretical ideas. The theory/model distinction is blurred. And, given the complexity of many social and demographic systems, the theoretical tool of choice becomes computer modeling or simulation. A particularly promising genre of simulation is agent-based modelling, which promises to link individual demographic behaviors to aggregate patterns, and to explicate the social – as distinct from stochastic – mechanisms underlying demographic dynamics.

This does not mean that empirical, statistical studies will become unimportant. Indeed, their importance may be all the greater, given a larger and stronger set of theoretical tools with which to interpret their findings. Nor does it mean that simpler models are obsolete. For some purposes, a simple model may be the model of choice. The ideal theoretical toolkit will contain a wide array of models – some old, some new; some mathematical, some verbal; some simple, some complex; some based directly on data, some more speculative; some explanatory, some more lawlike and predictive.[19] This inclusive approach to theory and models can only enhance the status of demography as science.

Old words in a language often lead to striking insights. In English, there is an old word, *theoric* (also spelled *theorick*), described as obsolete and archaic by the *Oxford English Dictionary*. Its first meaning is 'theory.' Its third meaning is: 'a

---

[18]An interesting exception is Doucet and Sloep (1992), whose book on mathematical modeling in the life sciences, includes a substantial discussion of the semantic school of philosophy, of which Giere and Cartwright are contemporary representatives.

[19]See Cartwright (1983) on two kinds of theory in physics. Newton's 'law' of universal gravitation describes the attraction of two bodies [ignoring other bodies], but does not give the mechanism underlying the attraction, nor explain the nature of gravitation. But few physicists would suggest it is not good theory.

mechanical device theoretically representing or explaining a natural phenomenon.'
Sixteenth century examples relate to astronomy. To many social scientists, the
separation between theory and a mechanical device is total. In Giere's model-based
view of science, there are three kinds of models: theoretical; visual; and physical,
that is, mechanical devices. Things have come full circle, back approximately to
where they belong.

References

Abbott, A. (1988). Transcending general linear reality. *Sociological Theory, 6*, 169–186.

Bangham, C. R. M., & Aquith, B. (2001). Viral immunology from math. In M. A. Nowak & R. M. May (Eds.), *Review of virus dynamics: Mathematical principles of immunology and virology* (Vol. 291). Oxford University Press, 2000, in *Science* [9 February 2001], p. 992.

Billari, F. C. (2003). In A. Prskawetz (Ed.), *Agent-based computational demography; using simulation to improve our understanding of demographic behaviour*. Heidelberg: Physica-Verlag.

Bracher, M., Santow, G., Morgan, S. P., & Trussell, J. (1993). Marriage dissolution in Australia: Models and explanations. *Population Studies, 47*, 403–425.

Burch, T. K. (2002). Computer modeling of theory: Explanation for the 21st century. In R. Franck (Ed.), *The explanatory power of models: Bridging the gap between empirical and theoretical research in the social sciences*. Dordrecht: Kluwer Academic Press. See also Ch.4 in this volume.

Burch, T. K., & Belanger, D. (1999). L'etude des unions en demographie: des categories aux processus. *Cahiers Quebecois de Démographie, 28*, 23–52.

Cartwright, N. D. (1983). *How the laws of physics lie*. Oxford: Clarendon Press.

Cartwright, N. D. (1999). *The dappled world: A study of the boundaries of science*. New York: Cambridge University Press.

Casti, J. L. (1997). *World-be worlds: How simulation is changing the frontiers of science*. New York: Wiley.

Coale, A. J. (1956). The effects of changes in mortality and fertility on age composition. *The Milbank Memorial Fund Quarterly, 34*, 79–114.

Coale, A. J. (1965). Factors associated with the development of low fertility: An historic summary. *United Nations world population conference, WPCAVP/194*, Belgrade.

Coale, A. J. (1973). The demographic transition. International Union for the Scientific Study of Population. *International Population Conference* (pp. 53–72).

Coale, A. J., & Hoover, E. M. (1958). *Population growth and economic development in low-income countries*. Princeton: Princeton University Press.

Coale, A. J., & Watkins, S. C. (1986). *The decline of fertility in Europe*. Princeton: Princeton University Press.

Courgeau, D. (2004). *Du groupe à L'Individu: Synthèse Multiniveau*. Paris: L'Institut National D'Ètude Démographiques.

Doucet, P., & Sloep, P. B. (1992). *Mathematical modeling in the life sciences*. New York: Ellis Horwood.

Edwards, D., & Hamson, M. (1989). *Guide to mathematical modelling*. Boca Raton: CRC Press.

Feeney, G. (1994). Fertility decline in East Asia. *Science, 266*, 1518–1523.

Friedman, M. (1953). The methodology of positive economics. In *Essays in positive economics* (pp. 3–43). Chicago: University of Chicago Press.

Giere, R. N. (1999). *Science without laws*. Chicago: University of Chicago Press.

Hedström, P., & Swedberg, R. (1998). *Social mechanisms: An analytic approach to social theory.* Cambridge: Cambridge University Press.

Hernes, G. (1972). The process of entry into first marriage. *American Sociological Review, 37,* 173–182.

Hobcraft, J. (2000). *Moving beyond elaborate description: Towards understanding choices about parenthood.* Paper presented at UN Economic Commission for Europe, Fertility and Family Surveys Flagship Conference, Brussels, Belgium.

Jandel Scientific. (1996). *TableCurve 2D: Automated curve fitting and equation discovery.* San Rafael: Jandel Scientific.

Keyfitz, N. (1971). Models. *Demography, 8,* 571–580.

Keyfitz, N. (1975). How do we know the facts of demography? *Population and Development Review, 1,* 267–288.

Lesthaeghe, R., & Vanderhoeft, C. (1997). *Ready, willing and able: A conceptualization of transitions to new behavioral forms.* Vrije Universiteit, IPD Working Paper, Interface Demography, Brussels.

McNicoll, G. (1992). The agenda of population studies: A commentary and complaint. *Population and Development Review, 18,* 399–420.

Meehan, E. J. (1968). *Explanation in social science: A system paradigm.* Homewood: The Dorsey Press.

Platt, J. R. (1964). Strong inference in scientific research. *Science, 146,* 347–353.

Turner, S. P. (1987). Underdetermination and the promise of statistical sociology. *Sociological Theory, 5,* 172–184.

Walker, A. (1997). *Modelmaker: User manual. Version 3.* Oxford: Cherwell Scientific Publishing.

Chapter 3
Computer Modeling of Theory: Explanation for the Twenty-First Century

3.1 Introduction

The words *theory, model, and explanation* are used in different ways by different writers. Complete agreement on their meanings among natural scientists, social scientists, philosophers of science, engineers and others seems unlikely, since meaning depends partly on context and on discipline-specific conventions. Accepted meanings often depend on subject matter, and on the purposes of research. In practice, a theory, model, or explanation – or a good theory, model, or explanation – for a physicist or chemist may differ in some respects from a theory, model, or explanation for a biologist, a meteorologist, or a demographer. These differences may appear all the greater if one looks at the use of models and theories in practical decision making, as in engineering or policy formation.

The question of which view of theory, models, and explanation is the 'correct' view seems less relevant than the question of which view promises to be more fruitful for mainstream social science. In this chapter I argue for the fruitfulness of an approach to theory building, modeling, and explanation which (a) emphasizes the abstract character of all theories and models, indeed of all human knowledge, and (b) judges the value of a model or theory pragmatically, in terms of the purpose for which it is being used. All scientific knowledge involves the abstract representation of concrete, real-world phenomena, and as such involves simplified representation of indefinitely complex realities. All knowledge distorts, since all knowledge simplifies. The crucial question is whether a model or theory, be it simple or complex, is adequate to some well-defined scientific purpose – prediction, explanation, or intervention.

Based on a presentation to the Centre Methodos Symposium on The Explanatory Power of Models in the Social Sciences, 14–17 November, 1998, Louvain-la-Neuve, Belgium; originally published in *The Explanatory Power of Models*, Robert Franck [ed.] Boston: Kluwer Academic Publishers, pp. 245–265.

© The Author(s) 2018

T.K. Burch, *Model-Based Demography*, Demographic Research Monographs,
DOI 10.1007/978-3-319-65433-1_3

An approach to theory, models, and explanation developed from these assumptions will have the following features:

1. Explanation is seen first and foremost as a logical exercise, assuming, of course, some empirically described phenomenon to be explained. Something is explained provisionally when it follows logically from a theory or model.
2. The propositions in a theory or model used in explanation are to be judged initially on their clarity, logical coherence and explanatory power, less on their origins. Propositions need not be, or be derived from, primitive axioms (as in economics). Nor must they be, or be derived from, empirical generalizations or verified empirical laws (as in the covering-law view of explanation). Theoretical propositions can express hunches, prejudices, or guesses, so long as they are clearly formulated and coherent. Models can contain unobserved or even unobservable variables.
3. The empirical question is not whether a given theory or model is 'true' or 'valid'. As suggested above, all theories or models simplify, that is distort and falsify the real world. The empirical issue is whether a logically sound model is close enough to some part of the real world to represent it with sufficient accuracy for some well-defined purpose. This is why the logical exercise mentioned just above (point 1) is only provisional. Given this relativity to purpose, no theory or model can be said to be absolutely better than another, even though scientific consensus at any point may favor one theory or model over others.
4. In social scientific explanation, theories and models may be more rather than less complex. There will be less emphasis on elegance and parsimony (theoretical aims inherited from medieval philosophy, early physics, and pure mathematics) in response to the complexity of social and historical phenomena. Simple models should not be abandoned, any more than classical mechanics has been abandoned in physics. They still are useful for many purposes, including teaching, and can provide well-developed building blocks for more complex models. But many social scientific and policy purposes will require more complex models.
5. Given (a) more complex theories and models and (b) the need for logical rigor in their manipulation (see point 1 above), natural language, logic and, analytic mathematics will be supplemented by computer languages in theoretical work. Apart from preliminary or simplified statements or sketches, theories and models will be stated in the form of computer code, or initially pseudo-code, using systems dynamics software, a programming language like R or C++, or some other suitable computer software.[1] Entailments, predictions, implications of the theories and models will be calculated by the computer, rather than inferred or eyeballed by the investigator.

---

[1]Computer systems for formal logic, with which I am not well acquainted, may be of service, although they have limited ability to deal with quantitative as well as qualitative reasoning. For an interesting sociological example, see Péli *et al.* (1994).

In the further development of these ideas, the words *theory* and *model* are used more or less interchangeably. Both are abstract representations of some part of the real world.

For some authors, a theory is often general, in the dictionary sense of 'involving only the main features rather than the precise details.' A model moves toward specification of details. Market theory says that a rise in price tends to reduce demand and to increase supply. A model of the theory would define the relationships more precisely by characterizing the appropriate curves (e.g., convex upward or downward) or by giving specific mathematical functions. But the difference is one of degree. Model, theory, and theoretical model – all are abstract representations of reality. The phrase *theoretical model* is an apt one, in that it emphasizes this fact.

Explanation, as noted above, involves the logical deduction of some concrete phenomenon or class of phenomena from a theoretical model that has been further specified to apply to particular real-world situation. Relevant historical or cultural context must be added in the form of concrete facts. Parameters in mathematical functions or algorithms must be given specific values. Whether the theoretical model used is appropriate to the phenomenon to be explained is a matter of judgement and of purpose. But the fact that a model is inappropriate to explain one phenomenon does not mean it is inappropriate for all – such a mismatch does not necessarily invalidate or falsify a model.

In a social scientific context, it is important to distinguish theoretical models from empirical or statistical models. The latter focus on the mathematical representation of a set of empirical observations or data, for example, a multiple regression model. Theoretical models represent theoretical ideas, which in turn are meant to represent some real-world system. Many computer simulation models, often confused with statistical models because of their technical and quantitative character, are better seen as theoretical models.[2]

But whatever concepts and terminology one uses, theories, models and explanations crafted using the above approach remain imaginative structures – created by the human mind - and in empirical science they must be related to the real world in some way. The logical empiricist tradition, which has so dominated late twentieth century social science, including demography, would speak of testing the validity or truth of theories and models, seeking to base them on empirical generalizations, and to reject models that fail to agree with the data.

A different approach is found in the writings of a few social scientists, notably in the work of the political scientist Eugene Meehan (1968), and in what has come to

---

[2]In demography, the notion that computer simulation is a way of working out the implications of theoretical ideas has been emphasized by Hammel and Wachter (see, for example, Wachter 1987; Hammel 1990). Note that a theoretical model can also be based on a fairly simple mathematical function, for example the exponential function applied to the growth of biological populations (cf. the use in physics of the parabola to represent the path of a projectile). The phrase *theoretical model* seems to occur more frequently among physical and biological than among social scientists. See for example, the title of Rowe (1994).

be known as the semantic school of the philosophy of science (see, for example, Giere 1999 or Cartwright 1999). Giere questions whether so-called scientific laws are in fact true. Cartwright views them as the product of models – which she describes as 'nomological machines'. Models and theories are not based on laws; they create them. Meehan thinks the search for laws in social science invites failure, since universal empirical generalizations are so rare. All argue, in different language, that the theoretical model (Meehan uses the word *system*) is the primary representational device in science. A good model is, in the words of Giere, 'true in the sense that an explicit definition is true.' Validity is a formal property of a model, relating to its logical clarity and internal consistency. The approach to empirical issues is more pragmatic, focusing on the fit between a theoretical model and some portion of the real world, with the adequacy of the fit judged in terms of the purpose of the analysis.

None of the key ideas in this chapter is novel, although in combination the approach they suggest is not common in day-to-day work in the social sciences. Typically, theoretical work is largely qualitative, discursive, and verbal, and empirical work consists largely of description and statistical modeling, often only loosely linked to theory. There remains a widespread conviction that a theory must rest on valid empirical generalizations, and that theories and models must be tested and verified or falsified.[3]

The equation of explanation with strict logical inference from *explicans* to *explicandum* is common enough in methodological and philosophical writings of those who adhere to an empirical science model of social science, as opposed to those who favor understanding or intuition. But it is encountered more in statements of methodological principle than in everyday work, where the logic often is informal, if not casual (see Platt 1964).

The notion that the origin of theoretical ideas or hypotheses is not so important so long as they are eventually compared to some part of the real world is classic Popper. A particularly forceful development of this view, as well as the equation of explanation with formal inference, is found in an early work of Meehan, *Explanation in Social Science: A System Paradigm* (1968) – a stimulating book that appears to have been neglected[4] – arguing against the covering law model of explanation. I refer to Meehan often because his ideas seem to me to clarify so many of the issues posed in the present volume, from the standpoint of a working social scientist. As

---

[3]In economics, the use of abstract models to analyse and explain is commonplace, but models and theories have tended to be restricted to those derived from a small set of axioms, and are often assumed to be both true and universally applicable. Empirical research serves a largely supportive role of the central ideas, although specific hypotheses are tested in the classic sense.

[4]I do not recall ever having come across reference to Meehan in works in sociology or social or economic demography. Nor does a perusal of indexes in several economics and sociology texts on methodology encounter his name. It would be unusual, of course, for someone in these disciplines to turn to a political scientist for methodological guidance. Like most distinctive human groups, social science disciplines are class-conscious and sometimes a bit snobbish.

noted above, more developed statements of these ideas are found in recent works by philosophers of science such as Giere (1999) and Cartwright (1999).

The move towards complexity in models and theories is well under way in many scientific fields. With the 'discovery' of chaos, it has become fashionable, but that does not mean it is mistaken. The quote that opens this chapter is representative of a changing, somewhat qualified outlook on simplicity as a scientific virtue (see also Waldrop 1992).

The idea of computer simulation or modeling of theoretical ideas is now commonplace in the physical and biological sciences, and would need no special attention were it not for the fact that it is still looked on with some suspicion in many social science circles.

The systems dynamics approach to modeling has a special history in social science, and has been roundly criticized, especially in connection with *The Limits to Growth* study (Meadows *et al.* 1972). My suggestion that we make more use of the software emerging from this tradition does not imply that we must accept all the ideas of 'general systems theory,' or that we should imitate some of the early misuse of the software. I view the software simply as a practical tool for the more rigorous statement and manipulation of theoretical ideas, a tool that goes beyond logic or analytic mathematics in power and flexibility. In any case, it is a tool that is accessible to the average demographer, who does not now have, and is unlikely to have in the future, the mathematical abilities of the average physical scientist or engineer, especially the ability to work with complex systems of non-linear equations.[5]

3.2   Explanation as Logical Inference

The influence of multivariate statistical methods has been so powerful in empirical social science that for many the word *explanation* tends to be equated with the phrase *accounting for variance*. X helps explain Y if it has a large and significant regression coefficient; a good explanation has a large R^2. This is a valid use of the word, but in many respects an impoverished one (see Abbott 1988; Lieberson 1985). Such an approach limits explanation to variables that are not only measurable but have actually been measured, if only indirectly (e.g., latent variables models). It tends to discourage, or at least often does not require, deep thought about process or mechanisms. It easily leads to atheoretical analysis; or at best theory is pared down to fit statistical models, in what might be called Procrustean empirical modeling.

---

[5]My thinking on these matters has been heavily influenced by Hanneman's *Computer-Assisted Theory Building: Modeling Dynamic Social Systems* (1988). For a comprehensive and mature treatment on the use of the systems dynamics approach, see Sterman (2000).

The idea of explanation as inference of the *explicandum* from a set of premises is common enough among some social scientists of a theoretical bent, such as mathematical economists, exchange theorists (see Homans 1967), and those who subscribe to logical empiricism and the 'covering law model of explanation.'

A particularly striking development of the idea is to be found in the work of Meehan noted above (Meehan 1968; see also Meehan 1981). Meehan dismisses the covering law approach to explanation (he cites Braithwaite, Hempel, and Nagel) and offers as an alternative what he terms the 'system paradigm of explanation'. Proposed at a time when computers and computer simulation were still in their infancy, his approach provides a convincing methodological foundation for computer modeling as a powerful tool for the statement and manipulation of behavioral theory.

Meehan characterizes the covering law or deductive paradigm of explanation as follows:

> An event is explained when it can be related to an established 'empirical generalization' or 'general law' according to the canons of formal logic; generalizations in turn are explained when they can be deduced from sets of 'higher' generalizations or theories. The structure is held together by the rules of formal logical inference. The elements of the structure, the empirical generalizations or laws, must be available before explanation is possible. If the relation is to be deductive, generalizations must take the form 'all A is B', or in some few cases 'n percent of A is B'. Other forms of generalization are not amenable to deductive inference. The generalizations, in other words, are established independently of the explanation; they are subject to 'empirical verification' or test (1968, p. 9). Meehan's characterization of the covering-law approach to explanation agrees with that of Miller (1987) who comments: 'Covering laws in the deductive nomological pattern must be, not just general, but empirical, subject to disconfirmation by observational data' (p. 19).

Meehan's criticism of the deductive approach is twofold: (a) '. . . the paradigm collapses or merges the logical and the empirical aspects of explanation. . .' (the classic problem of induction); and (b) '. . .the definition attaches no weight to the purposes for which explanations are sought or to the manner in which they are used' (1968, p. 10).

In practice, Meehan finds adherence to the deductive paradigm of explanation severely restricting for social science, since there are so few empirical laws or 'nomic empirical generalizations' of the sort the paradigm requires, which leads to a pessimistic view of the explanatory capacities of the social sciences. Meehan sees the situation not so much as a reflection of 'the weakness of social science' as of 'the limited usefulness of the deductive paradigm' (1968, p. 3).[6]

Simply stated, Meehan's notion of explanation of an observation or event involves: (a) creation of a logical structure of variables and their relationships, a structure which logically implies or entails the event; (b) demonstration that there is correspondence or 'isomorphism' between the logical structure and the real-world context in which the event is embedded.

---

[6]Meehan claims that the 'deductive paradigm' of explanation is in fact not actually used in the physical sciences, but has largely been made up by logicians. See 1968, pp.3–4.

In its emphasis on a 'formal logical structure', Meehan's approach bears some resemblance to traditional mathematical modeling, the axiomatic structure of modern economics, and the covering law model of explanation.[7] The difference lies in the origin and character of the propositions in the formal structure, to be discussed below.

The following summary statement by Meehan captures the spirit and essence of his approach:

> The instrument that makes explanation possible is here called a system. It is defined as a formal logical structure, an abstract calculus that is totally unrelated to anything in the empirical world. The system, as a system, says nothing whatever about empirical events; it generates expectations within its own boundaries (p. 48).

Expectations are generated through strict logical inference:

> Since the instrument used for explanation of empirical events must contain timeless or general propositions, and since it must generate expectations that can be warranted or justified, there is really no choice of instruments involved. Of all the structures that [one] can create, only a formal calculus can create warranted expectations. Given the axioms of a formal logical structure, certain conclusions are inescapable; if the axioms are accepted, the conclusions can be denied only by self-contradiction [. . .]. Barring errors in calculation, the entailments of a logical system are necessarily and indefeasibly true (p. 48).

Explanation is a form of applied mathematics or calculation, using a closed formal system (1968, pp. 62, 125). Meehan's system' is the equivalent of a theoretical model, as defined above.[8] In either case, it remains abstract. The system must be further specified (Meehan speaks of the formal calculus as being 'loaded') in order to apply to and explain a concrete event or class of events.

The notion of a computer template provides a contemporary analogy. A spreadsheet program for making a cohort-component population projection is an abstract algorithm. It must be 'loaded' with data for a particular country before it can be applied to predict or to explain past demographic dynamics. But first and foremost, it must be a logically and mathematically correct template. A similar idea is found in Miller's (1987) distinction between theories and 'event explanations': '. . . a theory is a description of a repertoire of causal mechanisms; a theoretical explanation, an explanation appealing to instances of such a repertoire' (p. 139).

A theoretical explanation that does not logically entail its explicandum, or a theoretical prediction that is not logically implied by its theoretical model, are non-starters. If an explanation is not logical, it is not an explanation. Many, perhaps most, social scientists would agree with this view in principle. But as Platt pointed

---

[7]Given the central place of deductive reasoning in his system paradigm of explanation, it is a bit awkward that his second name for the covering law approach to explanation, which he rejects, is the 'deductive paradigm'. What he is rejecting is the view that assessing the value of a theoretical model is solely a matter of logic, of deduction of hypotheses which are then tested against data.

[8]Meehan systematically avoids use of the word *theory* 'because of the ambiguity of common usage.' But he notes that in his approach, systems perform the same explanatory functions as theories, and comments that 'well-established systems should probably be called 'theories' if the concept is to be used at all.'

out many years ago (1964), in his classic chapter on 'strong inference', it often is neglected in everyday scientific work as researchers 'feel their way to conclusions' or investigate hypotheses 'loosely based on' or 'suggested by' theory. And, as noted above, explanation often is equated with explaining variance.

The origins of Meehan's ideas are somewhat obscure. His 1968 work, quoted above, makes no reference to philosophers of science with which he agrees – only those with which he disagrees. Later work (1981) contain passing reference to early proponents of the 'semantic' school of philosophy of science.

Recent works by philosophers of science, notably Ronald Giere's *Science Without Laws* (1999), share Meehan's abandonment of the logical positivist's search for scientific laws, which is seen as futile, even in the physical sciences. Nancy Cartwright (1983, 1999) writes of 'how the laws of physics lie', and argues that so-called scientific laws are derived from models – what she terms 'nomological machines' – more than from nature. Giere comments that most scientific laws are not universal, and that they are not even true: '. . . understood as general claims about the world, most purported laws of nature are in fact false' (1999, p. 24).

For Giere, the primary representational device in science is not the law but the model, of which there are three types: physical models; visual models; and theoretical models. Models are inherently abstract constructions that attempt to represent certain features of the real world. They are true only in the sense that definitions are true. The question of whether they are empirically true is irrelevant, since they cannot be. The world is too complex. The relevant question is whether they correspond to some part of the real world a] in some respects, b] to a sufficient degree, and c] for certain well-defined purposes.

Giere gives the example of the standard model for the earth-moon system. This model is adequate to describe and account for the moon's orbit around the earth and for putting a rocket on the moon, but is inadequate to describe the Venus-earth system. The prototype of scientific knowledge is not the empirical law, but a model plus a list of real-world systems to which it applies.

A model explains some real-world phenomenon if: (a) the model is appropriate to the real-world system in the three respects noted above; and (b) if the model logically implies the phenomenon, in other words, in the phenomenon follows logically from the model as specified to fit part of the real world. It would never occur to most physical scientists to add the second condition. But in social science, including demography, we are so accustomed to loose inference that its explicit statement is necessary.

With respect to evaluating a model's fit to a real-world system, Giere dismisses the notion of strict logical inference from data, as in Popperian falsification: '. . . the relative evaluation of rival paradigms is not something that can be reduced to any sort of logic. It is fundamentally a matter of choice by scientists acting as individuals within a scientific community' (1999, p. 119). And, 'Coming to hold that one model fits better than others is not a matter of pure reasoning or logical inference. Rather it is a matter of making a *decision*' (p. 7, emphasis in original).

But note that the prior evaluation – whether there is a logical connection between theory or model and an explicandum – *is* a matter of logic and inference. Logic cannot evaluate the empirical adequacy of several logically cogent theories or models. But it can dismiss a model that is not logically cogent, that is, that does not imply or entail the explicandum, what might be called 'logical falsification'.

3.3   The Origins of Theoretical Ideas Are Irrelevant

One of the best definitions of *theory* that I have encountered was in a small English dictionary in the library of The Netherlands Institute for Advanced Study in Wassenaar:

> Conceptions, propositions or formula [as relating to the nature, action, cause origin of a phenomenon or group of phenomena] formed by speculation or deduction or by abstraction and generalization from facts [exact reference unknown].

The definition properly does not limit theoretical ideas to one source or origin. Most important, it does not limit them to valid empirical generalizations, as in the covering law approach to explanation. Theoretical propositions arrived at 'by abstraction and generalization from facts' are included, but others sources of theoretical propositions are not excluded. In fact, it doesn't matter where one's ideas come from in science, so long as they are reasonably clear and coherent, relevant to the matter at hand, have explanatory power, and are subject to empirical evaluation.

This is a central theme in the work of Popper, who emphasizes the imaginative and creative character of theorizing and hypothesis formation, counterbalanced by a strict program of attempts at falsification. 'Bold ideas, unjustified anticipations, and speculative thought, are our only means for interpreting nature.... And we must hazard them to win our prize' (1959, p. 280).

This is also a central theme in the work of Meehan, as described earlier. If explanation in social science must rely on empirically valid generalizations ('covering laws'), its scope will be severely restricted at the outset and the explanatory enterprise will barely leave the ground. In his system paradigm of explanation, 'timeless or general propositions are assumed to belong to the logical rather than the empirical world' (1968, p. 32).

If an explanation does not require valid empirical generalizations as premises (along with relevant factual premises), it of course cannot contain statements which are clearly false. But one should be careful not to throw out the baby with the bath water. In demography, for example, the documentation of several instances (both nations and provinces) in which secular decline in aggregate fertility was *not* preceded by substantial mortality decline (Coale 1973) is commonly taken to invalidate classic 'transition theory' or any other explanatory theory to the extent that they assume such a time sequence is universal, or that mortality decline is a necessary condition for fertility decline. But the generalization applies to most historical cases in Europe and to virtually all recent non-European cases. And it should find a place in theories or explanatory models pertaining to the cases to which it applies (Giere's model plus the list of real-world systems to which it applies). It is too powerful a finding to discard because of exceptions.

This probably is the motivation behind past efforts to introduce probabilistic generalizations into covering law explanations. This is a difficult technical issue. But suffice it to say that the kind of strict logical inference that Meehan favors becomes more difficult with probabilistic statements. If A and B are positively but less than perfectly correlated and B and C are positively but less than perfectly correlated, it does not necessarily follow that A and C are positively correlated. Or if A causes B with moderately high probability, and B causes C with moderately high probability, the occurrence of A will lead to the occurrence of C with much lower probability – that is, there is a good chance that C won't happen at all.[9]

It is not clear how to reconcile the notion of explanation as strict logical inference with the introduction of non-universal, probabilistic premises, since explaining that something had a high probability of happening is not quite the same as explaining that it happened. One approach might be to keep theoretical models deterministic and therefore subject to strict logical inference, but to introduce stochastic elements into specific explanations. Meehan finesses the problem by urging resort to *ceteris paribus* assumptions, as does the more recent work by Cartwright (1999). Perhaps something deeper is at work, namely a backing off from the explanatory and predictive standards of 'celestial mechanics', which, when all is said and done, may not be quite suited to biological and human systems (Ekeland 1988).

3.4 Towards More Complexity

The influence of a traditional view of classical physics on our notions of good science is nowhere more evident than in the commonplace that theory should strive for elegance and simplicity. The physicist Steven Weinberg has written (1980): 'Our job in physics is to see things simply, to understand a great many complicated phenomena in a unified way, in terms of a few simple principles'. A hundred years earlier, J. Willard Gibbs had written: 'One of the principal objects of theoretical research in any department of knowledge is to find the point of view from which the subject appears in its greatest simplicity' (quoted in Tanford 1978). The idea has philosophical and theological origins with William of Ockham – after all, God is the one explanation for everything. It pervades physics from Newton right up to the present.

In social science, the self-conscious quest for elegant models is most pronounced in mainstream economics, based as it is on three basic axioms. A classic methodological reference is to Milton Friedman (1953), who not only favors explanation

---

[9]For an interesting probabilistic formalization of Coale's ideas on the 'necessary preconditions' of marital fertility decline, see Lesthaeghe and Vanderhoeft (1997).

with as few axioms as possible, but with human behavioral axioms that are counter-intuitive. That the quest for parsimonious explanation continues to influence thought is to be seen in a paper on fertility theory (Friedman *et al.* 1994). The authors argue that their theory of fertility is better than the standard microeconomic theory because it is based on only two axioms rather than three.

In sociology, Jasso (1988) holds to the reasonable view that other things equal, a theory that can explain many things with relatively few assumptions is better than one that requires more assumptions to explain the same things. There is a certain common sense to this way of thinking – why use a shotgun to kill a fly? But a reasonable notion of efficiency in explanation may become an obsession, with as much emphasis on simplicity as on explanation. Moreover, what will work in one field of study may not work in another. Only time will tell, but it may well be that biological and human systems are indeed more complicated than those studied by physicists and chemists. It already is clear that many natural systems are more complicated than those designed by engineers. Even within a discipline, demography, for example, some systems and models will be more complex than others. The exponential function applied to population growth is a relatively simple model. A model of the social, cultural, and economic changes involved in demographic transition (in turn involving mortality, fertility, marriage, and migration) will be appreciably more complex, except at the most general, almost tautological level, as will an individual-level model of demographic decision making.[10]

So, if the reality is more complex, then our theories and explanations also must be more complex, at least for some purposes This is the force of the quote from Rowe at the beginning of this paper. It is the theme of Wunsch's paper (1995) 'God gave the easy problems to the physicists'.

There seems little doubt that the sciences of the future will work with theories and models of greater complexity, and indeed this already is happening. The ultimate ideal of theoretical elegance no doubt will remain, based as it is on human aesthetics and common sense notions of efficiency. Simple models will be studied as sources of insight, will serve some explanatory purposes, and will remain the starting point for students. But for many purposes – for explanation, prediction, and practical application – useful theoretical models will be more complicated than we are accustomed to. The greater complexity will arise on several fronts. There will be more variables in models, including theoretically important variables for which empirical data are sparse or non-existent. The functional relationships will often be non-linear. The models will be inherently dynamic, with feedback processes. And there will be stochastic elements.

---

[10]It should be emphasised that the general principles regarding models and theories developed in this chapter are applicable to models of individual behavior as well as to aggregate social or demographic phenomena.

3.5 Manipulating Complex Systems

This greater complexity will strain the analyst's ability to derive logical implications of model assumptions using ordinary language and logic. Similarly, model manipulation will often exceed the capacity of analytic mathematics. The obvious tool for the manipulation of such complex models is numerical simulation by computer. In an introduction to an issue of *Science* on computers and fluid dynamics, the authors comment:

> Efforts to understand the formation of stars, the motions of ocean and atmosphere that control our weather, and other fundamental processes on Earth and in space face a double challenge. Data on these phenomena are often sparse, and they are governed by complex fluid motions. Thus they are tailor-made for study with a computer. (Hanson and Appenzeller 1995, p. 1353)

Gould and Tobochnik (1996), writing of computer simulation in physics, comment: 'Asking the question "How can I formulate the problem on a computer?" has led to new formulations of physical laws and to the realization that it is both practical and natural to express scientific laws as rules for a computer rather than in terms of differential equations' (p. 4).[11]

I have argued elsewhere (Burch 1997a) that demography – and by implication other fields of social science – faces a similar challenge, and need to pay far more attention to computer modeling, in both research and training, than has been the case up to now. Computer modeling is the only way to work with complex models while preserving logical rigor. The alternatives are rigorous simple reasoning or less than rigorous complex reasoning.

Meehan is cautious about how complex effective explanatory systems can be. His acquaintance with early examples of computer simulation apparently only underlined this caution:

> …logical limits preclude the development of large and cumbersome theories that contain a great many variables. Most of the complex structures that have been produced in the computer era are actually very weak and unreliable, and their internal operations simplistic. Good theories are likely to contain only two or three variables, with an elaborate set of limiting conditions. If the system is characterized by interactions among variables [feedback], those limits must be maintained. Calculi containing four variables with feedback are for all practical purposes impossible to calculate. If that number is increased to five, calculation becomes impossible in principle. This argues strongly against the development of theories containing dozens of interacting variables. (1981, p. 123)[12]

---

[11]The two are not mutually exclusive. Systems dynamics software and standard mathematical programs such as Mathematica, Maple, and Mathcad can solve differential equations numerically rather than analytically.

[12]Meehan quotes W. Ross Ashby's *Introduction to Cybernetics* (1963) to support this assertion. Ashby seems to be speaking of systems in which every variable directly affects every other: 'When there are only two parts joined so that each affects the other, the properties of the feedback give important and useful information about the properties of the whole. But when the parts rise to even as few as four, if every one affects the other three, then 20 circuits can be traced through them' (p. 54). It is uncharacteristic of contemporary systems modeling to posit direct causal links from each variable in the system to every other.

Such a view of early attempts at computer simulation is understandable given the ambitious character of some early models, notably, macroeconomic models of whole economies and 'world models', as in *The Limits to Growth*. With greater experience, we now understand that there are limits to the amount of substantive complexity that can be effectively dealt with even with the most modern computer hardware and software. There are limits to the intelligibility of overly complex models, limits to control over internal processes (we don't really know if the model is behaving the way we intended it too), and even limits to error-free programming.[13]

But computer modeling does allow for the rigorous manipulation of systems considerably more complex than those that can manipulated by means of traditional logic and analytic mathematics. These more complex systems can be dynamic (rather than static or based on equilibrium assumptions); they can contain non-linear relationships; and they can contain feedbacks and stochastic elements. Practical limits on the number variables no doubt exist, but they are much higher than the two or three variables that Meehan speaks of. It seems that modern computer modeling greatly extends the potential power of Meehan's 'system paradigm of explanation' – by expanding our ability to deduce, in strict logic, our explicanda from formal explanatory systems.

3.6   Relating Theoretical Models to the Real World

Meehan's explanatory system is a formal system in the same sense as plane geometry. It consists of well-defined variables and well-defined relationships between or among them (propositions), such that the system can be rigorously manipulated to infer implications or entailments. The variables do not need to relate to observables. The propositions do not need to have been empirically verified. They can themselves be formal; they can result from hunch or intuition; they can, but need not be, inspired by propositions widely accepted as empirical generalizations. The first requirement for an explanation is that the thing to be explained follows logically from the formal system. The second requirement is that the formal system, when 'loaded' or further specified to relate to a given empirical situation, is adequately 'isomorphic' with respect to that situation. It is not enough that the model's predicted outcomes match the explicandum; in some sense the whole model must match the whole empirical situation:

> When a system is applied to an empirical situation it is not enough to show that one particular entailment of the system can be found in the empirical situation. . .. The aim is to match the total explanatory system with an empirical situation so that all of the entailments of the system have empirical counterparts in observation. The goal in explanation is a

---

[13]But many of these problems can be minimized by a continuing effort at model improvement and replication.

perfect match or fit between a complete system and a description rather than a logical fit between a single event and a general proposition, as in the deductive paradigm. (1968, pp. 50–51)

Meehan is firm in his rejection of 'black box' explanations. An explanation must contain an account of the causal mechanism producing the outcome. It is not enough to show than an explanatory system can predict outcomes; Meehan makes a sharp distinction between explanations and forecasts. An explanation must relate to causes, and it must fit empirical reality in a broad sense:

> The nature of the isomorphism required is immutable and unambiguous. The whole structure must fit the observation. It does not suffice to show that some of the implications of the calculus appear in the observation. That result can be produced using false assumptions. But assumptions that are known to be false and to be imperfectly isomorphic to observation cannot be incorporated into theories. They are only useful for producing forecasts or predictions. The point is vital, particularly for criticism of much of the work in economics and econometrics. (1981, pp. 89–90, emphasis in original)

Unlike a prediction, which enables us to anticipate an outcome and adjust to it, explanation, given its clear causal structure, also provides a basis for intervention in a system and control of the outcome, at least in principle.

The meaning of Meehan's concept of isomorphism is not always clear.[14] Certainly no conceptual system or model can completely match a real-world system, with its infinite complexity. Speaking of the laws of nature, Giere notes that laws contain '. . . only a few physical quantities, whereas nature contains many quantities which often interact one with another, and there are few if any isolated systems' (1999, p. 24).[15] At times Meehan seems to be speaking of such a complete match. At other times, the emphasis seems to be on a correspondence between all the logical implications of the system, and specific empirical findings. He is concerned with accepting too readily a model that predicts a few empirical observations correctly, but not all or most.

Giere would view the requirement of 'perfect isomorphism' as too strong, and in any case unrealistic. The degree of fit need only be sufficient to one's purposes, in line with the three requirements noted earlier.

But there is no easy way to demonstrate isomorphism. This problem of how to assess the relationship between complex simulation models and empirical data has plagued the practice of computer modeling from the beginning, and has yet to be adequately resolved. It is one of the chief reasons why mainstream empirical social science has tended to hold simulation at arm's length, as being 'made up' rather than based directly on data, as are statistical models.

---

[14]In retrospect, his use of the word *isomorphism* is unfortunate, given its several highly technical meanings in mathematics. Wolfram Mathworld gives an informal definition that comes close to his idea: 'Informally, an isomorphism is a map that preserves sets and relations among elements.' Still, a phrase like *very close correspondence* or *similar form* (close to the Greek etymology) might have been more suitable.

[15]Clearly, any model of a system will have boundaries. Some variables are included, some excluded from the model. No model can include everything.

Insofar as they are supposed to refer to some part of the real world, computer models or simulations need to be empirically assessed in some way. This seems an obvious point, but it often has been overlooked by proponents of simulation, especially enthusiasts. Just because a computer model is complex and convincing, and produces plausible results, it is not therefore a realistic representation of some part of the world. That it produces results using a computer or produces results that are numerically precise (in table or graph) – even less does this guarantee the suitability of a model, despite a widespread mystique with respect to numbers and computers.

A strong tradition of computer modeling that can claim special relevance to social science problems is the 'systems dynamics' school, originating at MIT in the late 1960s and early 1970s, and associated especially with the names of Jay W. Forrester (author of such works as *Urban Dynamics*, 1969), and of Dennis L. and Donella H. Meadows – famous or infamous, depending on one's view – for *The Limits to Growth*. The systems dynamics school has generated a large literature, both general works and simulations of specific systems, and has helped foster the development of software specifically designed for the modeling of dynamic systems with feedback.[16]

It is characteristic of much of the literature of the system dynamics school that more attention is paid to the building of models than to their relationship to the real world. A basic hardback text from the MIT group (Roberts *et al.* 1983), for example, a work of over 500 pages, contains no chapter on testing, validation, parameter estimation, goodness of fit; indeed, these words don't even appear in the index. This exclusion apparently is deliberate. The authors include 'model evaluation' as one of the phases in the model-building process, and comment:

> ... numerous tests must be performed on the model to evaluate its quality and validity. These tests range from checking for logical consistency, to matching model output against observed data collected over time, to more formal statistical tests of parameters used within the simulation. Although a complete discussion of model evaluation is beyond the scope of the book, some of the important issues involved are presented in the case examples... (p. 9).

The main technique of model evaluation is the demonstration that the model fits one or more empirical time series of outputs. If the model can generate the output reasonably closely then it is considered a good model. Whatever the intent, it is hard for the reader to avoid the impression that testing a model against real world data is less interesting and less important than model building.

An earlier work from the same group (Richardson and Pugh 1981) makes clear that the emphasis on model building rather than model estimation or testing

---

[16]The original language developed by the MIT group is called Dynamo. More recent programs in the same genre include iThink, Powersim, Modelmaker, and Vensim. They all are designed to make it relatively easy to build and run models of complex dynamic systems with feedbacks. Essentially, they provide numerical solutions to difference/differential equations. Typically, graphical interfaces are used to define and specify models. Output is arrayed by time, which encourages dynamic thinking.

goodness of fit reflects a deep-seated attitude towards scientific and policy analysis, one somewhat at odds with traditional statistical methodology: 'The systems dynamics approach to complex problems. . .takes the philosophical position that feedback structures are responsible for the changes we experience over time. The premise is that dynamic behavior is the consequence of *system structure*' (p. 15, emphasis in original). That is, if one has the structure right, the details (e.g., specific parameter values) don't matter so much. And later:

> . . .experience with feedback models will convince the reader that model behavior really is more a consequence of structure than parameter values. One should therefore be more concerned with developing the arts of conceptualization and formulation than finding ultimate parameter selection methods. Our advice for beginners would be to estimate parameters with good statistics [data] but not Statistics [mathematical methods]. In the systems dynamics context the latter are a collection of power tools that just might cut off your intuition [p. 240].

In general, they are skeptical about the value of 'correlational approaches' and standard regression techniques (ordinary and generalized least-squares) when dealing with dynamic models with feedback (pp. 238–39).[17]

Validating a model in this tradition, as noted above, is achieved primarily by comparison of model output of key variables with 'reference behavior modes', essentially actually observed time-series measures of the phenomena of interest. But still the greater emphasis is placed on 'causal understanding' – how does the process really work? Regression equations, with coefficients attached to a set of distinct factors to reflect their relative importance, are viewed as uninformative, at least as a representation of process in an underlying system. In Abbott's (1988) words, they reject a 'representational' approach to linear regression models in favor of an approach that they feel accords better with our intuitions of how a system actually works.[18]

A later example in this tradition (High Performance Systems 1996) criticizes an econometric analysis of milk production, expressed as a function of GNP, interest rates, etc., because the model nowhere mentions cows, and a model of human births (as a function of birth control, education, income, health, religion, etc.) because the model nowhere mentions mothers (pp. 25–28).

Robert Hanneman pioneered in the application of systems dynamics to social and demographic modeling in *Computer-Assisted Theory Building: Modeling*

---

[17]They acknowledge development of more advanced statistical techniques that show '...promise for statistical estimation of parameters in systems dynamics models...,' but in general seem to prefer a 'bottom up' approach to parameter estimation as opposed to attempts to estimate parameters from data on the dependent variable, that is, the variable whose dynamic behavior is being modeled. One might view the increasing use of path analysis, simultaneous equations, and other structural equations modeling approaches as a move on the part of statistical modeling towards the systems dynamics tradition.

[18]I have not yet encountered a discussion in the systems dynamics literature of what Abbott termed the 'entailment approach' to regression, that is, the use of regression analysis to test whether linear relationships predicted by a behavioral theory or model are observed, making no claim that the linear equation 'represents' the system at work.

Dynamics Social Systems (1988). But sociologists and demographers have been slow to follow his lead, to adopt systems dynamics as a standard analytic tool.

More recent work suggests that the systems dynamics approach itself has matured. Sterman's 900-page text, *Business Dynamics: Systems Thinking and Modeling for a Complex World* (2000) is a prime example. He comments on the relevance of econometrics for systems modeling: '…[the] wise use of numerical data and statistical estimation is central to good systems dynamics practice, and more effort should be devoted to the use of these tools in simulation model development and testing. A whole chapter is devoted to this subject – 'Truth and Beauty: Validation and Model Testing' (pp. 845ff.).

Support for the value of the systems dynamics approach is also found in a careful re-examination of *The Limits to Growth* studies, *The Limits to Growth Revisited,* by Ugo Bardi, an Italian chemist (2011). Bardi argues convincingly that much of the criticism was based on misunderstanding of their purpose, to provide 'what-if' scenarios, not literal predictions. Some of the criticism was based on incorrect reading of tables. Seen from a modeling perspective, *The Limits to Growth* and subsequent updates were perfectly sound first attempt to model a very complex, but very important system of interrelationships among population, the economy, technology, and the environment. Greater understanding of these interrelationships and potential problems they may create may be said, without exaggeration, to be crucial to the survival of human society as we know it.

The intellectual history of the systems dynamics tradition remains to be written.[19] Based on an incomplete review of the literature, I would hazard the guess that most proponents are theorists at heart, more interested in ideas about how and why things work the way they do, and less interested in the technical details of measurement, statistical modeling, parameter estimation – the lifeblood of contemporary empirical research.

A central part of the problem is that there is no clearly defined or 'neat' processes for testing the fit of simulation models, processes analogous to goodness of fit measures for statistical models, of tests of significance and magnitude for coefficients attached to particular variables. Part of the difference arises from the fact that computer models may often contain variables for which there are no empirical measures. Another difference is that the computer model often assumes complex, non-linear functional relations between variables, and must postulate some value for key parameters, values which may not be firmly established through empirical research. A consequence is that it is often possible – or even easy – to modify a given model until it agrees with some empirical result, after the fact. That the model can yield predictions in close accord with empirical data is an important fact. But it does not prove that it is an appropriate model (much less the best model) for the data at hand. 'Correct' predictions can result from a model with incorrect assumptions

---

[19]An early and thoroughly negative assessment is by the mathematician Berlinski (1976). The economic and demographic critiques of *The Limits to Growth* are well-known.

and inputs. In any case, there may well be other models which predict the same empirical results as well or better.

My approach to this problem is to view the validation of a complex computer model of the sort I have been discussing as being closer to theory confirmation than to the estimation of statistical models, or the testing of one or a small set of specific hypotheses, as in many contemporary multivariate analyses. The process will be more like that described by Miller in his account of confirmation:

> Confirmation, I will argue, is the fair causal comparison of a hypothesis with its current rivals. A hypothesis is confirmed just in case its approximate truth, and the basic falsehood of its rivals, is entailed in the best causal account of the history of data-gathering and theorizing out of which the data arose. . . .. In arguments for hypotheses, as against textbook expositions of findings, the best scientists sound like honest, intelligent lawyers and like principled, mutually respectful people in engaged in political controversy (p. 155).

The overall process is thus a far cry from a chi-square or t test of a statistical model. The fact that a theoretical model agrees with some empirical data is important. But there also is the question whether the data adequately represent the part of the real world under investigation. In assessing theoretical models, unlike some specific empirical statistical analyses, definitive conclusions and closure are hard to come by. In any case, a theoretical model will always remain provisional, the best available until something better comes along.

But assessing a simulation model and estimating a statistical model are not mutually exclusive endeavors, even if they are different. The tension between the two approaches described above can be and needs to be reconciled, so that computer modeling leads to better empirical research and so that standard statistical methods may be of service in the evaluation of complex computer models. Several approaches can be mentioned.

A complex computer model or simulation can be tested in the classic way using the 'hypothetico-deductive' method. If the model is applied to a particular empirical situation, it predicts that certain empirical outcomes should be observable, perhaps a time series or a linear structure among variables. The failure to observe these outcomes leads to weaker acceptance if not outright rejection of the model as formulated and as applied to a particular case. Here the multivariate model is being used in the entailment sense (Abbott 1988). There is no thought that the statistical model represents the system or its mechanisms. Indeed, this use of statistics to test complex computer models may help avoid the very reification that Abbot is concerned with in the representational use of the general linear model.

An extension of this approach, used by Jacobsen and Bronsen (1995) to test a systems model of deviant behavior, might be called the 'multiple entailment' approach. They compare model predictions of deviant behavior in Israel not just with one or two empirical examples (time series of deviant behavior) but with as many as 15. That model predictions are in close accord with empirical time series in 12 of the cases studied is taken as strong evidence for the plausibility of model of deviant behavior and the more general theory underlying it, at least as applied to Israel. Jacobsen and Bronson do not claim proof, however, expressing a view that would be consistent with those of Giere or of Miller sketched just above.

Note that both the above approaches focus on comparing predicted output with empirical output. More comprehensive approaches to model validation are emerging, approaches that echo Meehan's use of the word 'isomorphism.' They are as concerned with the relation to empirical reality of the inputs and internal workings of the model as they are with the relation to empirical reality of outputs.[20]

Each element of the model is examined separately for its empirical or logical validity. For instance, in a simple model of fertility (see Burch 1997b, combining ideas from Easterlin's 'socioeconomic theory', and from Rosero-Bixby and Casterline's diffusion model), many of the inputs are of empirical data from surveys, and deal with well-defined concepts.[21] Others (e.g., natural fertility) can be estimated based on well-developed procedures in demography. Relationships among variables are often logically true (surviving children equals total children times survival probability), or seem to represent common-sense behavioral assumptions (e.g., that behavior is more apt to result from strong rather than weak motivation, or that behavioral responses to perceived external conditions are often delayed). At the end, only a few of the elements in the model are questionable or arbitrary, notably, the conceptualization and measurement of costs of fertility control. But overall, the model is close to reality at most points, as well as predicting empirical time series closely. Again, it is not proven, but its credibility and its applicability to one or more concrete cases is strengthened by a process of triangulation, or what Miller might refer to as a process of causal, comparative, and historical confirmation.

Hammel and Wachter have validated their SOCSIM model (a microsimulation model of household, family, and kinship) by showing that it can produce current population figures when run from 1900 to the present with the best available data for demographic input (see, for example, Wachter 1997; Wachter et al. 1997). This is similar to the approach taken by climate modelers, who try to predict current climate from long-term historical observations the presumed determinants, a task which has recently proven successful (R.A.K. 1997).

Recent versions of systems modeling computer software incorporate elements of this broader approach, in important steps towards reconciliation of the simulation and statistical approaches. ModelMaker and Vensim, for example, provide procedures for estimating a limited number of parameters in a model, given empirically observed output. Not all parameters in a complex model can be meaningfully estimated in this manner, and the procedure is not as cut and dried as least-squares. But, as in the case of my fertility model described above, when only a few parameters are unknown or in doubt, the procedure can be of great help.

Vensim also has a program feature which it calls 'reality check'. If we know certain things that must be true in the modeled system, we can specify them as

---

[20]Note that this approach is at odds with the view of theory testing expressed by Friedman (1953) in economics or by Jasso (1988) in sociology, in which a theory is to be judged by its predictions not by its assumptions.

[21]See Rosero-Bixby and Casterline (1967) and Easterlin (1975).

conditions and have the computer check whether they hold in model runs. As a simple example, a production model should produce zero widgets if the number of employees falls to zero. Some quantities in a model cannot increase without limit; others cannot drop below zero. If they do so, because of some complex set of interrelations within the model, then something is wrong with the model, and it must be re-worked. The model remains subject to common sense and sound scientific intuition.

The spirit of this approach to the evaluation of theories and models seems to me to accord with Giere's model-based view of science, which he terms *perspectival realism* (1999, pp. 212–15, 240–41).[22] He rejects reliance on the notion of *isomorphism,* interpreted strictly as a complete correspondence between scientific models and real-world systems.[23] He comments:

> ... models need only be similar to particular real-world systems in specified respects and to limited degrees of accuracy. The question for a model is how well it 'fits' various real-world systems one is trying to represent. ... 'fit' is not simply a relationship between a model and the world. It requires a specification of which aspects of the world are important to represent and, for those aspects, how close a fit is desirable (p. 93).

His last remark comes close to Meehan's emphasis on pragmatism in judging models and explanations – that is, judging them in terms of the purposes for which they will be used.

3.7   Concluding Comment

Computer modeling has been developed largely by mathematicians, statisticians, computer scientists, and engineers. It requires numerical inputs and specification of functional relations, and produces seemingly precise numbers and graphs. Not surprisingly, many social scientists associate computer modeling or simulation with quantitative, empirical social science, with 'number crunching.'

Of the many types of models that have been constructed, many justify this association. But, I would argue, the association is not a necessary one. For twenty-first century social science, one of the most fruitful application of computer modeling technologies will be to the statement, manipulation, and evaluation of our more promising complex theoretical models. This application does not represent as sharp a departure from past practice as may appear at first. Computer models of theories can be used to generate empirical predictions (implications, entailments) to

---

[22]Giere elaborates on this concept in *Scientific Perspectivism* (2006), focussing on color vision and scientific instruments.

[23]As noted earlier, some of Meehan's discussions of the concept seem to call for such complete correspondence. But his strong emphasis on judging a model in terms of the purpose for which it is constructed would suggest that isomorphism is a matter of degree, with the fit of a model good enough for some purposes but not others.

assess their applicability to real-world systems. Computer models can be used to explain, even if one takes the narrow covering law view of explanation, but even more powerfully if one takes a broader view of explanation, similar to those of Meehan, Giere or Miller, as sketched earlier.

Computer models can be used to generate precise numerical outputs. But working with them also tends to heighten one's awareness that the precise numbers are largely the result of one's assumptions. This can lead to a greater emphasis on broad qualitative results, an idea that has always characterized that quintessential tool of the hard sciences, differential equations.

The key point is that the computer and associated software has extended much more than our ability to do numerical computations. It has extended our powers of logical inference and reasoning. We can deduce the strict logical consequences or entailments of systems of propositions much more complicated than can be dealt with using logic or analytic mathematics.[24]

These systems will be richer and more realistic than those of modern economics, for example, based on mathematical deduction from a limited number of axioms, some of them behaviorally questionable. They will be more flexible and intuitive than those permitted by the covering law approach to explanation, requiring verified empirical generalizations before one can even begin. Such theoretical systems have always existed in social science, but in the past their statement has often been less than clear, their logical manipulation somewhat less than rigorous, and their empirical assessment problematic.

The newer approach will lay to rest the notion that one must 'let the facts speak for themselves' – an empiricist bias that can be traced to no less a figure than Newton – *Hypotheses non fingo*. It also will break free from an excessive concern with simplicity – a reductionist bias that can be traced to William of Ockham, and has been perpetuated by the dominance of a physics model of science. There will be less concern with where the assumptions in a theoretical system come from – empirical evidence, intuition, even fantasies – so long as they can be and eventually are subjected to rigorous empirical evaluation. If the theoretical systems become complex rather than simple and elegant, so be it, if that is the character of the reality being studied.

In short, the computer will enable twenty-first century social scientists to match the breadth and depths of their insights with expanded powers of logical inference, leading to a true marriage of theory and empirical research.

References

Abbott, A. (1988). Transcending general linear reality. *Sociological Theory, 6,* 169–186.
Ashby, W. R. (1963). *Introduction to cybernetics.* London: Chapman & Hall.
Bardi, U. (2011). *The limits to growth revisited.* New York: Springer.

---

[24]For an interesting illustration of the relative advantages of formal mathematical solutions and computer models, see Timpone and Taber (1998).

Berlinski, D. (1976). *On systems analysis: An essay concerning the limitations of some mathematical methods in the social, political, and biological sciences*. Cambridge, MA: MIT Press.

Burch, T. K. (1997a). Curriculum needs: Perspectives from North America. In D. J. Bogue (Ed.), *Defining a new demography: Curriculum needs for the 1990s and beyond* (pp. 47–56). Chicago: Social Development Center.

Burch, T. K. (1997b). *Fertility decline theories: Towards a synthetic computer model*. Discussion Paper 97–7. Population Studies Centre, University of Western Ontario.

Cartwright, N. D. (1983). *How the laws of physics lie*. Oxford: Clarendon Press.

Cartwright, N. D. (1999). *The dappled world: A study of the boundaries of science*. New York: Cambridge University Press.

Coale, A. J. (1973). The demographic transition. In International Union for the Scientific Study of Population. *International Population Conference, Liège* (pp. 53–72). Liège: IUSSP.

Easterlin, R. A. (1975). An economic framework for fertility analysis. *Studies in Family Planning, 6*, 53–63.

Ekeland, I. (1988). *Mathematics and the unexpected*. Chicago: University of Chicago Press.

Forrester, J. W. (1969). *Urban dynamics*. Cambridge, MA: MIT Press.

Friedman, M. (1953). *Essays in positive economics*. Chicago: University of Chicago Press.

Friedman, D., Hechter, M., & Kanmazawa, S. (1994). A theory of the value of children. *Demography, 31*, 375–402.

Giere, R. N. (1999). *Science without laws*. Chicago: University of Chicago Press.

Giere, R. N. (2006). *Scientific perspectivism*. Chicago: University of Chicago Press.

Gould, H., & Tobochnik, J. (1996). *An introduction to computer simulation methods: Applications to physical systems*. Reading: Addison-Wesley Publishing.

Hammel, E. A. (1990). *Socsim II* (Working Paper No.29). Department of Demography, University of California, Berkeley.

Hanneman, R. A. (1988). *Computer-assisted theory building: Modeling dynamic social systems*. Newbury Park: Sage Publications.

Hanson, B., & Appenzeller, T. (Eds.). (1995). Computers '95: Fluid dynamics. *Special Issue of Science, 269*, 1353.

High Performance Systems. (1996). *Stella: An introduction to systems thinking*. Hanover: High Performance Systems.

Homans, G. C. (1967). *The nature of social science*. New York: Harcourt, Brace, and World.

Jacobsen, C., & Bronson, R. (1995). Computer simulations and empirical testing of sociological theory. *Sociological Methods & Research, 23*, 479–506.

Jasso, G. (1988). Principles of theoretical analysis. Sociological Theory, 6, 1–20.

Lesthaeghe, R., & Vanderhoeft, C. (1997). *Ready, willing and able: A conceptualization of transitions to new behavioral forms* (Working Paper, Interface Demography). Vrije Universiteit Brussel.

Lieberson, S. (1985). *Making it count: The improvement of social research and theory*. Berkeley: University of California Press.

Meadows, D. H., Meadows, D. L., Randers, J., & Behrens, W. W., III. (1972). *The limits to growth*. New York: Universe Books.

Meehan, E. J. (1968). *Explanation in social science: A system paradigm*. Homewood: The Dorsey Press.

Meehan, E. J. (1981). *Reasoned argument in social science: Linking research to policy*. Westport: Greenwood Press.

Miller, R. W. (1987). *Fact and method: Explanation, confirmation and reality in the natural and social sciences*. Princeton: Princeton University Press.

Péli, G., Bruggeman, J., Masuch, M., & Ónualláin, B. (1994). A logical approach to formalizing organizational ecology. *American Sociological Review, 59*, 571–593.

Platt, J. R. (1964). Strong inference in scientific research. *Science, 146*, 347–353.

Popper, K. R. (1959). *The logic of scientific discovery*. London: Hutchinson & Co.

R.A.K. (1997). Model gets it right – Without fudge factors. *Science, 276*, 1041.

Richardson, G. P., & Pugh, A. L. (1981). *Introduction to system dynamics modeling with dynamo*. Cambridge, MA: Productivity Press.

Roberts, N., et al. (1983). *Introduction to computer simulation: The systems dynamics approach*. Reading: Addison-Wesley.

Rosero-Bixby, L., & Casterline, J. B. (1967). Modelling diffusion effects in fertility transition. *Population Studies, 47*, 147–167.

Rowe, G. W. (1994). *Theoretical models in biology: The origin of life, the immune system, and the brain*. Oxford: Oxford University Press.

Sterman, J. D. (2000). *Business dynamics: Systems thinking and modeling for a complex world*. Boston: McGraw-Hill.

Tanford, C. (1978). The hydrophobic effect and the organization of living matter. *Science, 200*, 1012.

Timpone, R. J., & Taber, C. S. (1998). Simulation: Analytic and algorithmic analyses of Condorcet's paradox—Variations on a classical theme. *Social Science Computer Review, 16*, 72–95.

Wachter, K. W. (1987). Microsimulation of household cycles. In J. Bongaarts, T. K. Burch, & K. W. Wachter (Eds.), *Family demography: Methods and their applications* (pp. 215–227). Oxford: Clarendon Press.

Wachter, K. W. (1997). Kinship resources for the elderly. *Philosophical Transactions of the Royal Society of London: Series B, 352*, 1811–1817.

Wachter, K. W., Blackwell, D., & Hammel, E. (1997). Testing the validity of kinship microsimulation. *Journal of Mathematical and Computer Modeling, 26*, 89–104.

Waldrop, M. M. (1992). *Complexity: The emerging science at the edge of order and chaos*. New York: Simon and Schuster.

Weinberg, S. (1980). Conceptual foundations of the unified theory of weak and electromagnetic interactions. *Science, 210*, 1212.

Wunsch, G. (1995). *God has chosen to give the easy problems to the physicists: Or why demographers need theory* (Working Paper No. 179). Institut de Demographie, Universite catholique de Louvain.

Chapter 4
Computer Simulation and Statistical Modeling: Rivals or Complements?

4.1 Introduction

Social science is rife with polarities, defined by the *Oxford English Dictionary* as 'the possession or exhibition of two opposite or contrasted aspects, principles, or tendencies.' There is the fundamental polarity inherent in all empirical science between data and theory—in John Locke's phrase, 'experience and reflection on experience.' There is a polarity between the micro and macro levels of analysis (Courgeau (2004) speaks of 'une opposition macro-micro') with at best partial synthesis of the two.

In some of the social sciences, notably sociology and political science, there are polarities between quantitative and qualitative research, between empirical research and critical analysis, and between value-free and explicitly ideological social science.

Less widely discussed are polarities involving different methodological traditions *within* quantitative social science. These affect many scientific disciplines, including demography. They have led to tension and at times hostility, thereby weakening empirical social science in its central tasks, and in its confrontations with post-modernist critics and old-fashioned radical positivists. Not least of these is the polarity between statistical modeling, viewed as the fitting of models to observational data, and computer modeling or simulation, viewed as an attempt to represent some portion of the real world, or some theory about the real world, in a way that goes beyond observational data. The statistician Adrian Raftery, paraphrasing C.P. Snow, refers to 'two main cultures of quantitative research – statistical modeling and deterministic simulation models...' noting that the proponents of the two approaches seldom interact (Raftery 2004).

Based on a paper presented at the 2005 General Assembly of the International Union for the Scientific Study of Population, Tours, France: Session 131, Epistemology in Demography and Sociology, Daniel Courgeau, Chair.

T.K. Burch, *Model-Based Demography*, Demographic Research Monographs,
DOI 10.1007/978-3-319-65433-1_4

In this chapter, I examine the last-mentioned polarity as it manifests itself in demography and related empirical social sciences. My central argument is that statistical modeling and computer simulation are best viewed as complementary not competing modes of analysis. I attribute much of the tension between the two approaches to a continuing misunderstanding of the interrelations among data, models, theory and reality, and to confusion about the epistemological character of different kinds of demographic analysis (Burch, 2003c and Chap. 2 above). Focus is on the failure to recognize that it is not so much the *form* of an analytic tool, but its *application*, the use to which it is put, that determines the epistemological character of an analysis.

Viewed in this light, much of the tension surrounding simulation and statistical modeling derives from the fact that the two approaches naturally tend toward different uses, simulation toward theoretical analysis, and statistical modeling toward empirical analysis. The polarity is at base the familiar polarity between theory and experiment – or, viewing science as a human institution, between theorists and empiricists – still very much unresolved in contemporary social science, but seen as a natural division of labor in more mature sciences.

To set the stage for the discussion, the next section presents a 2×2 table illustrating the crucial distinction between the form of an analytic tool and its uses or applications. I then consider the dichotomy between models of data and models of the real world (or theories about the real world), and suggest a softening of the earlier dichotomies, with examples of mixed forms of analysis. I conclude with a comment on the abstract, and therefore incomplete, character of all scientific knowledge, whether empirical or theoretical.

4.2   Analytic Tools and Their Disparate Uses

Much of the methodological confusion surrounding the epistemology of theory, models, and data can be clarified by distinguishing an analytic tool and the purpose for which it is being used. A simple two-by-two table can help. Figure 4.1 emphasizes the fact that the *same* mathematical or statistical tool can be used for *different* kinds of scientific analysis, that *different* tools can be used for the *same* purpose, and so on for the other two cells: *same/same* and *different/different*. The table can be used to classify demographic work, with examples readily available for each of the cells, although the distribution is far from even.

Cell a (*same/same*) might be thought of as containing stylized or stereotypical demographic analysis, in which the same analytic apparatus is used over and over for the same purpose. A classic example is the use of the cohort-component projection algorithm for population forecasting. This use has been canonized by governments and other official organizations, such as the United Nations Population Division and The World Bank. In demographic texts, the cohort-component

Tool or technique

	Same	Different
Same	**Same tool, same purpose:** *Example*: **conventional use of cohort-component model for population projection**	**Different tools, same purpose:** *Example*: **exponential, logistic, cohort-component, systems dynamics, etc. models for population projection**
Different	**Same tool, different purposes:** *Example*: **use of cohort-component model for forecasting/projection, prediction, prospective analysis, or computer experiment [Romaniuc, 1990]**	**Different tools, different purposes:** *Example*: **statistical models for data analysis, differential equations for theoretical analysis**

Purpose labels the rows (Same / Different).

Fig. 4.1 Analytic tools and their uses

technique is routinely presented as the standard forecasting method, sometimes the only method.

This has resulted in comparability among population forecasts by governments and other agencies, and insured a kind of correctness in procedure. But it also has discouraged exploration of other possible approaches to population forecasting, the use of *different* tools for the *same* purpose. The identification of population forecasting with cohort-component forecasts is a form of what Oeppen and Wilson (2003) have termed reification in demography - the confusion of an abstract measure or model in demography with the underlying real-world process to which it pertains.[1] The continued use of the same technique, and virtually only that technique, for the same purpose is not inherently fallacious, but it tends to lead to reification by sheer repetition and habit. We tend to develop tunnel vision.

For population forecasting, cell b (*same* purpose/*different* tools) would include, as well as cohort-component projection: the Leslie matrix; the exponential and logistic functions, and their extensions (common in population biology and ecology); systems models for projection (e.g., with feedback from outcomes to inputs).

---

[1]Abstractions in the standard cohort-component projection model include its deterministic and linear character, the absence of feedbacks or interrelations among input variables, and the absence of any but core demographic variables (no environmental, economic or socio-cultural variables).

In the beginnings of modern population forecasting in the early decades of the twentieth century, a variety of methods was explored, before the cohort-component approach became dominant almost to the point of monopoly (de Gans 1999; Burch 2003a and Chap. 10 below). Only recently has the field begun once again to explore alternatives to the standard model, such as the addition of feedbacks, socio-economic and environmental variables, and stochastic inputs (with confidence intervals on outputs).

Another classic example of the use of different tools for the same purpose is the use of both the stable population model and cohort-component projection to clarify the effects of changing mortality, fertility and migration on population age structure. Each approach yielded the same general conclusions (e.g., the centrality of fertility decline in population aging). But each shed distinctive light on various facets of the problem. And some problems were more tractable using one approach rather than the other. Transient dynamics and the role of migration, for example, were easier to study using the projection model.[2]

The stereotypical approach to population forecasting and other demographic analyses - the tendency to identify one tool with one specific use – has also had the result that cell c (*same* tool for *different* purposes) is not as full of examples as might be desirable. The regular presentation and use of the cohort-component projection algorithm for projection, for instance, helped obscure its value for other applications. Romaniuc (1990) has provided the most systematic exposition of this point in his discussion of the standard projection model as 'prediction,' 'simulation,' and 'prospective analysis.' In general, he views the uses of the algorithm as being ranged on a continuum, from the most realistic (prediction) to the least realistic (simulation). Burch (2003b and Chaps. 8 and 9 below) has developed the same line of thought with respect to the life table, arguing that at base it is a theoretical model of cohort survival, with the description of period mortality rates only one of its uses. But current demography texts tend to remain in cell a – the projection algorithm is for forecasting; the life table is for measuring current mortality.

There is nothing novel in the idea that a given analytic tool can be used for several different purposes. Coleman begins his classic work on mathematical sociology (1964) by outlining four major, and different, uses of mathematics in science. The idea is implicit in the adoption of mathematics by so many different disciplines and in the use of some mathematical concepts in so many different substantive contexts. Witness the exponential function, used to study radioactive decay, population growth, interest rates and discounting, and fixing the time of death by body temperature, to mention only a few. In demography, the exponential

---

[2]The habit of thinking in terms of many different tools for the same general purpose is common among demographers when it comes to measurement (cf. the large variety of measures of fertility), but not so common when it comes to other kinds of analysis. The idea of a 'toolbox' of theories and models is central to the model- based view of science among philosophers (see Giere 1999, 1988). It is found in the work of some empirically inclined social scientists See Coleman (1964) on 'sometimes-true theory'; Meehan (1968); Keyfitz (1975). The more influential doctrine of scientific procedure has been logical empiricism, which aims toward discovery of the one true theory.

is usually presented as a 'technique,' even though many of its actual uses are speculative and theoretical in character—doubling times, *reductio ad absurdem* projections (e.g., human population for the next 2000 years at 1.5% per annum).

But some tools are closely wedded to particular kinds of analysis, and this leads to cell d (*different* tools for *different* purposes). Statistical models, for example, are designed for analyzing data, for summarizing and describing data sets, including relationships among variables. But they are not so useful for the statement of theoretical ideas or the representation of real world systems. For this, one needs tools that can deal with unobserved entities or unmeasured variables in a way that goes beyond simply combining them in an error term.

4.3   Modeling Data and Modeling Ideas About the Real World

A key distinction is between models of a set of empirical observations (data) and models of a set of ideas about real-world processes. Wickens (1982) provides a nice statement of the point, noting that 'statistical models describe what the data look like, but not how they came about,' and proceeds to suggest ways for 'interpreting the data through a description of the mechanisms that underlie them' (p. 9; see also Hedström and Swedberg 1998). There is a sense in which data are outcomes of a partly 'black box' whose inner working must be modelled in some other way.

The most common multivariate statistical models such as linear regression and its refinements are often interpreted as though they represent underlying real-world processes. But, as Abbott (1988) has argued convincingly, such an interpretation typically involves the fallacy of reification, the invention of a 'general linear reality,' a social world that is linear and largely atemporal. Abbott distinguishes this 'representational' interpretation of linear models from their more appropriate 'entailment' use: if a theory or hypothesis is sound, then I should find a certain statistical structure in a relevant data set. But now statistical modeling is being used not to state some theoretical idea, but to test it. Traditional statistical analysis is pre-eminently a tool of empirical research.[3]

---

[3]A qualification is needed on this point, based on the recognition of two very different kinds of theory in science. Cartwright's (1983) finds a common distinction in physics between 'phenomenological' and 'fundamental' theory. The former deals with empirical regularities and 'laws' (e.g., Newton's law of falling bodies), without delving very deeply into explanatory mechanisms. Coleman (1964, pp. 34–52) makes a related distinction between 'synthetic' and 'explanatory' theory. Insofar as statistical analysis yields findings of strong empirical regularities, even universal relationships, it can provide the building blocks of a theoretical system. This has been precisely the logical empiricist program for science. But in the human sciences, strong empirical laws are sufficiently rare that some other approach to theory development is required (see Meehan 1968). Theory must ultimately be based on empirical research, but, in the face of culture and history and

The differential equation, by contrast, is pre-eminently the tool of theory. Lotka puts it as follows:

> In the language of the calculus, the differential equations display a certain simplicity of form, and are therefore, in the handling of the theory at least, taken as the starting point, from which the equations relating to the progressive states themselves, as functions of time, are then derived by integration (1956, p. 42).

In a footnote, he adds: 'In experimental observation usually (though not always) the reverse attitude is adopted.' The study of data on the progressive states of a system over time or at a point in time (as is often the case in contemporary social science) is a matter of statistical analysis.

As I have argued elsewhere, the infrequent use of differential equations in demographic research may be due in part to demography's relative lack of interest in theory (Burch 2011, and Chap. 5 below).

Cell d (*different* tools, *different* purposes) has occasioned more than a little confusion regarding the uses of statistics and modelling, including differential/ difference equations models. Much of the confusion stems from a mistaken notion that multivariate statistical analysis can yield essentially theoretical propositions as results. As noted earlier, Abbott (1988) has cogently argued against this idea, typified in his quote from Blalock (1960) that 'These regression equations are the "laws" of science' (p. 275), a statement firmly rooted in logical empiricism. Abbott's review of the differing fortunes of Blalock's *Social Statistics* (featuring multiple regression) and Coleman's *Introduction to Mathematical Sociology* (featuring differential equations) suggests the popularity of Blalock's view. Coleman's work had gone out of print by the time Abbott wrote; Blalock's text was regularly reprinted and published in new editions. The notion that theory essentially moves beyond the data has been resisted by many quantitative social scientists.

A similar confusion is found in some writings of the systems dynamics school of modeling, based on the pioneering work of Jay Forrester at MIT. In several of their works, representatives of this school extol the superiority of systems dynamics modeling over the use of statistical analysis, as if the two served the same scientific function. In one recent manual, multiple regression is held up to ridicule (for an elaboration, see Burch 2002, and Chap. 3 above). But there is little recognition that most of their systems dynamics models were in fact theoretical, in the sense of speculative and untested. Although they contain some data and often try to reproduce some data series as output, they are not fundamentally empirical. They were often criticized by empiricists, who found them fanciful, and by theorists, who found them lacking in firm theoretical grounding. As Hummon (1990) remarks of computer simulation, 'Applications in the past have tended to focus on large, complex systems. Simulation models of complex organizations, cities, the world environmental system, were the standard fare. Of course, coherent theories for these

---

an absence of universal generalizations, it does not simply flow from it through the application of inductive logic. See the contemporary theoretical physicist Roger Newton (1997) on theory as an act of the creative imagination.

phenomena did not exist' (pp. 65–66). He goes on to note that more recent applications of computer modeling to theory construction are more focused, often tied to existing theoretical models.

4.4 Hybrids and Mixed Forms: Revisiting the Dichotomies

The distinction developed in the previous section is important but it is not absolute. One should think of it in terms of the emphasis or even spirit of a particular analysis. Is it mostly about the data, or is it mostly about the theoretical ideas? Some analyses lie at one or the other pole, for example, regression analysis of data with few if any guiding theoretical ideas, or at the opposite extreme, pure theoretical speculation oriented only casually toward empirical observation.

The advance of any science involves an ever closer intermingling of data and theory. Theory must ultimately be evaluated in terms of its ability to explain or predict empirical observations. And data, at least in a scientific context, is meaningful only if it is collected with an eye to theoretical development. Recent developments in statistics, theory and computer modeling have tended to blur the distinction and promote healthy intermingling.

Some statistical models, for example, have moved a little closer to theoretical models. Structural equations models such as path analysis are a case in point. When properly used, they are fit only after one has formulated at least a primitive model of the process at hand. Assumptions must be made about temporal ordering, causal linkage, and direct and indirect effects. A path model begins to unravel the complex process that links outputs to inputs. They are rudimentary mechanistic models. Such models remain largely statistical and empirical, however, insofar as they include only variables that have been measured (at least indirectly, as in factor analysis, latent variables, and similar techniques).

By the same token, computer modeling as theoretical elaboration has begun to incorporate elements of statistical analysis. The development of stochastic population projections is a case in point (see, for example, Raftery *et al.* 1995; Lee 1999; Keilman *et al.* 2000).

These blends can require a re-examination of categories like *stochastic* and *deterministic*. Consider a largely deterministic systems model that has been slightly modified by the addition of random terms to one of the key relationships ($y = (f)x + a$, where a is some sort of random term), and by the inclusion of one or more conditional statements involving such a 'randomized' variable. This could represent a threshold, such that very different outcomes result from the variable being above or below the threshold. An example might be differential equations models of species extinction once the population declines below a certain size. Now it is a case of a random event triggering a qualitatively different response in an otherwise deterministic model. Do we call such a model deterministic or stochastic?

Another example of a movement of computer modeling toward statistics can be found in more recent incarnations of dynamics systems software, characterized earlier as somewhat hostile toward statistical methods. GoldSim, a relatively new product, emphasizes the addition of random terms to model variables (as described just above), and the running of multiple simulations to yield both average values and variance of results. Recent versions of older software such as ModelMaker and Vensim emphasize statistical tests for goodness of fit to the data. More importantly, they include optimization routines to find some parameter values that yield the best fit (with already known parameter values fixed, at least within given ranges). Statistical methods are being used to specify some key elements of a complex model. But many elements, perhaps the majority, remain beyond the ken of empirical observation. One has a theoretical model that is partly estimated statistically.

The emerging field of computational modeling (agent-based or rule-based models) provides many more examples of an intermingling of determinism and chance (in demography, see Billari and Prskawetz 2003). In earlier micro-simulation such as Monte-Carlo models, events occur mainly by chance, according to various probability distributions (but see some early models of family and household formation, in which kinship rules play a central part; see, for example, Wachter, 1987). In agent-based models, chance still operates at many points. But central to most models are strong behavioral rules which are determinative, that is, not subject to chance.

4.5   Concluding Comments

Our conventional views of empirical social science need revision. Demography and mainstream empirical sociology need to develop a more sophisticated approach to theoretical models. We need to reconsider the superordinate position we have granted highly flawed and limited statistical analyses, which have regularly been used to 'disprove' perfectly sound and useful theory. Statistical analysis may be closer to the data, but that does not necessarily mean it is closer to reality (see Chap. 2 above). A carefully crafted theory or model, which can include unmeasured, even unmeasurable variables, may be a better representation of reality for many purposes.

Demographers and other highly quantitative social scientists often think of statistical analysis of data as solid and hard-headed, firmly grounded in reality – in sharp contrast to the verbal speculation of theorists or the 'made-up' numbers of simulators. But the epistemological differences between theory, modeling and statistical analysis are not as great as our conventional thinking would have it. Statistical analysis is not the bedrock it often is taken to be.

Empirical data sets which we subject to statistical analysis are abstract repre-sentations of concrete reality; they are partial, selective, over-simplified depictions of some complex concrete real-world system. The data set does not constitute theory in any meaningful sense, but it often is shaped by the influence of implicit theoretical assumptions as to what data are important. There is no such thing as pure empirical description. There always is selection. Each datum is empirical, and real to the extent of its precision, but the assumption that the overall data set represents an object or system is just that, an assumption.

The standard multivariate statistical models also are highly abstract creations of the human mind. They assume a specific mathematical structure among a limited set of variables, whether that structure exists in the real world or not. If they are thought to represent the world, they are almost certainly grossly over-simplified representations, which is not to say that they may not be useful for some purposes. But an abstraction—say, a linear or log-linear model—added to an abstraction—a data set as described above—does not yield absolute truth about the concrete world. Like theory, they are selective and partial representations. They may be useful for some purposes, but that does not make them true. If such multivariate models are viewed, on the other hand, as 'entailments' of some well-developed theory, then they become analogous to experimental results. They do not of themselves explain anything; they only indicate that an explanatory theory has some plausibility.

These limitations of statistical analysis of data are the basis for the notion of the underdetermination of theory by empirical research (see Turner 1987). A striking statement of the problem is provided by Bracher *et al.* (1993). After a state-of-the-art analysis of unusually rich survey data, they comment: 'However detailed and comprehensive the 'explanatory' factors that we have had at our disposal, they are, after all, only dim reflections of the possibly unmeasurable factors that keep marriages together or drive them apart. . .' (p. 423). It is precisely the role of theory to go beyond such dim reflections.

But, as suggested above, the two kinds of work are not so much diametrically opposed as lying toward the opposite ends of a continuum of human attempts to describe and understand the real world of human behavior. All human knowledge, including empirical statistical analyses, is a human invention, a construct. Like theory or modelling, it is selective, abstract, limited, incomplete, provisional—in short relative, not absolute. There are important differences among different kinds of social scientific knowledge and the processes that generate them. But their fundamental epistemological character is the same. Our scientific convictions often are held as absolutes, as fundamentally true. In fact, scientific knowledge can aspire at best to 'realism without truth' (Giere 1999).

References

Abbott, A. (1988). Transcending general linear reality. *Sociological Theory, 6*, 169–186.

Billari, F. C., & Prskawetz, A. (2003). *Agent-based computational demography using simulation to improve our understanding of demographic behaviour*. Heidelberg: Physica-Verlag.

Blalock, H. M. (1960). *Social Statistics*. New York: McGraw-Hill.

Bracher, M., Santow, G., Morgan, S. P., & Trussell, J. (1993). Marriage dissolution in Australia: Models and explanations. *Population Studies, 47*, 403–426.

Burch, T. K. (2002). Computer modeling of theory: Explanation for the 21st century. In R. Franck (Ed.), *The explanatory power of models: Bridging the gap between empirical and theoretical research in the social sciences* (pp. 245–265). Boston: Kluwer Academic Publishers. See also Ch. 3 in this volume.

Burch, T. K. (2003a). The cohort-component population projection: A strange attractor for demographers. In J. Fleischhacker, H. A. de Gans, & T. K. Burch (Eds.), *Populations, projections and politics* (pp. 39–58). See Ch.10 in this volume.

Burch, T. K. (2003b). *The life table as a theoretical model.* Paper presented at annual meetings of the population Association of America, 1–3 May 2003, Minneapolis, Minnesota. See Ch. 8 in this volume.

Burch, T. K. (2003c). Data, models, theory and reality: The structure of demographic knowledge. In F. C. Billari & A. Prskawetz (Eds.), *Agent-based computational demography* (pp. 19–40). Heidelberg: Physica-Verlag. See Ch. 2 in this volume.

Burch, T. K. (2011). Does demography need differential equations? *Canadian Studies in Population, 38*, 151–164. See Ch. 5 in this volume.

Cartwright, N. (1983). *How the Laws of physics lie.* Oxford: Clarendon Press.

Coleman, J. S. (1964). *Introduction to mathematical sociology.* New York: The Free Press.

Courgeau, D. (2004). *Du Group À L'Individu: Synthèse Multiniveau.* Paris: Èditions de L'Institut National D'Études Démographiques.

De Gans, H. A. (1999). *Population forecasting 1895–1945: The transition to modernity.* Dordrecht: Kluwer Academic Publishers.

Fleischhacker, J., & de Gans, H. A. (2003). In T. K. Burch (Ed.), *Populations, projections and politics: Critical and historical essays on twentieth century population forecasting.* Amsterdam: Rozenberg Publishers.

Giere, R. N. (1988). *Explaining science: A cognitive approach.* Chicago: University of Chicago Press.

Giere, R. N. (1999). *Science without laws.* Chicago: University of Chicago Press.

Hedstrom, P., & Swedberg, R. (1998). *Social mechanisms: An analytic approach to social theory.* Cambridge: Cambridge University Press.

Hummon, N. P. (1990). Computer simulation in sociology. *Journal of Mathematical Sociology, 15*, 65–66.

Keilman, N., Pham, D. Q., & Hetland, A. (2000). Why population forecasts should be probabilistic: Illustrated by the case of Norway. *Demographic Research, 6*, 409–453.

Keyfitz, N. (1975). How do we know the facts of demography? *Population and Development Review, 1*, 267–288.

Lee, R. (1999). Probabilistic approaches to population forecasting. In W. Lutz, J. Vaupel, & D. Ahlburg (Eds.), *Frontiers of population forecasting.* Supplement to volume 24, Population and Development Review (pp. 156–190).

Lotka, A. J. (1956). *Elements of mathematical biology.* New York: Dover Publications. (First published in 1924 under the title Elements of Physical Biology).

Meehan, E. J. (1968). *Explanation in social science: A system paradigm.* Homewood: The Dorsey Press.

Newton, R. (1997). *The truth of science: Physical theories and reality.* Cambridge, MA: Harvard University Press.

Oeppen, J., & Wilson, C. (2003). On reification in demography. In J. Fleischhacker, H. de Gans, & T. K. Burch (Eds.), *Population, projections and politics* (pp. 113–129).

Raftery, A. E. (2004). See relevant section of personal web page at: http://www./stat.washington.edu/raftery/research/dsm.html

Raftery, A. E., Givens, G. H., & Zeh, J. E. (1995). Inference from a deterministic population dynamics model for bowhead whales. *Journal of the American Statistical Association, 90*, 402–416.

Romaniuc, A. (1990). Population projection as prediction, simulation and prospective analysis. *Population Bulletin of the United Nations, 29*, 16–31. See also revised version in Canadian Studies in Population 30[2003] 35–50.

Turner, S. P. (1987). Underdetermination and the promise of statistical sociology. *Sociological Theory, 5*, 172–184.

Wachter, K. W. (1987). Microsimulation and household cycles. In J. Bongaarts & T. K. Burch (Eds.), *Family demography: Models and their applications* (pp. 215–227). Oxford: Clarendon Press.

Wickens, T. D. (1982). *Models for behavior: Stochastic processes in psychology.* San Francisco: W.H. Freeman.

Chapter 5
Does Demography Need Differential Equations?

5.1 Introduction

The predator-prey equation is one of the most famous differential equations of all time. It is central to discussions of population growth in population biology, and appears regularly in application-oriented textbooks on differential equations. It figures prominently in the work of one of the founders of modern demography, A. J. Lotka. Indeed, another name for the model is the Lotka-Volterra equation, after its co-discoverers.[1]

More profoundly, as applied to the humans, it is a reminder that we too are part of nature, as both predator and prey. The model does not apply strictly to humans, since as omnivores we have escaped the fate of species dependent on a single food supply. Nor are we successfully singled out as prey – a preferred food source – for some other species. But the model is embedded in our population dynamics. An argument could be made that our predatory behavior has been both a cause and a result of our long-term sustained population growth. And, there have been occasions when human populations were decimated by micro-organisms, notably the Black Death in the fourteenth century and HIV-AIDS today.

Despite all this, the predator-prey model is seldom discussed in contemporary demographic literature, whether textbooks, compendia, or research papers. What is the explanation for this neglect of such an important theoretical population model? This essay attempts a tentative answer by discussing two related questions:

The first question is: Why has demography made relatively little use of differential equations? I take the fact as evident, but give some specifics in the next

---

Based on a presentation at the Center for Studies in Demography and Ecology, University of Washington, Seattle (20 February 2004), in a seminar series on simulation and modeling organized by Martina Morris; originally published in *Canadian Studies in Population* 38 (2011) 151–164.

[1]Vito Volterra (1860–1940) was an Italian mathematician and physicist known for his contributions to population biology and to the study of integral equations.

© The Author(s) 2018
T.K. Burch, *Model-Based Demography*, Demographic Research Monographs,
DOI 10.1007/978-3-319-65433-1_5

section. The question relates to demography generally, not just to the highly specialized sub-field of mathematical demography, where the use of differential equations is more common, although not as common as one might suppose. The question assumes that differential equations should be and are a basic tool in empirical science, and that demography is or aspires to be an autonomous science, not just a branch of applied statistics. The former assumption will be re-visited later; the latter assumption, I believe, needs no further discussion.

The second question is a more specific version of the first: Why has demography made so little use of modern software – readily available and easy to use – for modeling complex dynamic systems with feedback? I am thinking of systems dynamics software such as Dynamo, Stella, Vensim, and ModelMaker. Designed to provide numerical solutions to systems of differential/difference equations, this software provides an accessible scientific tool for those with limited grounding in mathematics. Again, it seems evident that systems dynamics software is rarely used by demographers.

These questions identify gaps in our discipline, gaps that ought to be filled. The relative absence of the use of standard differential equations strikes me as difficult to remedy, since it relates to a deep and widespread lack of mathematical training of demographers, and a lack of early training is not easily made up later. I am speaking here mainly of North American demography, since the situation in, say, Italy or France is different. And I am speaking mainly of general demography and social demography rather that economic demography, where mathematical theory and simulation are much further developed.

The failure to use systems dynamics software would be relatively easy to remedy, since it is designed to be user-friendly, and requires little in the way of mathematical sophistication. Computer mathematics packages such as Maple, Mathematica, Derive, and Mathcad, which include routines for solving differential equations, can also help in this regard. But they assume a higher level of mathematical competence.

The basic remedy lies in the training of future demographers. Again impressionistically, it seems that training in mathematics and in computer modeling/simulation skills specific to social science do not yet occupy the place they deserve in our demographic curricula, whether undergraduate or graduate. This, in turn, is related to contemporary demography's preoccupation with statistical modeling of census and survey data, and a relative neglect of substantive theoretical models.[2]

---

[2]This problem is neither new nor confined to demography. The British biologist Maynard Smith commented in 1968: 'It is widely assumed – particularly by statisticians – that the only branch of mathematics necessary for a biologist is statistics. I do not share this view. I am concerned with those branches of mathematics – primarily differential equations, recurrence relations and probability theory – which can be used to describe biological processes' (Smith 1968: 1). On the respective roles of theoretical computer models and statistical models in demography, see Burch (2005) and Chap. 4 in this volume.

5.2   Predator-Prey and Other Differential Equations in Demographic Literature

Predator-prey. A JSTOR search of 24 population studies journals on the terms 'predator-prey' and 'Lotka-Volterra' yields less than two dozen citations. In most of these, the term or concept is discussed only in passing. In a few cases, predator-prey equations are used to study the interactions between two human populations (Keyfitz 1965; Hudson 1970). Keyfitz, in a study of marriage and the two-sex problem in population models, begins with a quote from Volterra to the effect that the study of a population in isolation '... is inadequate, no matter how elaborate the model may be, when the population in question is in effective ecological contact with some other population' (Keyfitz 1965: 276). Hudson uses the predator-prey model to study population growth and migration in a two-region (metropolitan/non-metropolitan) system. Interestingly, Hudson is a geographer, not a demographer. The JSTOR search reveals virtually no articles dealing at length with the interactions of humans with non-human species.

The neglect of the predator-prey equation in demography is a special case of a broader neglect of the use of differential equations, as is evident from a quick survey of the literature.

Differential equations in texts. Demography is not particularly rich in textbooks, since publishers are reluctant to deal with a relatively small undergraduate market. Nevertheless, a review of a fair sample of recent and older works turns up few instances of the use of differential equations. This is so of substantive texts, such as John Weeks's popular undergraduate text, but it also is true of more technical works. One searches in vain for differential equations in older works, such as Barclay's *Techniques of Population Analysis*, or Shryock and Siegel's *Methods and Materials of Demography*.

An authoritative recent work by Preston *et al.* (*Demography: Measuring and Modeling Population Processes,* 2001) uses differential equations in only a few places, notably in discussing exponential growth and the force of mortality. Exceptions may be found in specialized works by mathematical demographers, or the journal *Mathematical Population Studies*. But, as noted earlier, this body of work stands somewhat apart from the demographic mainstream – substantive demography, especially social demography – whereas differential equations appear to be central to substantive exposition in many other disciplines.

Differential equations in journal articles. There are only a handful of mainline demographic papers in which differential equations play a central role, or even appear. A notable exception is a paper by Hernes (1972) on marriage. Hernes presents a differential equation of the first marriage curve, based on behavioral assumptions of: (a) some initial level of 'marriageability;' (b) an exponential decline of marriageability with age; (c) pressure to marry based on the proportion in a cohort already married; and (d) limits to marriage due to declining availability of partners. His behavioral reasoning leads to a relatively simple and easily understood differential equation. The behavioral assumptions have become outmoded by subsequent events (notably the rise of extramarital sex, divorce, and cohabitation), but it was a strong beginning. However, the Hernes model was largely ignored by demographers, with only a few exceptions, and the Coale-McNeil model (Coale and McNeil 1972) became canonical.[3] I compared the two in a 1993 paper (Burch 1993. See also Chap. 6), noting that Hernes's model was more elegant, fit cohort data just as well, and had more behavioral content. The Coale-McNeil model, of course, still has the merit of modeling other aspects of the marriage process, such as culturally defined statuses and waiting times.

Another example is a paper by Rosero-Bixby and Casterline (1993) on fertility decline in Costa Rica. They develop a differential equation model for the diffusion of family planning use, and its impact on fertility over time. It is a compartment model – with women moving from non-motivated, to motivated but not using family planning, to using family planning – with elements of point-source and interaction diffusion in variants of the basic model. Their paper is cited occasionally, but does not seem to have inspired replication or further development.

More examples could be found, but there are not many. As a rule, empirical/quantitative articles consist of statistical analysis of data, and theoretical articles are not stated in rigorous, formal language; the few that have been are more apt to resort to formal logic than to mathematics and tend to be relatively static.

5.3 Lotka's Patrimony

Many demographers, especially mathematical demographers, would agree that Alfred J. Lotka is one of the founders of modern demography. And although we claim to be his intellectual descendants, it is interesting how little of his scientific patrimony we have accepted – stable population theory, reproduction rates, and, more recently, the demography of kinship, inspired by his pioneering work on the prevalence of orphanhood by age. Much else has been left behind. Lotka, of course, was not just a demographer. His early training was in the physical sciences, primarily chemistry and biology. He became active in demographic circles later, including at early meetings of the International Union for the Scientific Study of Population. His work best known to demographers is entitled *Demographic Analysis, With Special Reference to the Human Species*. This monograph is in fact the second part of a larger work entitled *Analytic Theory of Biological Associations*. The first part, seldom referenced by demographers, is entitled simply *Principles* (see Lotka 1934/1939).[4]

---

[3]It is worth noting that Hernes' paper did not appear in an obscure journal but rather in *The American Sociological Review,* a leading sociological journal.

[4]Bibliographies in authoritative contemporary works such as *Mathematical Demography: Selected Papers* (Wachter and LeBras 2013; Preston *et al.* 2001) include reference to the second part but not the first.

On p. 8 of *Principles* one encounters the differential equation

$$dX_i/dt = F_i[X_1, X_2, \ldots, X_n, P, Q]$$

Lotka introduces it as a general statement of the principle that the rate of increase of any component in a system is a function of the quantity of all other components in the system plus parameters defining the characteristics of each component P, as well as other parameters Q that 'serve to complete the definition of the state of the system' (Lotka 1934: 8).

Later, Lotka begins a chapter entitled 'Biological Stoichiometry' with the following statement, introducing a *system* of differential equations: 'In asserting that at each instant the rate of growth of each species in the system depends on the size of that species and of all the other species present, as well as on parameters *P* and Q, we have already noted that the analytic expression of this very general proposition takes the form...' – a system of *n* differential equations follows (see Fig. 5.1). Shortly after, the system is abbreviated by dropping the parameters P and Q, on the grounds that the characteristics of species and of the environment ('climate, topography, etc.') change little over relatively short periods (Lotka 1934: 32–33).

Here, the human species is firmly embedded in a biological system consisting of many other species. His framework is essentially a systems framework. The scope of the systems he envisions is shown in a complex diagram of the interrelations of fish populations and their food supplies (Lotka 1934: 37, Table 2). Lotka was thinking in terms of systems well before the systems concept became popular 30 or so years later.

Later in the chapter, he presents equations for two species in interaction, the 'predator-prey equations,' and develops an expression for the logistic curve, then thought of as a 'law' of population growth. In every case, the development is in terms of differential equations, sometimes leading to an analytic solution, sometimes not. But the differential equations frame the discussion.

In his earlier work, *Elements of Physical Biology* (1924), some of these ideas are developed in greater detail, including the extension of the two-interacting-species model to three or more,[5] as well as a description of several types of two-species interaction other than as predator-prey. One of his examples relates to humans' relationship to domestic animals such as cattle and poultry, which we breed and nurture to eat.[6]

---

[5]Stella, student-oriented systems dynamics software, provides an interesting game in which the student is challenged to bring three interacting populations (deer, wolves, and grass) into equilibrium. The near impossibility of doing so is a powerful demonstration of the effects of non-linearity in systems. A similar challenge is posed in the agent-based modeling software NetLogo, in one of its tutorials.

[6]A recent collection of classic papers on mathematical demography (Wachter and LeBras 2013) contains no index entry for *predator-prey*, nor do the authoritative texts by Preston *et al.* (2001) and by Wachter (2014). Hanneman's (2005) online text, by contrast, contains a whole section on

Fig. 5.1 Lotka's system of differential equations

$$dX_1/dt = F_1[X_1,X_2, \dots ,X_n , P, Q]$$

$$dX_2/dt = F_2[X_1,X_2,\dots ,X_n , P, Q]$$

$$\dots$$

$$dX_i/dt = F_i[X_1,X_2, \dots ,X_n , P, Q]$$

$$\dots$$

$$dX_n/dt = F_n[X_1,X_2, \dots ,X_n , P, Q]$$

5.4   Lotka the Human Demographer

In the second part of *Analytic Theory...,* Lotka begins:

> Species exist in mutual relationships with one another, such that it is true to say that it
> would be impossible to make a well-rounded study of a species without taking account of
> the large number of other species which influence it in one way or another. (Lotka 1939: 5)
>> He continues:
>> However, there exist among the internal factors of a population of living beings (such as
>> natality, mortality, growth, etc.) a large number of relationships which permit and even
>> demand a special study, without the necessity at each step of taking explicit account of
>> other species occupying the same locale. This study, in fact, constitutes a well-defined body
>> of research and of results, which we take up in the present volume, with particular attention
>> to the human species, for which we possess an abundance of data. (Lotka 1939: 5)

This comes close to a description of demography as we know it.

Lotka divides the study of human populations into two parts. One he terms *demographic analysis,* a branch of mathematics (i.e., analysis) applied to human population dynamics, to discover and state necessary relations among demographic variables. He distinguishes this from a second part of demography, which he calls *statistical demography,* the statistical study of relationships among demographic variables. The two branches seem to be related as theory and empirical research.

5.5   Lotka the Theorist

Lotka assumes the importance of empirical research – he is, after all, a scientist – but clearly thinks it is not enough:

> ... one will find more satisfying to the spirit that knowledge more complete, or at least
> deeper, which one obtains when one has succeeded in taking account of not only the
> empirical relationships, whose physical causes and logical reasons escape us ... but also the
> *necessary* relationships [imposed by the laws of logic and of physics] among the quantities
> describing the state of and the changes in a population. (Lotka 1939: 6)

---

the predator-prey model. This is a reminder that systems dynamics software makes it relatively easy to work with systems of differential equations, even for those who are not mathematicians.

It appears that Lotka was at heart a theorist. And he considers differential equations to be a fundamental tool of theory. In *Elements of Mathematical Biology,* he writes:

> In the language of the calculus, the differential equations display a certain simplicity of form, and are therefore, in the handling of the theory at least, taken as the starting point, from which the equations relating to the progressive states themselves, as functions of the time, are then derived by integration. (Lotka 1956: 42)

He adds in a footnote: 'In experimental observation usually (though not always) the reverse attitude is adopted.' Demography typically uses the integral rather than the original differential equation.

The Hernes model mentioned earlier (see also Chap. 6 below) provides a nice illustration. The differential equation is simple and transparent. Its integral, giving proportion married by age in a cohort, is more complicated and harder to intuit, but more useful for fitting cohort data on proportions married by age.

One wonders whether Lotka contemplated a third part to *Analytic Theory...,* which would have revisited his system of equations, discussed at length in the earlier monograph, to study relationships between human populations and other species. But clearly demography has focused on the more limited study of human population as defined above. In doing so, we have left behind a large part of Lotka's intellectual heritage, including: (a) a strong emphasis on theory as well as empirical, statistical research; (b) regular use of differential equations as a natural tool for the theoretical study of process; and (c) the study of the interrelationship between human and non-human populations.

A student of demography could go far in the field without ever being taught to think of the human species as both predator and prey. We study diseases as causes of death, not as a manifestation of micro-organisms using human bodies as habitat. We study fish as a natural resource, not so much as a population on which we prey, although this is changing with the disappearance of many stocks. Joel Cohen notes in a paper on population projections: 'Other species are recognized explicitly only in the recent innovation of quantifying the devastating impacts of HIV and AIDS' (2003: 1172).

As noted above, Hernes and Rosero-Bixby and Casterline used differential equations to study processes and systems that demographers study regularly – cohort behavior, multi-state systems, and diffusion. Lotka and others (notably biological ecologists) use them to study processes and systems that we have largely ignored.

In other cases, we have studied certain systems, but only in a limited, technical way. The logistic model is a case in point. In ecology and in differential equations texts, it is introduced as a differential equation. In demography, it typically is presented simply as a mathematical curve (the analytic solution of the differential equation), invariably identified as a technique for population projection. As such, it is rejected in favor of the standard cohort-component technique, partly because it deals only with total population, not with the components of growth. In an obvious sense this is partly so, but in another sense it is not. When ecologists (e.g., Wilson and Bossert 1971) discuss the logistic curve, it is derived from assumptions relating to the relationships among population density, fertility, and mortality. In demography, the logistic is simply a population projection tool. In ecology, it is a theoretical model.

What is the explanation for our relative lack of interest in multi-species models? Human ethnocentrism, perhaps? There is a large element of exceptionalism in our view of our place in the natural world. The introduction to *Demographic Analysis and Synthesis: A Treatise in Population* (2005), a four-volume work of nearly 3000 pages, states that the treatment is limited to human demography, partly because the material on those is already so vast, but also

> '...to highlight its singularity. Humans are not just statistical units, simple living beings, or merely social creatures like bees and ants.... In Aristotle's phrase, man is a *political animal*, thinking and influencing his or her own individual and collective destiny, which situates the study of population dynamics clearly in the field of social science *rather than* biology. ' (p. xxvi, emphasis added)

Granted there is room for different emphases in the study of bees and ants versus humans, there is ever-increasing evidence of overlap between biology and the sciences of human behavior. Humans *are* a biological species.

In 'Population dynamics of humans and other animals' (1987), Ronald Lee struck a better balance, arguing that density-dependent phenomena that affect most non-human species also affect humans, although indirectly.[7]

Another possible explanation for a neglect of differential equations is the fact that a large proportion of practicing demographers, especially social demographers, simply do not know the mathematics of differential equations, even the low level of knowledge necessary to understand the predator-prey equations.

Other disciplines, notably biological ecology or population biology, have continued to develop Lotka's insights and equations, including the systematic study of inter-species relationships. Gotelli's introductory text (1998), for example, devotes about 50 out of 200 pages to the topic.

5.6   Abbot on Coleman vs. Blalock

Andrew Abbot, in his stimulating paper 'Transcending general linear reality' (1988) suggests a similar neglect of differential equations as a tool in empirical sociology. He notes the domination of quantitative sociology by multivariate statistical analysis based on the general linear model. In a footnote, he compares citations to Blalock's 1960 text *Social Statistics* (featuring the use of regression) to Coleman's (1964) text *Introduction to Mathematical Sociology* [featuring the use of differential equations]. In the period 1966–1970, there were 162 citations of Blalock vs. 117 of Coleman; by 1980, it was 117 vs. 24, and by 1984, it was

---

[7]No mention is made of the predator-prey equation, but given his central thesis, this was not particularly relevant.

104 vs. 15. He notes that Coleman's work has never been reprinted. He attributes the dominance of regression analysis to its 'commodification' in easy-to-use packages.

Abbot makes the useful distinction between the 'representational' interpretation of regression models ('My model represents the social system') and the 'entailment' interpretation ('If my theory is correct, then I should get certain results in my regression model'). One is largely descriptive of relationships among measured variables; the other is oriented towards testing theory. Abbot considers the representational interpretation a case of reification, the positing of a 'general linear reality' based on a highly abstract empirical model.

Blalock presented regression clearly as a tool of empirical research, although, in keeping with the logical empiricist doctrine of the time, he viewed the resulting empirical generalizations as 'laws,' and therefore as the essential foundation blocks for theory. Coleman tends to see differential equations as a theoretical tool used to 'represent' dynamic systems. Either tool can be used in Abbot's entailment mode.

The impact of 'commodification' is difficult to judge. But it is worth noting that the commodification of differential equations also occurred relative early – Dynamo was developed in the 1960s and became commercially available soon after. In the same year that Abbott wrote, Robert Hanneman published a book urging sociologists to consider Dynamo as a tool for modeling dynamic social systems (Hanneman 1988).[8] And the major mathematical software packages (Mathematica, Maple, Mathcad, Matlab) regularly expanded their utilities for solving differential equations. Why did empirical sociology and demography buy so much of the one commodity and not the other?

Several possible answers to the first question suggest themselves:

1. Differential equations are not necessary or particularly useful for the study of most issues of greatest interest to demographers. Other analytic methods have been more fruitful.
2. The average demographer has little competence in the use of differential equations. That level of mathematics has not been required for entrance into, or successful completion of, most graduate programs.
3. Demography has avoided substantive areas that essentially require the use of differential equations, including non-linear equations.
4. Differential equations are more a theoretical than an empirical tool, and demographers have never given high priority to theory, as opposed to data and techniques.

---

[8]Hanneman has continued the use of systems dynamics software in an online work entitled *Spatial Dynamics of Human Populations: Some Basic Models*, (2005). (http://faculty.ucr.edu/~hanneman/ spatial/index.html). He has switched from the now obsolete Dynamo software to Berkeley Madonna, developed with U.S. government support. An interesting but rare use of a systems dynamics approach by economist-demographers is to be found in the Wonderland project of Sanderson *et al.* See Sanderson (1994).

I would argue that #1 is questionable. Why should a tool that has proven so fruitful in other sciences be of little use to demography? Answer #2 lies at the heart of the problem: Demographers generally were not schooled in differential equations, so we didn't try to use them, and avoided topics that required their use even at the most elementary level (as with predator-prey).

5.7   Systems Dynamics Software

In light of (2) in the previous section, one can ask a second question: Why has demography not taken advantage of systems dynamics software? It enables the 'mathematically challenged' to construct and work with models of complex systems with feedbacks, in effect, systems of differential equations. And it necessarily orients thinking towards dynamics and process, not just cross-sectional recursive relationships.

The invention of systems dynamics software is generally attributed to an engineer, Jay Forrester, who applied engineering principles of feedback and control to social systems. His first work, *Industrial Dynamics*, was published in 1961. *World Dynamics* appeared in 1971 and became the basis for the influential and controversial book *The Limits to Growth* by Meadows *et al.* (1972). The MIT systems dynamics school has generated a large literature, both general works and simulations of particular systems, and has stimulated the development of other software packages with similar structure and aims.[9]

It is characteristic of much of the literature of the MIT group that more attention is paid to the building of models than to their relationship to the real world. A basic hardback text from the MIT group (Roberts *et al.* 1983), for example – a work of over 500 pages – contains no chapter on testing, validation, parameter estimation, or goodness of fit; indeed, these words don't even appear in the index. This exclusion apparently is deliberate. The authors include 'model evaluation' as one of the phases in the model-building process, and comment:

> [N]umerous tests must be performed on the model to evaluate its quality and validity. These tests range from checking for logical consistency to matching model output against observed data collected over time, to more formal statistical tests of parameters used within the simulation. Although a complete discussion of model evaluation is beyond the scope of the book, some of the important issues involved are presented in the case examples. (Roberts *et al.* 1983: 9)

The main technique of model evaluation is the demonstration that the model fits one or more empirical time series of outputs. If the model can generate the output reasonably closely, then it is considered a good model. But it is not 'proven,' of course. To assume so is to commit the fallacy of affirming the antecedent.

---

[9]The Wikipedia article on *systems dynamics software* lists more than 30 versions.

Whatever the intent, it is hard for the reader to avoid the impression that evaluating a model's fit to real world, or at least to data, is less interesting and less important than building the model.

An earlier work from the same group makes clear that the emphasis on model building rather than model estimation or testing goodness of fit reflects a deep-seated attitude towards scientific and policy analysis, one somewhat at odds with traditional statistical methodology:

> The systems dynamics approach to complex problems takes the philosophical position that feedback structures are responsible for the changes we experience over time. *The premise is that dynamic behavior is the consequence of system structure.* (Richardson and Pugh 1981, p. 15)

That is, if one has the structure right, the details (for example, specific parameter values) don't matter so much. And later:

> …experience with feedback models will convince the reader that model behavior really *is* more a consequence of structure than parameter values. One should therefore be more concerned with developing the arts of conceptualization and formulation than finding ultimate parameter selection methods. Our advice for beginners would be to estimate parameters with good statistics (data) but not Statistics (mathematical methods). In the systems dynamics context the latter are a collection of power tools that just might cut off your intuition. (Richardson and Pugh 1981, p. 240)

In general, they are skeptical about the value of correlational approaches and standard regression techniques, especially when dealing with dynamic models with feedback (Richardson and Pugh 1981, pp. 238–239).

Validating a model in this tradition, as noted above, is achieved primarily by comparison of model output of key variables with 'reference behavior modes,' essentially observed time-series measures of the phenomena of interest. But still, the greater emphasis is placed on causal understanding: how does the process really work? Regression equations, with coefficients attached to a set of distinct factors to reflect their relative importance, are viewed as uninformative, at least as a representation of process in an underlying system. In Abbott's terms, they reject a 'representational' approach to linear regression models in favor of an approach that they feel accords better with our intuition of how a system actually works.

A later example in this tradition criticizes an econometric analysis of milk production, expressed as a function of GNP, interest rates, etc., because the model nowhere mentions cows; and a model of human births (as a function of birth control, education, income, health, religion, etc.) because the model nowhere mentions mothers (HPS 1996: 25–8). Much of these early texts seemed almost hostile to statistical research in the social sciences.

Substantive research using the systems dynamics approach was heavily criticized by social scientists and others. A special target was Forrester's 'world model,' the basis for *The Limits to Growth*. The model was so large and complex that some questioned whether it could be meaningful.[10] It went beyond what could be

---

[10]Similar criticisms were made of early macroeconomic models, some of which contained scores of variables and hundreds of equations.

intuited, and was so large that there was high risk of programming errors, functional misspecification, and wrong parameters. Despite the size of the model, as my former colleague Tom Wonnacott constantly reminded me, the resource module contained no variable for price. Although a best-seller, *The Limits to Growth* was dismissed by many economists, demographers, and others.

A recent re-evaluation of *The Limits to Growth* studies (Bardi 2011) suggests that much of the early criticism was misplaced, based on misunderstanding of the purpose of the simulations or, in some cases, outright errors in describing the models or their results. And, he notes that some of central projections of the studies have been borne out by subsequent events.

There is a special reason why demographers might criticize this body of work. Population projections are done in an unconventional way and use unconventional language. The absolute numbers of births and deaths flowing into and out of a population per unit of time are referred to as *rates* (per unit of time) – a perfectly good usage in calculus and common in ecology, but at odds with demographic usage. The relative numbers of births and deaths are referred to as *fractional rates*. And the number of deaths is calculated by dividing population by average lifetime (life expectation at birth from a life table), instead of using the crude death rate (the rough equivalence obtains, of course, only in the stationary population model). Instead of surviving an age group to the next older age group using survival ratios, age-groups remain in place, as it were, with deaths being subtracted, and population 'aging in' from the age group below, and 'aging out' to the age group above. For a 5-year age group, for example, it is assumed that, apart from deaths, one fifth will move to the next-highest age group, with one fifth of the next-lowest age group moving in. The language and procedure strike the average demographer as improper, and suggest a lack of understanding of population dynamics. By convention, they are indeed incorrect, and a student who used this approach on a demographic techniques exam probably would get a failing grade. But in fact, given identical input, the systems dynamics procedure can generate projections by age and sex that do not differ appreciably from those produced by the standard cohort-component projection technique. Both approaches, of course, contain approximations.

The intellectual history of systems dynamics remains to be written. But my impression is that some early excesses and some disciplinary rivalries (Forrester, after all, was an engineer who did not 'convert' to economics or demography) gave a perfectly sound approach and its associated software a bad name. In talking to colleagues about Dynamo, I remember getting a distinct impression that reputationally it was 'lower-class' software. But I think we may have thrown the baby out with the bathwater.

Although still generally ignored by demographers and many other quantitative social scientists, the systems dynamics approach has continued to develop, and is now widely taught and used in other circles. Nearly 50 years of practice have led to greater balance and sophistication, such that many earlier critiques – including some of my comments above – have less relevance or force.

One indication that systems dynamics has come of age is its inclusion in the recently released Wolfram System Modeler software package. While relying heavily on Modelica, it also provides a separate systems dynamics utility, with most of the main features of older software, such as the graphic interface for the initial definition of a system. Clearly, Wolfram thinks that various forms of systems modeling, including the relatively accessible systems dynamics approach, are as important to contemporary scientific research and policy analysis as mathematics and programming, both of which are covered in their older software, Mathematica.

More direct evidence that systems dynamics has come of age is found in the work of John D. Sterman, Professor of Management at the Sloan School of Management, Massachesetts Institute of Technology. His 900+ page textbook – *Business Dynamics: Systems Thinking and Modeling for a Complex World* – develops the systems dynamics approach in detail, and with great common sense and balance. And while oriented to business, it includes scientific examples, including some demographic models.

Sterman's central argument is not that systems dynamics models can represent real-world systems perfectly, but only that they can often do so better than the 'mental models' that we inevitably develop and use in analysis and practice. Our mental models typically are overly simple, linear, relatively static, and unable to think effectively about feedback and delays. Similar limitations affect many of our multivariate statistical, econometric, and demographic models, which are single equation, linear or log-linear, static, without feedback or delays.

But unlike some earlier proponents of systems dynamics discussed above, Sterman has a healthy respect for statistics. In discussing the estimation of model parameters, he notes: 'The basic choice is formal statistical estimation from numerical data, or judgmental estimation' (Sterman 2000, p. 867). He continues: 'Systems dynamics modelers are well-advised to study econometrics and other approaches to formal parameter estimation. It is essential to know how the important regression techniques work, what their maintained hypotheses and limitations are, and when each tool is appropriate' (p. 868). This is a far cry from the complaint that a regression equation on milk production fails to mention cows. Judgement comes into play when there are no reliable statistical measures, direct or indirect, on a variable thought to be important. The systems dynamics tradition prefers to make an informed guess rather than to omit that variable altogether, relegating it to the error term.

So why has demography – or sociology, for that matter – not taken greater advantage of these tools? In addition to the possible answers given earlier to the more general question, the following come to mind:

1. There are inherent flaws in the systems dynamics approach and associated software[11];

---

[11]There are clear limitations, of course, but the same could be said of standard demographic methods and of statistical modeling.

2. Demographers were put off by the exaggerated claims of early systems dynamics modelers, and by their seeming indifference, and even hostility, towards statistical research in the social sciences;
3. We dismissed their population models because they did not use the 'correct' approach and terminology, that is, the canonical approach in demography;
4. Quantitative social scientists in general often viewed systems modeling as second-rate empirical work, dealing with made-up numbers instead of hard data. Social theorists, on the other hand, assumed it was 'number crunching,' since it relied on the computer and dealt with numbers and quantitative relationships. Thus, a valuable tool fell through the cracks.

5.8 Concluding Comment

Demography is a wonderful discipline. I have come to think of it as a better discipline than is generally recognized, because we have not codified and presented it in the most effective way. And clearly, I think it might be an even stronger discipline if it had assimilated the regular use of differential equations in general, and systems dynamics software in particular. The latter would have allowed those of us who lack a thorough grounding in mathematics to work with relatively complex systems of differential equations. This is not just for the sake of using them, but to help us with thought processes that need help. Their use would encourage us to think more about dynamics and process, and not just cross-sectional relationships and equilibria. They could help us think better about complex social and demographic systems containing non-linear relationships and feedbacks. They could help us introduce more clarity in our theoretical models (for example, transition theory) typically stated in words and manipulated by everyday logic. And they could introduce these intellectual habits to our students – even sociology undergraduates who typically know little mathematics.

The use of differential equations could also help us to extend our discipline to consider topics previously neglected. It would help us to develop a richer portfolio of population growth models, beyond the exponential, stable, and projection models. We might begin to renew a serious interest in the logistic, which in the very long term may apply to human population after all (see Lee 1987). We could learn about the Allee effect[12] from our biological cousins in ecology; in almost 60 years in the field, I had never heard about this in demography, yet it would seem to have relevance to our past and future. We would be better equipped to study interactions among humans and other species, to finally recognize and accept the fact that we are both predator and prey.

---

[12]The discovery that in some biological species the initial response to population growth and increasing density may be an increase in the birth rate and a decrease in the death rate – just the opposite of the assumptions underlying the logistic model – and similar to some historical cases of human population dynamics. See Allee *et al.* (1949).

In all of this, we must get over a common confusion referred to several times above, a confusion of differential equation models with empirical work. They are not a substitute for statistical investigation, qualitative description, or other forms of empirical study. Rather they are a tool for the construction and exploration of the theory and theoretical models that attempt to explain our empirical findings. Demography is generally thought to be rich in data and technique, and poor in theory. I have suggested elsewhere (Burch 2003a, b) that we have more and better theory than is generally thought. But our body of theory could be richer still if we were to take advantage of both classic (differential equations) and contemporary (systems dynamics software) tools for the statement and manipulation of theoretical ideas about demographic processes.

References

Abbott, A. (1988). Transcending general linear reality. *Sociological Theory, 6*, 169–186.

Allee, W. C., Emerson, A. E., Park, O., Park, T., & Schmidt, K. P. (1949). *Principles of animal ecology*. Philadelphia: W. B. Saunders.

Bardi, U. (2011). *The limits to growth revisited*. New York: Springer.

Blalock, H. M. (1960). *Social statistics*. New York: McGraw-Hill.

Burch, T. K. (1993). Theory, computers and the parameterization of demographic behavior. In *IUSSP international population conference, Montreal 1993*. (Vol. 3, pp. 377–388). Liege: IUSSP. See also Ch. 6 in this volume.

Burch, T. K. (2003a). Data, models, theory and reality: The structure of demographic knowledge. In F. C. Billari & A. Prskawetz (Eds.), *Agent-based computational demography: Using simulation to improve our understanding of demographic behaviour*. Heidelberg: Physica-Verlag. See also Ch. 2 in this volume.

Burch, T. K. (2003b). Demography in a new key: A theory of population theory. *Demographic Research, 9*, 263–284. See also Ch. 1 in this volume.

Burch, T. K. (2005). Computer simulation and statistical modeling: Rivals or complements? Paper presented at Session 131 (The Epistemology of Demography) of the General Assembly of the International Union for the Scientific Study of Population. Tours, France. Available at http://www.iussp.org/Erance2005. See also Ch. 4 in this volume.

Burch, T. K. (2016). Review of U. Bardi. The limits to growth revisited. *Canadian Studies in Population 43* 160–162.

Coale, A. J., & McNeil, D. (1972). The distribution by age of the frequency of first marriage in a female cohort. *Journal of the American Statistical Association, 67*, 743–749.

Cohen, J. E. (2003). Human population: The next half century. *Science, 302*, 1172–1175.

Coleman, J. S. (1964). *Introduction to mathematical sociology*. New York: Free Press.

Forrester, J. W. (1961). *Industrial dynamics*. Cambridge, MA: MIT Press.

Forrester, J. W. (1971). *World dynamics*. Cambridge, MA: MIT Press.

Gotelli, N. J. (1998). *A primer of ecology* (2nd ed.). Sunderland: Sinauer Associates.

Hanneman, R. A. (1988). *Computer-assisted theory building. modeling dynamic social systems*. Newbury Park: Sage Publications.

Hanneman, R. A. (2005). *Spatial dynamics of human populations: Basic models*. http://faculty.ucr.edu/~hanneman/spatial/index.html

Hernes, G. (1972). The process of entry into first marriage. *American Sociological Review, 37*, 173–182.

HPS/High Performance Systems. (1996). *Stella. An introduction to systems thinking*. Hanover: High Performance Systems.

Hudson, J. C. (1970). Elementary models for population growth and distribution analysis. *Demography, 3*, 361–368.

Keyfitz, N. (1965). On the interaction of populations. *Demography, 2*, 276–288.

Lee, R. D. (1987). Population dynamics of humans and other animals. *Demography, 24*, 443–465.

Lotka, A. J. (1956). *Elements of mathematical biology*. New York: Dover Publications. First published in 1924 as Elements of Physical Biology.

Lotka, A. J. (1998). *Analytical theory of biological populations* (Translated with an introduction by D.P. Smith and H. Rossert). New York: Plenum Press. Translation of *Théorie Analytique des Associations Biologiques. Première partie, Principes; Deuxième partie, Analyse dé mographique avec application particulière à l'espèce humaine. Paris: Hermann & Cie, 1934,1939*.

Meadows, D. H., Meadows, D. L., Randers, J., & Behrans, W. W., III. (1972). *The limits to growth*. New York: Universe Books.

Preston, S. H., Heuveline, P., & Guillot, M. (2001). *Demography: Measuring and modeling population processes*. Oxford: Blackwell Publishers.

Richardson, G. P., & Pugh, A. L. (1981). *Introduction to systems dynamics modeling with dynamo*. Cambridge, MA: Productivity Press.

Roberts, N., Anderson, D., Deal, R., Garet, M., & Shaffer, W. (1983). *Introduction to computer simulation: The systems dynamics approach*. Reading: Addison-Wesley.

Rosero-Bixby, L., & Casterline, J. B. (1993). Modeling diffusion effects in fertility transition. *Population Studies, 47*, 147–167.

Sanderson, W. C. (1994). Simulation models of demographic, economic, and environmental interactions. In W. Lutz (Ed.), *Population, development, environment: Understanding their interactions in Mauritius* (pp. 33–71). Berlin: Springer.

Smith, J. M. (1968). *Mathematical ideas in biology*. Cambridge: The University Press.

Sterman, J. D. (2000). *Business dynamics: Systems thinking and modeling for a complex world*. McGraw-Hill Higher Education.

Wachter, K. W. (2014). *Essential demographic methods*. Cambridge, MA: Harvard University Press.

Wachter, K. W., & LeBras, H. (Eds.). (2013). *Mathematical demography: Selected papers* (2nd revised edition). Heidelberg: Springer.

Wilson, E. O., & Bossert, W. H. (1971). *A primer of population biology*. Sunderland: Sinauer Associates.

Part II
Some Demographic Models Re-visited

Chapter 6
Theory, Computers and the Parameterization of Demographic Behavior

6.1 Introduction

This is a story of two demographic models – their structure, rationale and interpretation, goodness of fit, and reception by demographers. The story raises interesting questions about demography – the structure of the discipline and its scientific community, attitudes toward theory and scientific methodology, and paths of future development. The two models are the Coale-McNeil (1972) and the Hernes (1972) models of first marriage. Developed at roughly the same time, the models have experienced rather different fates. The Coale-McNeil model has entered the standard repertoire of technical demography. It has been 'canonized,' as that term is used in a recent essay on culture by Griswold (1987) – that is, accepted by 'that elite group of specialists who may legitimately talk about value' (p. 11).

The Hernes model, by contrast, was largely ignored by mainstream demography until recently. It is not mentioned in the United Nations *Manual X* in the section on 'Nuptiality Models,' and is mentioned only briefly if at all in many other treatments of marriage in recent demographic literature.

Yet by ordinary scientific standards, the Hernes model does not seem inferior to Coale-McNeil. In some respects, it might even be judged a more elegant and well-rounded piece of scientific work. How can one explain its relative neglect? After a closer look at the two models, I return to this question below, suggesting that part of the answer lies in a predilection of mainstream demography for certain styles of work, with emphasis on measurement and the technical side of modelling, and a tendency to neglect issues of behavioral theory. More than is commonly realized, demography is two disciplines, one a branch of applied statistics dealing with population, the other a branch of social and behavioral science, focusing on

---

This chapter is a slightly revised version of a paper presented at the International Population Conference, Montreal, 1993. See International Union for the Scientific Study of Population, *International Population Conference, Montreal, 1993*, Vol. 3, pp. 377–388.

© The Author(s) 2018

T.K. Burch, *Model-Based Demography*, Demographic Research Monographs,
DOI 10.1007/978-3-319-65433-1_6

demographic behavior and aspiring to the development of behavioral substantive theory.

Viewed in terms of textbook social scientific methodology, mainstream demography's relative neglect of theory weakens its stature as a science. But recent methodological writings offer new and different views of the scientific enterprise, and suggest better prospects for abstract analytic theory in demography and other social sciences. A comparison of the two models of first marriage illustrates the issues as they pertain to contemporary demography.

6.2 The Coale-McNeil Model

The Coale-McNeil marriage model was first presented in two papers in the early 1970s (Coale 1971; Coale and McNeil 1972). The discussion here is based primarily on Coale's informal account of the model's development in a special issue of *Population* dedicated to Louis Henry (Coale 1977).[1]

The fundamental equation of first marriage risk for those eventually marrying in a cohort is given by:

$$g(a) = (0.1946\Theta/\gamma)\exp[(-0.174/\gamma)(a - a_0 - 6.06\gamma)] \\ - \exp[(-0.288/\gamma)(a - a_0 - 6.06\gamma)] \tag{6.1}$$

Where θ is the proportion who will eventually marry, a_0 is the age at which marriage first begins, and γ is '...the scale factor expressing the number of years of nuptiality in the given population which are equivalent to 1 year in the standard population' (U.N. 1983, pp. 22–23). The numerical constants in this expression were derived by fitting an earlier form to a standard schedule of first marriage based on 1865–1869 Swedish data.

Coale characterizes the process leading to the model partly as trial and error. It began with the realization that empirical curves of proportions ever-married could be made virtually identical by means of three transformations (Coale 1977, p. 132), adjusting for the earliest age at which the proportion visibly departs from zero (taken as a new origin), the proportions eventually marrying (determining a new vertical scale, from 0 to 1), and the steepness with which the curve rises over the period of most rapid increase (determining a new horizontal scale). This led to the conclusion that there was 'a common pattern of first marriage frequencies' (Coale 1977).

---

[1]Key elements of the model were developed by Griffith Feeney in the summer of 1971 (see Feeney 1972) and shared at a meeting that same summer. Coale and McNeil fully acknowledge Feeney's contribution.

The next step was to find a functional form that could represent this common pattern. Experiments with various forms (initially a double exponential function) led to Eq. 6.1. Along the way, Coale began to look for a behavioral interpretation:

> I expressed dissatisfaction with the double exponential risk function on the grounds that it did not provide any evident basis for an intuitive understanding of first marriages. In other words, it did not suggest a theory or model of nuptiality. One cannot infer what kind of individual behavior, or what form of social influence, causes the risk of first marriage (setting aside those who never marry) to follow a double exponential. (Coale 1977, p. 140)[2]

Griffith Feeney suggested an interpretation in terms of a normally distributed age of entry into the marriage market, and an exponentially distributed delay, or waiting time, between entry and marriage. Subsequent theoretical and mathematical work showed that *'First marriage consists of arriving at an age of marriageability (an age with a distribution that is approximately normal), followed by passage through 2 or 3 stages,* the probability of passage to the next stage being approximately constant within each stage' (Coale 1977, p. 144, italics in original). Coale tentatively identifies the stages in a Western context as dating, meeting the future spouse, engagement and finally first marriage. He acknowledges a similar conceptualization of the marriage process in several papers by Henry, but apparently was not aware of these in the early stages of his work.

Rodriguez and Trussell (1980) reformulated the Coale-McNeil model to give an expression with three parameters representing the mean and standard deviation of age at marriage among those who marry, and the proportion who ever marry.

6.3 The Hernes Model

The development of Hernes's model (1972) seems to have taken a somewhat different course than the Coale-McNeil model.[3] An initial step is the conceptualization of first marriage as a diffusion process within a cohort. The pace and extent of this diffusion are determined by several factors: an initial level of 'marriageability' characterizing the cohort; a rate at which marriageability declines with age; increasing social pressure to marry as the proportion of the cohort already married increases; and decreasing availability of potential mates as the proportion already married approaches its ultimate value.

These behavioral assumptions lead to a 'non-homogeneous diffusion' model expressed by the differential equation:

---

[2]Coale's interest in finding a behavioral rationale for the model suggests a distinction between the approach in his early work and its later treatment by the demographic community.

[3]I say 'seems' because a discussion of the Hernes model cannot benefit from a first-person account as contained in Coale (1977).

$$dP_t/dt = Ab^t(1 - P_t)(P_t) \tag{6.2}$$

The parameter A refers to the initial marriageability; b is a constant of deterioration. P_t is the proportion married at time t years from the beginning of the marriage process. The last two terms in Eq. 6.2 express the shortage of suitable mates as the proportion not yet married $[1 - P_t]$ becomes small, and the social pressure to marry as the proportion married $[P_t]$ increases. The product of these two terms reaches a maximum when P_t is 0.5.

The parameter A is defined by Hernes as individual 'marriage potential' and is assumed to be the same for every member of the cohort – thus 'average initial marriageability.' He does not fully elaborate on this concept, which combines notions of motivation, eligibility or capacity, and the cultural value of marriage. Marriage potential is assumed to decline geometrically with age by a factor $b < 1.0$. Upon integration, Eq. 6.2 yields what Hernes describes as an 'unwieldy' expression, which has no simple behavioral interpretation – the behavioral concepts are reflected in the differential equation.[4]

Hernes fits Eq. 6.2 to cohort data from a 1960 U.S. census publication (U.S. Bureau of the Census 1968), for two cohorts of men and woman, for whites and non-whites. He also shows that marriageability is higher but decreases more rapidly with age for more highly educated white women than for the less educated.

6.4 Canonization Versus Relative Neglect

In subsequent years, the Coale-McNeil model become the standard model of first marriage, while the Hernes model was largely neglected by mainstream demography. As noted already, Hernes's model was not mentioned in U.N. *Manual X*. Newell (1988) included it in his bibliography but did not discuss it further. Trussell and Reinis (1989) did not include it in an extensive bibliography on age at first marriage and at first birth, in a paper in which the Coale- McNeil model is featured. Keyfitz (1985), with characteristic comprehensiveness, gave Hernes several paragraphs. But overall, relative to Coale-McNeil, the Hernes model was ignored by demographers. Many otherwise well-informed demographers had never heard of it.[5]

Published work on Hernes's model has been concerned largely with its formal or statistical properties, evaluating goodness of fit compared to other models, or using it to complete incomplete marriage cohort experience. Virtually no use has been made of his model to study *substantive* issues relating to first marriage (for

---

[4]The resulting expression is unwieldy mainly by comparison with the original differential equation, and is no more so than the Coale-McNeil equation.

[5]Anecdotal evidence. I became aware of the Hernes model by accident, reading the article that immediately preceded it in the journal.

example, following up on his lead on educational differentials). Nor has there been much effort to develop his theoretical insights into the first marriage process, some of which now seem dated, but which certainly provided promising leads.[6]

How can one explain the fate of Hernes's work? The most obvious explanation – overall scientific merit – would not seem to be the answer, although clearly this is a matter of subjective judgement. In terms of the usual evaluative criteria. Hernes stacks up rather well against Coale-McNeil.

Goodness of Fit Although I know of no systematic, rigorous comparison of the goodness of fit of the two models across a wide array of empirical data, published evidence and my own experience point to the conclusion that both models fit first marriage curves very well. Hastings and Robinson (1973) used Hernes to fit data on several U.S. cohorts, with relatively small errors for most of them (formal measures of goodness of fit are not reported). Diekmann (1989) concludes, based on German and U.S. data, that Hernes performs well when compared with several other models of the class evaluated (diffusion models). He comments:

> ...the Hernes model complies quite well with the observations while the log-logistic model yields a middling approximation to the data. However, it should be noted that the two-parameter log-logistic model is a more parsimonious parameterization than the three-parameter Hernes model. (p. 39)

He adds: 'Both models are not merely descriptions of observed data but also have considerable theoretical appeal' (p. 39). Diekmann does not consider the Coale-McNeil model in this paper, which focuses on diffusion type models; he categorizes Coale- McNeil as a 'latent state' model.

In a direct comparison of Hernes and Coale-McNeil, Malakar (1987) concludes that Coale-McNeil provides a better fit to Indian data. But the data used are relatively poor, and in the main comparison (his Table 2) Hernes fits female (but not male) data as well as or better than Coale-McNeil.[7] Measures of error are relatively small for both models.

Trussell and Reinis (1988) rely on Coale-McNeil for a comparative analysis of data from 41 WFS surveys. But they report enough problems with fitting the data (including proportions ever marrying exceeding 1.0), that one wonders why they did not consider other possible models.

Parsimony and Tractability Hernes's mathematical function is, if anything, the more elegant of the two. The differential equation is simple, flows directly from behavioral reasoning, and is transparent – that is, its behavioral interpretation is easy to see in the function itself. The Coale-McNeil convolution of normal and exponential functions probably is harder for most people to intuit or visualize. And

---

[6]There also has been a general lack of interest in the behavioral rationale for the Coale-McNeil model. Possible complementarities in the behavioral underpinnings of the two models (and consequent possibilities of synthesis) seem never to have been noted.

[7]I take Malakar's reported goodness of fit measures at face value, although I have been unable to reproduce his parameter values for the Hernes model using Mathcad's nonlinear fitting function.

its derivation and presentation involve: a novel definition of the standard demographic notion of risk; transformations of origins, horizontal and vertical scales; and discussion of convolutions of infinite series of exponential functions. Hernes simply fits the solution to his differential equation to the data, assuming only a reasonable starting point (comparable to Coale-McNeil's a_0). Hernes's equation has a closed-form solution; the Coale-McNeil risk function does not.[8] Formally, both models have three parameters, but Coale-McNeil has four additional numerical constants relating to a standard schedule of first marriage risk. In applications of Coale-McNeil, 'Normally, the proportion single in age group 50–54 may be considered an estimate of...the proportion who will never marry' (U.N. Manual X, p. 23); the Hernes model need not assume, but generates, meaningful asymptotic values, given observations up to age 50 or so.[9]

Behavioral Content The Coale-McNeil model might be characterized as 'semi-behavioral.' Its parameters relate primarily to formal properties of the fitted function – starting point, asymptotic value, level relative to the Swedish standard curve (in the Rodriguez-Trussell re-parameterized version (1960), the mean and standard deviation of age at marriage). They are not closely tied to or descriptive of the underlying process posited, that is, the series of waiting times.[10]

The notion of *waiting times* is itself as much formal as behavioral insofar as little is said about why there is delay in moving from one stage to another. Coale links the conceptualization to such social institutions as dating and engagement, but these ideas are not reflected directly in the model.[11]

The Hernes model, by contrast, deals with notions of motivation, social pressure, eligibility for marriage, and supply of mates. And, these behavioral concepts are reflected in the form of the model and in its parameters, although admittedly the parameter A confounds measures of factors the behavioral theorist would prefer to keep separate.

Logical Inference As noted above, Coale expressed concern with finding a theoretical rationale for the Coale-McNeil model, but appears to have been quickly satisfied by Feeney's suggestions and the work of Henry, both relating to a 'waiting times' conceptualization of the first marriage process. Neither in the original work

---

[8]In the sense that the integral of the risk function cannot be expressed in terms of elementary functions.

[9]In my experience, estimating parameters for Hernes is easier than for Coale-McNeil using the nonlinear least-squares utility in Mathcad. With Coale-McNeil, the process often breaks down due to numbers beyond the capacity of the program $[10^{-308}$ to $10^{308}]$. I do not know if this is a problem with other techniques or software.

[10]Feeney's (1972) model, based on a similar conceptualization of the process, is more graphic, in that it yields as parameters a mean age of entry into the marriage pool, a mean waiting time in the pool, and a mean age at marriage.

[11]There is a potential link with a large economics literature on search processes and assortative mating, but to my knowledge this link has not been developed in the demographic literature on first marriage. But see Goldstein and Kenney (2001).

nor in its applications by others has there been much interest shown in the possibility of alternative conceptualizations of the marriage process.

Keyfitz (1985), in an uncharacteristic logical lapse, goes along with Coale's relaxed acceptance of the 'waiting times' theory: 'The closeness of fit of the convolution to the observed data for this and other populations confirms their behavioral model' (p. 180). Trussell and Reinis (1989) comment more accurately: 'Subsequent research has done little to either confirm or deny the behavioral interpretation of the Coale/McNeil model' (p. 132). Hernes (1972) also takes the more correct view of the situation, avoiding the logical fallacy of affirming the antecedent:

> The general problem with our type of analysis is that the fit between the observed and calculated curve of first marriage is not a strong test of the model.... [I]t is hard to tell whether the resulting estimates actually reflect the causal forces involved. The model, which contains the common wisdom we began with, is clearly admissible by the data. But by the above analysis, we have not eliminated other causal processes that might generate curves of cumulative marriages with the same rough shape. (pp. 180–81)

This comment might be thought to have all the more force when the theoretical rationale for a model is provided after the fact, as in the case of Coale-McNeil.

6.5   The Sociology of Demography

If their relative scientific merits[12] do not explain the different receptions accorded the two marriage models, what does? There are, of course, personal and institutional factors at work. Coale was located at a major demographic research institute, and had been at the center of the international demographic community as represented by International Union for the Scientific Study of Population. He continued to develop the model, and to promote its use. Hernes, by contrast, apparently wrote no more on the subject,[13] and did not pursue a full-time career in social science research. At last report, he held a cabinet post in the Norwegian government.

But some part of the explanation must lie with the intellectual character of the discipline of demography. A recent quote from Newell's (1988) discussion of Coale- McNeil can serve to illustrate the point:

> Coale (1971) and Coale and McNeil (1972) go to considerable lengths to try to identify a plausible behavioral explanation of the marriage process which is consistent with the double exponential form of the model. They conclude that such a form is probably a

---

[12]As assessed by this writer, of course. It is quite possible that I have overlooked some flaws or practical disadvantage in the Hernes model, or failed to see some additional virtues or advantages in Coale-McNeil.

[13]It is worth emphasizing the fact, however, that his article was published in what is generally considered the leading sociological journal in North America, if not the world. There is no question of inaccessibility in an obscure journal.

consequence of first marriage consisting of a series of stages.... This rationalization is, however, unimportant for practical purposes. One is generally only concerned with the model's ability to fit a wide range of experience, not with its ability to reflect the underlying processes involved'. (p. 169)

Even with due regard for context (namely, a book on demographic techniques) and qualifying phrases ('for practical purposes'), it is difficult not to see in this quote a certain abdication of scientific aspirations, insofar as science is conceived of as an attempt at explanation. Process and mechanisms do not matter so much; one is content to leave the 'black box' black.

The Newell quote may be particularly blunt, but the attitude it seems to reflect is widespread in the demographic community. It would not be too-hard to document the fact that many demographers are concerned almost entirely with measurement, description, statistical modeling and the formal aspects of forecasting. There are others, many of whom would consider themselves social demographers or economic demographers rather than just demographers, who are particularly interested in explanation, and therefore in theory.

There are different ways of thinking about this situation. Perhaps it reflects a normal process of specialization and division of labor within a complex scientific field (cf. theoretical and experimental physics). Or perhaps the division has gone too far, leaving demography schizoid. There are almost 'two demographies,' one a branch of applied mathematics/statistics, focusing on measurement and formal modelling, greatly concerned with high degrees of precision, and relatively neglectful of causal explanation or theory.[14] This brand of demography is often, but not always, practiced in a governmental or quasi-governmental context. The other demography is a branch of social or behavioral science, concerned with explanation of demographic phenomena (and therefore with substantive behavioral models and theory), and somewhat more tolerant of measurement error. This brand of demography is often but not always practiced in universities or free-standing research institutes.

Differing attitudes toward error in demographic measurements may be taken as hallmarks of the two demographies. The government context of much demographic work often dictates great concern with precision. The central task of a government statistical office is to collect good data, and the results are often politically sensitive. A change of 0.3 percentage points in an unemployment rate can have major political consequences. And millions of dollars were spent in legal battles over the accuracy of the 1990 U.S. census, presumably in part because many more millions of dollars were thought to be at stake. This governmental view of precision is often carried over into more academic demography, where it may have less justification except insofar as the quest for accurate measurement becomes an end in itself. In his book on demographic methods, Smith (1992) expresses reservations about a particular method because it involves data accurate 'only to two or three significant digits' (p. 84). In his Table 4.5, calculations are carried out to five

---

[14]The idea of 'two demographies' is elaborated on by McNicoll (1992) and by Olsen (1988).

decimal places. Given errors in basic demographic data, perhaps only two or three significant digits may be justified. And from a scientific theoretical point of view, such precision may not be particularly important.

The problem is an old one, the classic comment that of Norbert Wiener, as quoted by Morgenstern: 'Economics is a one or two-digit science' (Morgenstern 1963). His point: there are few if any substantive propositions in economics (at all but the lowest level of generality) that would be verified or falsified depending on results in the third or fourth significant digit or decimal.[15] This would be truer of behavioral demography, which has much less carefully-honed general theory.

Another view of situation described above, however, is that the theoretical aspirations of much academic demography are futile. John Q. Stewart, in a defense of some of his descriptive work on population potential, once defined science as 'the search for non-obvious regularities in the visible world.' Recent methodological writings in sociology have begun to question the feasibility of going much beyond that, suggesting that theoretical progress based on the adjudication of two or more competing theories by means of empirical research may be a chimera (Turner 1987). Turner attributes this view to Karl Pearson, for whom '...theory, in the positivist sense of an articulated logical structure, had no place' in science, and whose recommendation was '...to abandon the goal of theory in social science in favor of amassing correlational sequences...' (p. 179), what we might now call empirical generalizations. In this light, a neglect of theory may represent scientific common sense.[16]

In the context of the case study presented in this chapter, there are two main problems with this abstemious approach to theory. *First,* if 'One is generally only concerned with the model's ability to fit a wide range of experience...,' then recent developments in computerized curve-fitting may have downgraded much of demographic modeling to a clerical task. Finding a good fit to a given data set is now a trivial exercise. To give but one example, a product such as TableCurve (software from Jandel Scientific) can fit over 3,000 curves to a typical demographic data set (such as first marriage data) in a matter of seconds. Some of them might fit the data better (measured by R^2, F, or mean square error) than either Coale-McNeil or Hernes. Many of them are linear forms (in the parameters), with several uninterpretable parameters. But this doesn't matter if 'One is generally only concerned with the model's ability to fit etc....'

Finding a curve that will fit 'a wide range of experience' admittedly is a more difficult task in general, but relatively easy for a phenomenon that has tended up until now to be fairly stable over time and space (for example, first marriage, which has strong biological underpinnings), and takes a characteristic pattern – it begins at

---

[15]While this view still seems valid, it may need to be qualified to take account of measurement error in complex multivariate models now commonplace in social science, as well as other forms of propagation of error generally.

[16]The point about 'one or two digits' might still apply, however, since it is hard to think of empirical generalizations that would stand or fall on third or higher digits.

around age fifteen, is monotonic, and cannot exceed 1.0 but usually reaches 0.9 or so.

Finding a curve with behaviorally interpretable parameters is much more difficult, of course, but now one is becoming concerned with 'its ability to reflect the underlying processes involved,' in short, with theory. Finding the good-fitting curve with a theoretical rationale is the aim of mainstream social science, in contrast to the Pearsonian variant mentioned above.

Finding the model with a good theoretical rationale may also be important for purposes of measurement and prediction, even if one is only concerned with its 'ability to fit a wide range of experience.' Another reason why modeling without theory is problematic is that, if we don't know *why* a model fits a wide range of experience, we have many fewer clues as to *whether* it will continue to fit data outside that range, whether in the future or for hitherto unobserved cases. Extrapolation to other cases or beyond a range of observation remains extrapolation, whether it is based on a simple linear model, a double exponential, or a modified Gompertz. Only theory can hope to tell us whether the extrapolation is justified.

Successes to date with modeling first marriage may be partly fortuitous, and the radical changes in patterns of union formation over the last decades will require new and different models. Later home-leaving, cohabitation, and the delay and avoidance of legal marriage may lead to unprecedented low levels of proportions ever-married, and may lead to a curve of first marriage risk with opposite skewness, or even conceivably bi-modal curves with respect to age. Suitable curves will differ depending on the inclusion or exclusion of informal unions.

A graphic example of this kind of 'structural shift' is given by Fig. 6.1, which shows non-family 'headship' rates (incomplete cohort experience) for several cohorts, based on data from four Canadian censuses (1971–1986). The data are based on an unchanging census concept of 'head,' so that the changes in pattern are not artefactual. A similar structural shift can be seen in cohort data on female rates. In either case, a function that fit older cohort experience quite well would do poorly when applied to younger cohorts, and this will eventually be reflected in cross-sectional data.[17]

The comparison with first marriage is not perfect, since accession to and relinquishment of 'household headship' are compound events, functionally related to more elementary events such as home-leaving, marriage, divorce, and widow[er]hood. But the general point is clear: mathematical models that fit well in the past may not fit well in the future. And our ability to anticipate this is based very much on a theory-based understanding of why the model fits. Well-formulated theory may be the most practical thing of all.

---

[17]It may be possible to find a functional form that would represent the varied patterns of both older and younger cohorts, but it would be considerably more complicated than functions like Coale-McNeil or Hernes, to capture the non-monotonic character of the curves for younger cohorts.

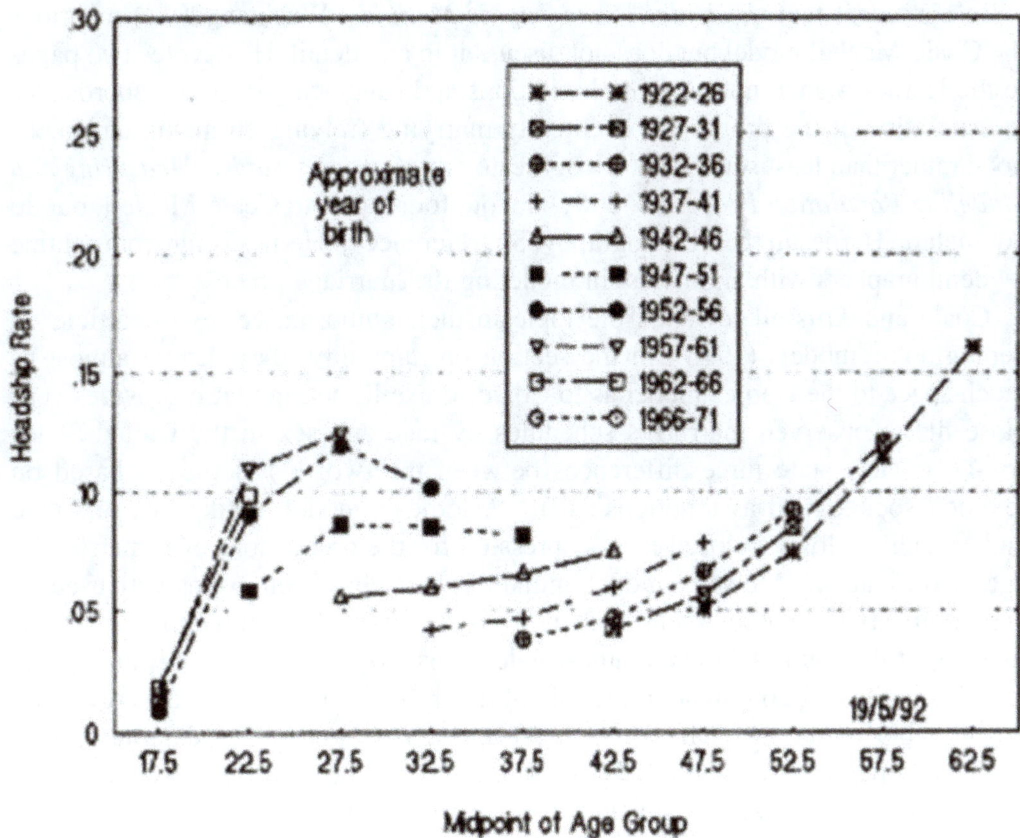

Fig. 6.1 Headship rates by age, non-family households Canadian cohorts, 1922–1926 to 1966–1971

6.6 Afterthoughts and Updates

The paper reprinted in this chapter is the earliest in the collection. It reflects the status of the Hernes model in demography at the time, nearly 25 years ago. It also reflects an early stage in my intellectual development, as I moved away from positivism and logical empiricism and worked to assimilate the 'semantic' or 'model-based' view of science, and to apply it to demography. Demographers are now better acquainted with the Hernes model, which is more often cited, used in research, and featured in textbooks on demographic methods.

A prime example is a 2001 paper by Goldstein and Kenney (2001) entitled 'Marriage delayed or marriage foregone? New cohort forecasts of first marriage for US women.' The authors use both the Hernes and the Coale-McNeil models to study patterns by cohort, educational level and race. The two models '...give essentially identical estimates when based on the same data' (p. 512). Unlike earlier papers, Goldstein and Kenney move beyond the issue of goodness of fit, and discuss their statistical results in light of microeconomic theories of marriage and of assortative mating.

In his recent text, *Essential Demographic Methods,* Wachter (2014) mentions the Coale-McNeil model but does not discuss it in any detail. He devotes two pages to the Hernes model, noting some limitations and suggesting different approaches to estimation of the proportion eventually marrying (relying on maximum likelihood rather than least squares; p. 215). Preston *et al.* (*Demography: Measuring and Modeling Population Processes,* 2001) devote four pages to Coale-McNeil, but do not include Hernes in their bibliography. So, reference to Hernes is far from routine by demographers with an interest in modeling the marriage process.

Coale and Trussell revisited the topic in their authoritative review article on demographic models (1996). In the section on nuptiality, they devote almost as much space to the Hernes model as to Coale-McNeill, noting that it provides very close fits to observed marriages schedules by race and sex in the United States (p. 477). They state three differences between the two: (1) Hernes is based on 'explicit sociological assumptions'; (2) '…Hernes's model, unlike that of Coale and McNeill, allows a closed-form expression for the proportions ever married by age'; (3) Coale and McNeil's model, unlike Hernes's has been extensively used by demographers.' They comment further: 'Hernes's model is both simple and intuitively appealing; it has deserved and still deserves more attention by demographers (p. 477). A closing comment on the role of theory in the kinds of models reviewed (presumably including marriage models) appears to represent a departure from Coale's earlier view as quoted above, where he '...expressed dissatisfaction with the double exponential risk function on the grounds that it did not provide any evident basis for an intuitive understanding of first marriages. In other words, it did not suggest *a theory or model* of nuptiality' (Coale 1977, p. 140, emphasis added). In an overall characterization of the models, Coale and Trussell note: 'The models are descriptive and were never intended to be anything else. No deep theory, or even shallow theory, underlies the search for empirical regularities. In contrast, the discovery of empirical regularities can stimulate the search for underlying causes' (1996, p. 483). But they comment further that '…finding a mathematical expression to represent a demographic process is not an end in itself. The models are valuable because they can be used to make broad inferences about behavior or, more commonly, to build a technique for estimating basic demographic indices for populations with limited or defective data' (p. 483).

Read together the above quotes suggest ambivalence about the role of theory in demographic research. One might try to develop theory eventually, but the main tasks for the demographer are empirical research, modeling, measurement and estimation. There is but a qualified interest in theory.

Part of the problem, perhaps, is that many of us have had an outdated and inappropriate view of what theory is and how it works. The 'search for empirical regularities' is key; they are the building blocks of theory, not just a stimulus for theoretical thinking. And by the doctrine of falsification, we search for one best theory, the scientific equivalent of monotheism. My own writing in this sometimes reflects these older views of theory. The comparison of the two models comes close to suggesting that we adopt Hernes *rather than* Coale-McNeil. I now firmly believe in the 'toolbox' approach to theory and models, and the centrality of purpose in evaluating a given model. The two models are qualitatively different, one a diffusion model, the other a 'latent states' or waiting-time model. Their behavioral content is different, giving different perspectives on the first-marriage process. For some purposes, the Coale-McNeill model may be better than Hernes in the attempt to gain insight into certain aspects of marriage behavior and its causes. But still, if one is not concerned with social and behavioral explanation, if one is only interested in fitting empirical data on first marriage, then Hernes would seem the better choice – it's simpler, more intuitive, and fits most empirical data equally well.

References

Coale, A. J. (1971). Age patterns of marriage. *Population Studies, 25*, 193–214.

Coale, A. J. (1977). The development of new models of nuptiality and fertility. *Population [numero special], 32*, 131–152.

Coale, A. J., & McNeil, D. (1972). The distribution by age of the frequency of first marriage in a female cohort. *Journal of the American Statistical Association, 67*, 743–749.

Coale, A. J., & Trussell, J. (1996). The development and use of demographic models. *Population Studies, 50*, 469–484.

Diekmann, A. (1989). Diffusion and survival models for the process of entry into marriage. *Journal of Mathematical Sociology, 14*, 31–44.

Feeney, G. (1972). *A model for the age distribution of first marriage* (Working Paper No. 23, 31pp). Honolulu: East-West Population Institute.

Goldstein, J., & Kenney, C. T. (2001). Marriage delayed or marriage foregone? New forecasts for US women. *American Sociological Review, 66*, 506–519.

Griswold, W. (1987). A methodological framework for the sociology of culture. *Sociological Methodology*, 1–35.

Hastings, D. W., & Robinson, J. G. (1973). A re-examination of Hernes's model on the process of entry into first marriage for United States women, cohorts 1891–1945. *American Sociological Review, 38*, 138–142.

Hernes, G. (1972). The process of entry into first marriage. *American Sociological Review, 37*, 173–182.

Keyfitz, N. (1985). *Applied mathematical demography* (2nd ed.). New York: Springer-Verlag.

Malakar, C. R. (1987). On recent developments of marriage models and their application to Indian nuptiality. *Genus, 43*, 93–101.

McNicoll, G. (1992). The agenda of population studies: A commentary and complaint. *Population and Development Review, 18*, 399–420.

Morgenstern, O. (1963). *On the accuracy of economic observations* (2nd ed.). Princeton: Princeton University Press.

Newell, C. (1988). *Methods and models in demography*. London: Belhaven.

Olsen, R. J. (1988). Review of 'Models of marital status and childbearing,' by M. Montgomery & J. Trussell. In O. Ashenfelter & R. Layard (Eds.), *Handbook of labor economics. The Journal of Human Resources 23*, 577–583.

Preston, S. H., Heuveline, P., & Guillot, M. (2001). *Demography: Measuring and modeling population processes*. Oxford: Blackwell Publishers.

Rodriguez, G., & Trussell, J. (1980). *Maximum likelihood estimation of Coale's model nuptiality schedule from survey data* (WFS Technical Bulletin No. 7). London: World Fertility Survey.

Smith, D. P. (1992). *Formal demography*. New York: Plenum Press.

Trussell, J., & Reinis, K. I. (1989). Age at first marriage and age at first birth. *Population Bulletin of the United Nations No. 26* (pp. 126–194). New York: United Nations.

Turner, S. P. (1987). Underdetermination and the promise of statistical sociology. *Sociological Theory, 5*, 172–184.

United Nations, Department of International Economic and Social Affairs. (1983). *Manual X: Indirect techniques for demographic Estimation* (Population Studies #81). New York: United Nations.

Wachter, K. W. (2014). *Essential demographic methods.* Harvard University Press.

Chapter 7
Estimating the Goodman, Keyfitz and Pullum Kinship Equations: An Alternative Procedure

7.1 Introduction

In a pioneering paper, Goodman *et al.* (1974) presented a general analytic system for studying the relationships between mortality and fertility and kin numbers. For stable populations with varying regimes of fertility and mortality, they provide formulas to calculate average numbers of kin, by category of kin, for females of various ages.

Of great substantive importance was their demonstration of the strong relationship between kin numbers and fertility levels for all categories of kin except ascendants in the direct line. The general relationship, obvious after the fact, was not widely recognized before their work [more attention had been devoted to the effect of mortality on kinship], nor had it been quantified even roughly. The relationship, combined with current low levels of fertility in many societies [for example, Italy with a total fertility rate of 1.3, or about 0.65 daughters born per woman] points to a continuing decline in numbers of kin for the average person in the future, and probably an associated decline in the importance of family and kinship in everyday life.[1]

The potential importance of this finding can be illustrated by a mental experiment. Suppose China's 'one-child' policy were perfectly realized, with no one having more than one birth. In a generation or two, collateral kinship would

---

The research underlying this chapter was carried out while I was Visiting Professor, Dipartimento di Scienze Demographiche, Università degli Studi di Roma, at the kind invitation of Prof. Antonella Pinnelli. Originally published in *Mathematical Population Studies* 5 (1995) pp. 161–170.

[1]A major qualification of this statement relates to the potential role of high levels of divorce and remarriage in supplying an individual with 'new' kin – step kin – in addition to those resulting from first marriage and birth.

© The Author(s) 2018

T.K. Burch, *Model-Based Demography*, Demographic Research Monographs,
DOI 10.1007/978-3-319-65433-1_7

disappear: there would be no brothers or sisters, aunts or uncles, nieces or nephews, or cousins—only, parents, grandparents, child, and grandchild.

Despite its substantive importance, their approach has not seen much further development [for example, by the inclusion of data on proportions married, or the relaxation of the stable population assumption] or widely used for the exploration of substantive questions relating to kinship (with the major exceptions of Goldman 1978, 1984 and Coresh and Goldman 1988). One practical barrier has been the difficulty of estimating the integral equations in which the basic relations are stated, equations containing up to quadruple integrals.

In their original paper the authors comment: 'Ordinarily, we cannot evaluate the $l(x)$ and $m(x)$ functions for arbitrary values of x, since the data are usually collected for 5-year age intervals' (p. 24). To estimate the equations, they develop finite approximations of the multiple integrals, programmed in Fortran by Pullum. In its original form, this Fortran code ran to more than ten single-spaced pages. It has been used in the later work by Goldman, and more recently by Keyfitz (1986), in an analysis of Canadian kinship numbers. But such code, written by someone else, is often difficult to master or to modify correctly.

This note illustrates an alternative procedure for evaluating the kinship integrals, using computer software developed since their paper first appeared. The procedure allows one in effect to 'evaluate the $l(x)$ and $m(x)$ functions for arbitrary values of x.' It involves a minimum of programming, yields results that agree well with the Pullum approximations, and has the advantage, both scientific and pedagogical, of working directly with the theoretical equations rather than with long finite approximation algorithms. Theory and computation are more closely linked.

The procedure involves two steps: (1) analytic expressions are found to represent empirical data on age-specific fertility and survivorship; (2) these expressions are substituted into the theoretical integral equations for kin numbers [with appropriate arguments and limits of integration], which are then evaluated numerically.

In the present note, the first step has been accomplished using TableCurve, an automated curve-fitting package using standard algorithms for linear or non-linear fitting.[2] Any general-purpose curve-fitting routine could be used. TableCurve has the advantage, for this application, that the user does not have to supply a functional form ahead of time, although user-defined functions are an option. The program has a built-in library of over 3500 functions, and can successfully fit most sets of demographic data by age or duration.[3]

The resulting analytic expressions and parameter estimates are used solely to represent particular schedules of age-specific mortality and fertility. They do not

---

[2]Systat, Richmond, California.

[3]The ability of computer curve-fitting packages such as the one used here to find functions to represent demographic data is a matter for further empirical investigation, To date I have encountered only a few cases of demographic data for which TableCurve could not find a function that fits reasonably close. An example: data on age-specific householder rates [female and non-family] from recent Canadian censuses, rates which rise to around age 30, decline, and then rise again in later life.

have, nor need they have for this application, any theoretical rationale or interpretation for their parameters. The only requirement is a close fit to the data at hand. Of course, if functional forms better grounded either in mathematics, empirical research, or substantive theory are available, their use in this application would be possible and desirable.

The second step uses the numerical integration capabilities of Mathcad, a numerical mathematics package.[4] Again, other mathematics packages could be used, so long as they can evaluate multiple integrals. Mathcad has an advantage that basic formulas are entered and appear [on the screen and in hardcopy] in standard mathematical notation, tying the calculations more closely to theoretical equations. Note, however, that the results still are based on underlying numerical approximation procedures not unlike those of Pullum'.[5]

The procedure is illustrated for children and grandchildren for 1981 Canadian data, and the results compared with those in Keyfitz (1986). Since both techniques start with data for 5-year age intervals to approximate theoretical integrals, neither can be said to yield 'correct' estimates of kin numbers, so that Keyfitz's results cannot serve as an absolute standard against which to judge the new procedure proposed. In any case, the agreement is close,[6] and the choice between the two computational techniques can be made on other grounds – ease of application, transparency, and flexibility.

Canadian 1981 age-specific fertility rates from Keyfitz (1986) were modified by adding zero values at ages 10 and 52.5, and fit by TableCurve.[7] Perfect fits were given by high-order polynomials, with eight to ten parameters. But for convenience in further use, more compact functions, with three or four parameters, were examined. The following function was chosen[8]:

---

[4]PTC Inc., Needham, Mass.

[5]It is conceivable that expressions for fertility and survivorship could be found that would lead to closed-form solutions of the kinship equations. But these still would not be exact solutions given the approximation involved in the underlying data.

[6]As it should be, given that both are using essentially the same data and similar numerical approximation procedures. The small differences observed presumably relate to small differences in input [for example, treatment of extreme ages of fertility or survivorship, age indexing, etc.] and in numerical procedures.

[7]For fitting, age-specific fertility rates were associated with the mid-points of their respective age intervals. This clearly involves error, especially in the intervals 10–14 and 45–49. With more information [e.g., data on births by single-years of age], average ages instead of midpoints could be used. Or one could simply assume that the rate for 10–14 should be associated with some age greater than 12.5. But such refinements are not necessary for present purposes.

[8]For readability, only three digits are given for parameter values. For accurate graphing of these functions more digits may be needed, especially if the function is non-linear. See Note to Appendix A.1

$$f(x) = e^{(a+[bx\sqrt{x}]+c\sqrt{x})}$$
$$a = -35.1 \quad b = -0.122 \quad c = 9.66$$

When the resulting function $f(x)$ is integrated over the same reproductive span as given by the original data (ages 10–50), the total fertility rate agrees with that computed in the usual way to within 0.1%. As well, visual inspection and conventional measures of goodness of fit suggest that f(x) provides a reasonable fit to the fertility data at hand. To repeat, that is the only goal for the present application. No theoretical or substantive claims are made for the resulting functions; we use them as approximating functions, defined by TableCurve as '...nothing more than an equation which is used to represent X-Y data' (Systat 2002, pp. 20–1).[9]

To eliminate small non-zero values of f(x) outside the reproductive ages, the function is redefined by inserting conditions on x which evaluate the function as zero when x is less than 10 or greater than 52.5. The function is also re-defined to adjust for the sex ratio at birth [since the kinship equations relate to one-sex, stable population models], yielding m(x), a maternity function for female births.

A similar curve-fitting procedure was applied to L_x values from the 1981 abridged life table for Canada [the data used by Keyfitz] to fit a survivor function.[10] In this case, four parameter functions were required to get an adequate fit. The chosen function:

$$s(x) = a + \frac{b}{1 + e^{\frac{c-x}{d}}}$$
$$a = -0.741 \quad b = 5.66 \quad c = 84.4 \quad d = -8.85$$

As with the fertility function, conditions on x were inserted to assure that the curve behaves properly at ages outside the range of observation.[11] And, the values were adjusted to take account of the 5-year intervals of the original L_x data, yielding a survivorship function p(x) (See Appendix A.1).

---

[9]The parameters relate to geometric properties of the graph – intercept, height, center, and width. But they have no further meaning in terms of a theory of kinship.

[10]The same L_x data were used for the sake of comparability. Given the continuous formulation of the present approach, fitting l_x values from the complete life table at ages 0,5...100 would have been more natural.

[11]With TableCurve, one can zoom out to see the behavior of a fitted function well outside the range of observation, and can quickly calculate predicted values for arguments outside that range. But this further step [for example, requiring zero survivors beyond some maximum age] seems warranted given the somewhat blind/mechanical procedure of curve-fitting. A skilled mathematician, of course, might define a function with the correct asymptotic properties.

Start of reproductive period: a = 0   **Age of ego: a = 0,20…80**

Daughters born by age a:

$$B_1(a) = \int_a^a m(x)\,dx$$

Living daughters at age a:

$$BL_1(a) = \int_a^a p(a-x)m(x)\,dx$$

Granddaughters born by age a [y = 0…50, defining a new age range for the daughter generation]:

$$B_2(a) = \int_a^a [\int_a^{a-x} p(y)m(y)\,dy]\,m(x)\,dx$$

Living granddaughters at age a:

$$BL_2 = \int_a^a [\int_a^{a-x} p(y)m(y)p(a-x-y)\,dy]\,m(x)\,dx$$

Fig. 7.1 Estimating Kin Numbers

7.2 Estimating Kin Numbers

Figure 7.1 defines the Goodman, Keyfitz and Pullum equations for daughters born, living daughters, granddaughters born and living granddaughters by age a of an average woman [ego]. The fertility and survivorship functions $m(a)$ and p(a) are as defined above. Given these equations and function definitions, Mathcad evaluates the integrals (see Appendix A.2). The results are given in Fig. 7.2.

Estimates by the proposed procedure are in close agreement with those of Keyfitz (1986), presented for comparison. Agreement is to within 1.1 per 100 kin for all categories and ages. The largest relative errors are for daughters and living daughters at age 20 of the reference woman – about 15%. These presumably relate to differences in procedures for dealing with fertility rates in the earliest ages of childbearing. But notice that the substantive story is not appreciably different, 6 or 7 daughters born per 100 women by age 20.

7.3 Discussion

The differences between the results of the proposed computational procedure and those produced by the Pullum algorithm are negligible, within the bounds of error of the original data. Moreover, the results are precise enough for any likely substantive use to which they might be put, given that they relate to a highly abstract model of kinship [a one-sex stable population model, with no input for marriage patterns].

Number of Kin per 100 Women

Age	Daughters	Living Daughters	Granddaughters	Living Granddaughters
Results from equations in Figure 1:				
20	7.4	7.3	0	0
40	80.5	79.2	1.8	1.8
60	81.3	79.7	51.8	50.9
80	81.3	77.0	64.9	63.7
Results from Keyfitz [1986]:				
20	6.3	6.3	0	0
40	80.4	79.5	1.9	1.9
60	81.3	79.7	50.9	50.3
80	81.3	77.6	64.9	63.9

Fig. 7.2 Comparison of estimates

The general approach used above clearly has applications to other areas of population mathematics. The approach is not entirely novel, but until recently it was impractical and beyond the capabilities of many researchers. Finite sums using grouped data became conventional. Writing as recently as 1985, for example, Keyfitz could note correctly with respect to an expression for the intrinsic growth rate r: 'no direct use can be made of a continuous form like (5.1.4) – it must be converted to the discrete form for calculations' (1985, p. 115), and more generally: 'Although the stable age distribution is easier to think about in the continuous version, application requires a discrete form' (1985, p. 81).

Due to recent developments in computer software, this is no longer the case. As illustrated above, it is now relatively easy to find continuous functions to represent many demographic data sets, and to do direct numerical evaluation of integrals and other analytic expressions. In some contexts, working with analytic expressions for processes such as fertility, survivorship and marriage may be a more effective way to derive numerical results than traditional finite sums. At the very least, one now has a choice.

Approximating functions also can be effective for interpolation and – with due caution – extrapolation.

The suggested procedure is a reminder of Hakkert's (1992) argument that many standard demographic algorithms were derived for purposes of hand calculation, and may need to be revised to make greater use of modern developments in statistics and computer software.[12]

---

[12]Caswell (1989) makes the interesting historical observation that much of Leslie's (1945) paper on matrices in demography is spent developing transformations suited to hand calculation, transformations now largely outmoded by the computer.

As with any use of computerized 'black box' procedures, of course, one must balance the potential advantages in ease, speed and flexibility of computation against the possibility of unrecognized pitfalls leading to seriously incorrect results. In the case at hand, for example, it would be easy to select a survivorship function that rises after age 100 or so. The careless use of such a function in the kinship equations would lead to meaningless results for some kinship categories. Computer mathematics software is at best a partial substitute for mathematical skill, and no substitute at all for thoughtful analysis.

Finally, it should be emphasized once more that in this approach, the analytic expressions are used solely to represent *specific sets of* data. Fertility schedules for a high-fertility population might lead to different functions being selected. The discovery of *general* analytic expressions for such processes, especially expressions with theoretically meaningful parameters, is another, more difficult and more important task.

Appendices

Appendix A: Tablecurve Output for Fit of Survival Curve

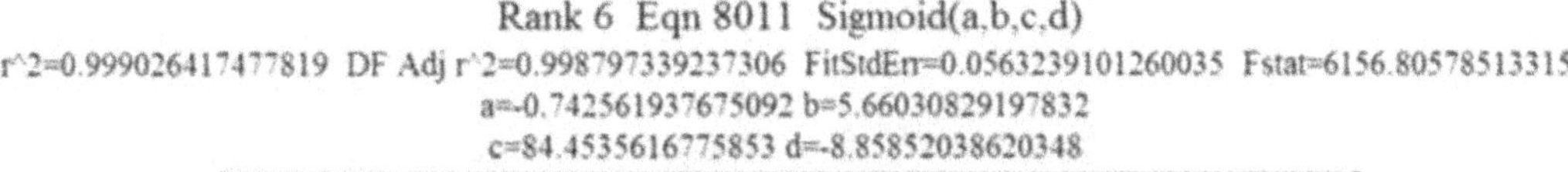

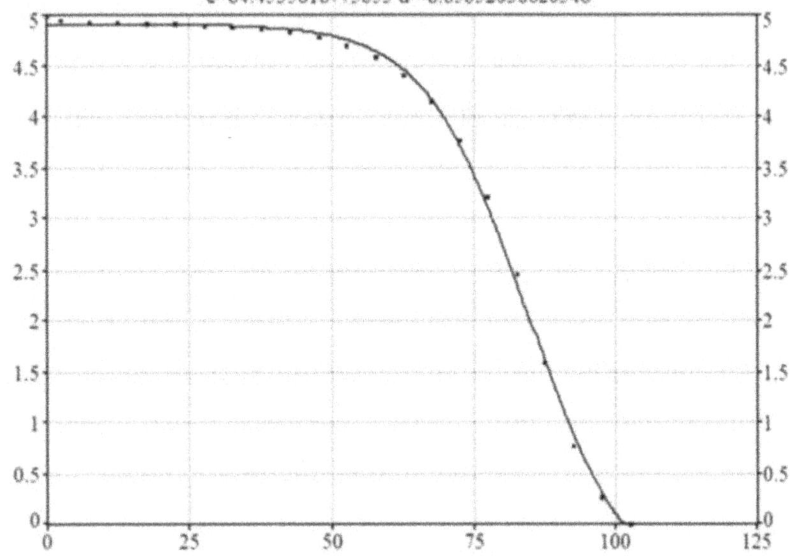

Note. This is a facsimile of the TableCurve graphic output for the function fit to L_x data, to represent survivorship. Parameter values and measures of goodness of fit are given to 15-digit accuracy. This is not justified by the accuracy of the basic data. But if one wishes to graph the function independently of TableCurve, many digits may be required to get an accurate graph, for example, with the correct range or specific values of y. Other output, not shown here, gives summary statistics and confidence intervals for parameters.

Appendix B: Facsimile of Mathcad Worksheet for Kin Numbers

Note: In Mathcad, this would be a live worksheet, with results recalculated after changes to numbers, expressions, etc., as in a spreadsheet. Notation inconsistency: P(x) and S(x) are the same as p(x) and s(x) used in text earlier.

Start of reproductive period : $\alpha := 0$ Age of ego : $a := 0, 20 .. 80$

Fertility functions:

$$a := -35.134315 \qquad b := -0.122003 \qquad c := 9.656093$$

$$f(x) := e^{[a+(b \cdot x \cdot \sqrt{x})+c \cdot \sqrt{x}]}$$

$$m(x) := f(x) \cdot 0.4867 \cdot (x \geq 10)(x \leq 50)$$

(Female births only; range limited to 10 to $-$ 50 by conditions on x)

$$p := -0.741013 \qquad q := 5.658693 \qquad r := 84.446801 \qquad s := -8.853886$$

$$S(x) := p + \frac{q}{1 + e^{\left[\frac{-(x-r)}{s}\right]}}$$

$$p(x) := \frac{S(x) \cdot (x \geq 0) \cdot (x \leq 100)}{5}$$

(Range limited to 0 to $-$ 100 by conditions on x)

$$a := 0, 20 .. 80 \qquad\qquad x := 0 .. 100$$

Daughters born by age a	Daughters living at age a
$B1(a) := \int_{\alpha}^{a} m(a)\,da$	$BL1(a) := \int_{\alpha}^{a} P(a-x) \cdot m(x)\,dx$

B1(a)=	BL1(1)=
0.000	0.000
0.074	0.073
0.805	0.792
0.813	0.770

Age range for daughter generation $y := 0 .. 50$

$$B2(a) := \int_{\alpha}^{a} \left(\int_{\alpha}^{a-x} P(y) \cdot m(y)\, dy \right) \cdot m(x)\, dx \qquad BL2(a) := \int_{\alpha}^{a} \left(\int_{\alpha}^{a-x} P(y) \cdot m(y) \cdot \right.$$

$$\left. P(a - x - y)\, dy \right) \cdot m(x)\, dx$$

B2(a)=
0.000
0.000
0.018
0.518
0.649

B2(a)=
0.000
0.000
0.018
0.509
0.637

References

Caswell, H. (1989). *Matrix population models*. Sunderland: Sinauer Associates.

Coresh, X., & Goldman, N. (1988). The effect of variability in the fertility schedule on numbers of kin. *Mathematical Population Studies, 1*, 137–156.

Goldman, N. (1978). Estimating the intrinsic rate of increase of a population from the average number of older and younger sisters. *Demography, 15*, 499–508.

Goldman, N. (1984). *Fertility, mortality and kinship*. Paper presented at annual meetings of Population Association of America, Minneapolis.

Goodman, L., Keyfitz, N., & Pullum, T. (1974). Family formation and the frequency of various kinship relationships. *Theoretical Population Biology, 5*, 1–27. See also 1975 Addendum, *Theoretical Population Biology* 8: 376-381.

Hakkert, R. (1992). *Computing in demographic analysis: Beyond paper and pencil algorithms*. Paper at IUSSP/NIDI Expert Meeting on Demographic Software and Computing, The Hague, 29 June–3 July, 1992.

Keyfitz, N. (1985). *Applied mathematical demography* (2nd ed.). New York: Springer.

Keyfitz, N. (1986). Canadian kinship patterns based on 1971 and 1981 data. *Canadian Studies in Population, 13*, 123–150.

Leslie, P. H. (1945). On the use of matrices in certain population mathematics. *Biometrika, 35*, 213–245.

Nagnur, D. [Statistics Canada]. (1986). *Longevity and historical life tables, 1921–1981 [Abridged], Canada and the Provinces*. Ottawa: Ministry of Supply and Services.

Statistics Canada. (1984). *Life tables, Canada and the Provinces, 1980–1982*. Ottawa: Ministry of Supply and Services.

Chapter 8
The Life Table as a Theoretical Model

8.1   Introduction

The life table is most commonly thought of as a summary measure of period age-specific death rates, and typically is described as such to students and to the public – thus the term *ordinary* life table. This life table also is characterized as describing the hypothetical survival experience of a *synthetic* or *fictitious cohort*, subject to current death rates over an imagined lifetime.

A second interpretation views the life table's numbers as a description of the stationary population model, built up by a succession of birth cohorts of the same size, all of which experience the same age-specific death rates. Sometimes the last two interpretations – synthetic cohort experience and stationary population – have been confounded in the same table, with some column headings referring to cohort experience and others to the population model.

Less common than the ordinary or period life table is the cohort or generational life table, based on the actual historical experience of a real birth cohort. In either case, the life table is viewed primarily as a measurement device summarising observed death rates.

Shryock and Siegel's (1973) discussion of the life table is representative. At the outset, they note that 'A life table is designed essentially to measure mortality...,' and 'Life tables are, in essence, one form of combining mortality rates of a population at different ages into a single statistical model. They are principally used to measure the level of mortality of the population involved' (II: 429). They distinguish period and cohort tables by the reference year[s] involved, with a discussion and abbreviated example of a real-cohort table (446–447). All discussion is of life tables based on actual, observed data. There is no mention of life tables based on hypothetical data. They note that 'In general, unless otherwise specified, the term 'life table' is used...to refer to the current life table' (429).

More recent treatments in demographic texts do not differ appreciably from Shryock and Siegel, although there is more discussion of applying the 'life table

T.K. Burch, *Model-Based Demography*, Demographic Research Monographs,
DOI 10.1007/978-3-319-65433-1_8

concept' to other demographic processes, notably in event-history analysis. But the emphasis continues to be on the period mortality table as a measurement model. Most detailed examples are of such a table. I have found no treatment which begins with or emphasizes the completely general concept of the diminution of a cohort by some kind of attrition event.

There is historical justification for this emphasis, since the majority of published life tables have been and continue to be period tables – official life tables prepared by government statistical agencies, 'standard' tables used by insurance firms, and collections published in the U.N. *Demographic Yearbook*. Such tables have also formed the basis for several sets of 'model life tables.'

8.2   Another Perspective on Life Tables

A more fruitful approach, I submit, is to view the life table as a completely general theoretical construct, with many applications and empirical interpretations, of which current mortality measurement is only one.[1] The identification of the life table with the ordinary life table is a case of cultural lag. In the view of Wilson and Oeppen (2003), it is an example of reification, the fallacy of identifying an abstract, general idea with one of its concrete realisations.[2]

At the most general level, the life table expresses an abstract concept of the survival experience of some kind of cohort in the face of some kind of decrement or attrition-event. It is an *abstract model* of cohort survival. In the case of mortality, the model is that of a birth cohort being diminished by death according to some schedule of mortality until the last member is dead. For divorce, the model is that of a cohort of marriages or of married persons, being diminished by divorce over duration or age. This general idea can be expressed in words as a *verbal model*, or visually by means of a state diagram, a compartment model, or a flow diagram – a *visual model*.

In these forms, the model can only suggest a few limited ideas about the processes involved: over time/age some number or fraction of members of the original cohort will move from one state to another [life to death, married to divorced]; the survival curve, at least for these kinds of events, must be monotonic decreasing. And some or all of the cohort will eventually experience the event – all for death, some for divorce.[3]

---

[1] For an earlier statement of the value of differing interpretations and uses of the same demographic algorithm, see Romaniuc (1990). See also Burch (2005) and Chap. 4 above.

[2] Among philosophers, the concept of *reification* seems to have taken on slightly different meanings since A.N. Whitehead spoke of the 'fallacy of misplaced concreteness.' But all contain the central notion of a confusion of abstract entities with concrete reality.

[3] There is the additional issue of other events to which a cohort might be at risk, for example, the attrition of single persons by first marriage or death. This chapter discusses mainly single-decrement models, but the ideas extend easily to more complex survival tables.

The abstract concept can be further specified as an *algorithm*, a computational procedure expressed in a series of steps described verbally, in a set of equations, or in computer code. The algorithm assumes some set of death rates or probabilities of dying by age, or probabilities of some other attrition event, but need not specify these. The result is a template, an empty box that can be filled in many ways.

The most common realization of the life table, as noted above, is as measurement model, using as input observed period or real cohort age-specific death rates. Based as it is on actual data, this table in some sense answers the question 'What has actually happened?' In the case of a real cohort mortality table, the measurement is straightforward, and the table becomes a depiction of the actual lifetime experience of the cohort as it occurred in historical time. In the case of period mortality, interpretation is far from straightforward. The data underlying the table are real, but the process depicted is not, since it is a process that has not been and will never be experienced by any concrete group of human beings. In any case survival occurs in real time, and phases like 'this year's life expectancy' and 'current survival' are at best shorthand, at worst misleading. In the real world, average person-years lived in a given calendar year cannot exceed 1.0; realisation of average life expectancy requires a lifetime, real or imagined. The ordinary life table is thus measurement, but it also is a form of modeling or simulation [see below].

For purely descriptive purposes of current mortality levels, demography might have done just as well to adopt Schoen's (1970) suggestion to use the geometric mean as an age-standardised measure of age-specific death rates. Of course, there are other useful applications of the ordinary life table – survival ratios, for example – and these work well enough as long as its fictitious character is properly taken into account. Often it is not, as in frequent statements in the press and by students, equating the current e_0 with 'how long a baby born this year can expect to live.' This is confusion of an abstraction, the period life-table, with concrete future reality.

8.3   From Measurement to Simulation

Given the fact that demographers have been so completely comfortable with the fictions involve in the ordinary life table, it is surprising that we have not also been more comfortable with another application of the basic algorithm, as simulation or modeling, using whatever set of death rates that suit one's purpose. These rates can be observed rates, imaginary but plausible rates, or fanciful rates that serve some analytic purpose. Such a life table deals with the question 'What would happen if. . .?'

In a surprisingly sophisticated treatment for a text over 50 years old, Barclay (1958) graphs a comparison of an ordinary survival curve with the straight line that would result from equal numbers of deaths at each age. He mentions, but does not illustrate, the result of a constant proportion of deaths at each age, a negative exponential survival curve.

But there is no limit to the range of scenarios that might be explored in this way, for an increased understanding of survival processes and their implications. What would the survival curve look like if human beings were immortal? If the resulting horizontal straight line seems trivial, consider the position-time graph of a stationary object presented in an introductory physics text, in the discussion of straight-line motion. Rather than being trivial, this is a matter of starting at the beginning, with the simplest case, especially important for students. The simplest case also serves as a natural reference point for all others.

What-if scenarios can be played off the ordinary life table. How much would e_0 change if all deaths before 30 were eliminated? What would the survival curve look like if a typical set of q_x's were experienced by a cohort in reverse order [with the proviso that no $q_x = 1.0$]? The result is a reminder that the species could not survive with such a mortality pattern, combined with our relatively low fertility [compared to plants or many insects], and the long period of infant/child dependency. It's a reminder of how much of our social structure and culture is a result of overlapping generations.

Of current interest is the revised period life table proposed by Bongaarts and Feeney (2002), based on the age-specific mortality rates that would have been observed in the absence of any secular trend in mortality. Without trying to judge the deeper issues involved, I would note that their life table involves all the fictions involved in the ordinary period life table, plus the added fiction that mortality is not changing over time when in fact it is. Their argument does not seem to me to justify dismissal of the standard life table as biased. Both are abstract models, not concrete descriptions of anything. It's more a question of which fiction to use for which purpose.

In any event, with a willingness to imagine data, the life table model becomes a much more versatile scientific tool than when it is tied so closely to empirical data. It allows demographers and students of demography to undertake more active and imaginative analyses of decrement process, to engage in computer experiments about cohort experience.

The life table often is seen as a prediction model, forecasting future mortality experience of a population or cohort. The question at issue here is 'What will happen in the future?' Whether the life table is correctly interpreted in this way depends. In the case of the ordinary period life table, forecasting over a few following years is safe, assuming mortality is changing slowly. To interpret the life expectancy at birth as a prediction of the average length of life of persons currently being born – not uncommon in journalistic accounts – is misleading. Their length of life will depend on the next century or so of changing death rates.

A truly predictive life table, which is not yet in common use, would be based on age-specific death rates or probabilities of death by age, which have themselves been forecast far enough into the future to cover the mortality experience of living cohorts, but also those yet to be born. It would be in effect a generational life table projected into the future.[4] Such a life table could be constructed for any birth cohort.

---

[4]To my knowledge, there are not many examples of such tables. One is Vallin and Meslé (2001).

For those already alive, it would be a hybrid of past and future experience. In such a future-oriented life table, the phrase *expectation of life* takes on more meaning specifically as a real expectation for the future, not measures on the imaginary lifetimes of a synthetic cohort. In accord with the best contemporary practise of mortality forecasting, life table measures could be given with error bounds. Such a life table, giving a realistic account of future mortality, would seem to be more useful for many kinds of demographic analysis that now rely on period tables.

Such life tables or their equivalent must surely underlie many official government population forecasts, but they seem seldom to be published as being of interest in their own right. The published and publicized life tables from government statistical agencies invariably are period tables, which are then duly misinterpreted by the press.

Interestingly, the suggestion to make more use of tables based on forecasts of future rates dates back to at least 1917 in Knibbs' appendix to the 1911 census of Australia. Knibbs termed it a 'fluent life table.' The suggestion was strongly reiterated by Dublin and Speigelman in a paper at the 1941 meetings of the Population Association of America (Dublin and Spiegelman 1941; contains reference to Knibbs). The failure of the discipline to implement these suggestions must have something to do with our fundamental preference for empirical data, which, rightly or wrongly, we equate with hard-rock reality. Simulated or modelled results are often viewed as fanciful – made-up data.

Finally, the basic life table can be extended to relate to the mortality, not of one cohort, but of a succession of fictitious cohorts of the same size, across a century or more, all subject to the same mortality schedule. The life table becomes a population model, specifically the stationary model. Combine with this an unchanging set of age-specific fertility rates and one has a stable population model, expressing in numerical terms some basic elements of stable population theory.[5]

8.4 Modeling as Theory

Granted that the basic life or survival table model can take many forms, is it a theoretical model, or theory? There are several justifications for such language. It accords with practice in some of the most successful disciplines, notably physics. If Newton's law of falling bodies is theory, then so is the life table. Newton's equation is an abstract model of a point mass falling in a vacuum with only two bodies in interaction. It can be used to approximate a concrete case with the insertion of a parameter for the force of gravity. But this parameter is not constant – even on earth it differs by location, altitude and other factors. Similarly, the algorithm for the life

---

[5]Some would say that the *theory* resides in the underlying equations, whereas a specific numerical example is to be called a *model*. Clearly there are differences between the two forms, but they are differences of specificity rather than of basic epistemological status.

table must be specified by insertion of a set of death rates. There may be no 'law of mortality,' but there is a limited range of life expectancies; and life table functions have similar shapes.[6]

Mortality data and life-table functions also can be represented by approximating functions (see Chap. 7), but these will be more complicated that Newton's law; instead of one parameter, they typically will require three or more. But the difference between these demographic functions and Newton's equation is quantitative not qualitative. Both are abstract models that approximate real-world phenomena.

This accords with the views of an increasing numbers of philosophers of science, in what has come to be known as the 'model-based' view of science (see especially Giere 1999, 2006; Teller 2001). In this approach, the basic element of science is not the law but the model, seen as a formally true abstract representation of some portion of reality. The most common type of model is the theoretical model, expressed in words, mathematical equations, or, increasingly, in computer code. The word *theory* can refer to a very general model or to a collection of smaller, more specific models, as in the phrase 'theory of harmonic oscillators' in physics, a collection of models dealing with objects such as springs and pendulums. In this latter sense, the life table is a theoretical model, an abstract representation of some aspects of the survival of a cohort.[7]

For the model-based school, the empirical question regarding a theoretical model is not whether it is true, but whether it applies to some part of the real [or at least observed] world closely enough, in certain respects, for a certain purpose. Thus, the ordinary life table is 'true' in this sense, and works well as a summary of current age-specific death rates. Whether it works well enough as an indicator of some current underlying mortality conditions not reflected accurately in current rates is a matter of current controversy. Clearly, it does not work well as a prediction of future mortality over the next century.

Closer to home, justification for viewing the life table as theory can be found in two prescient papers by Keyfitz (1971, 1975) in which he argues that most of what we reliably know about population dynamics comes from our use of models rather than empirical data, that models are the basis of our understanding. At many points, he uses the terms *model* and *theory* interchangeably. Also of interest is the fact that he does not distinguish between formal demographic and behavioral models; all have the same epistemological status.

But these are arguments from authority. The best argument for adopting this view of the life table is that it would be good for the discipline. Demography needs all the theory it can get if it is to be a science and not just a branch of applied statistics. In fact, we have much good theory, but we have tended not to recognise it

---

[6]These facts are the basis for model life tables, and for attempts to define a mortality function, the Gompertz curve, for example.

[7]An interesting question regarding demographic usage is why we regularly speak of 'stable population theory' but refer to the cohort-component projection model as a 'forecasting technique.' Both are abstract representations of population dynamics.

as such. If the life table is theory, then so is the exponential growth formula, the stable model, the projection model, indeed much of so-called formal demography. This is not a word game. Such models give rigorous substantive insight into how populations and cohorts behave. And that is theory.

A systematic approach to the life table as a general model and many different specific realizations would in time help lessen the confusion that surrounds many of our models. The ordinary life table is better understood and less liable to misinterpretation if it is put in the context sketched above, which underlines its abstract and hypothetical character. This would be especially important to our students. And if we didn't reify the ordinary life table, then perhaps we could do a better job of explaining current results to journalists and the public. But even battle-hardened demographers are not immune to confusion, as is seen in the current discussions of the Bongaarts-Feeney modified life table.

Finally, there is much to learn from the life table through computer experiment as well as through its use for straightforward calculation with the usual data. Such work is scientific analysis as opposed to measurement, which is a prelude to scientific analysis, an essential prelude but a prelude nonetheless.

The model-based view of science has another important general implication for demography. If much of formal demography is theory, it also is the case that we can reinterpret many of our older, often rejected, behavioral models as perfectly good abstract theoretical models that may or may not fit a concrete case well enough for a specific analytic purpose. Much that we have rejected is perfectly good theory.

The two re-interpretations combined point to demography as a discipline with a rich body of theories about how populations work, not just a body of techniques or a branch of applied statistics.

References

Barclay, G. W. (1958). *Techniques of population analysis*. New York: Wiley.

Bongaarts, J., & Feeney, G. (2002). How long do we live? *Population and Development Review, 28*, 13–29.

Burch, T. K. (2005). Computer simulation and statistical modelling: Rivals or complements. Paper at International Union for the Scientific Study of Population, General Assembly, Tours, France; Session #131, Epistemology in Demography and Sociology [Daniel Courgeau, organiser]. See also Ch. 4 above.

Dublin, L. I., & Spiegelman, M. (1941). Current versus generation life tables. *Human Biology, 13*, 439–445.

Giere, R. N. (1999). *Science without laws*. Chicago: University of Chicago Press.

Giere, R. N. (2006). *Scientific perspectivism*. Chicago: University of Chicago Press.

Keyfitz, N. (1971). Models. *Demography, 8*, 571–580.

Keyfitz, N. (1975). How do we know the facts of demography? *Population and Development Review, 1*, 267–288.

Romaniuc, A. (1990). Population projection as prediction, simulation and prospective analysis. In *Population bulletin of the United Nations* (pp. 16–31). New York: United Nations 29.

Schoen, R. (1970). The geometric mean of the age-specific death rates as a summary index of mortality. *Demography, 7*, 317–324.

Shryock, H., & Siegel, S. (1973). *The methods and materials of demography*. Washington, DC: US
    Government Printing Office.
Teller, P. (2001). Twilight of the perfect model model. *Erkenntnis, 55*, 393–415.
Vallin, J., & Meslé, F. (2001). *Tables de mortalité francaises pour les XIXe et XXe siècles et
    projections pour XXIe siècle*. Paris: Collections INED.
Wilson, C., & Oeppen, J. (2003). On reification in demography. In J. Fleischhacker, H. A. De
    Gans, & T. K. Burch (Eds.), *Populations, projections and politics* (pp. 113–129). Amsterdam:
    Rozenberg Publishers.

Chapter 9
Cohort Component Projection: Algorithm, Technique, Model and Theory

9.1 Introduction

If a student were to ask a North American demographer where to find a detailed treatment of population projections, chances are he or she would be sent to a text on demographic 'techniques' or 'methods,' or urged to take a course on 'technical' demography. If the student were to look in a standard introductory textbook on population, or take a course on 'population problems' or on 'behavioral' or 'substantive demography,' chances are he or she would be exposed to at best a cursory treatment of population projections, mentioning their use in population forecasting or prediction.

I have come to think that the sharp distinction between formal or technical demography on the one hand, and substantive or behavioral demography on the other, has been mistaken. The relegation of the population projection algorithm, along with many other measures and models, to the category *techniques*, devalues them as scientific knowledge. The standard projection algorithm, of course, is a technique and a computational procedure. But when rightly viewed, it is more than that. It is a powerful substantive model of core population dynamics. At a basic level, it tells us clearly and accurately how populations work. When viewed in the light of newer ideas in the philosophy of science, the population projection model is nothing less than a demographic theory. The philosopher of science Ronald Giere recently has written of physics:

> The problem is not with current scientific theories of the world, but with current theories... of what it is to acquire good scientific theories of the world. As is typically the case for individuals, our collective self-knowledge lags behind our collective knowledge of the world. (Giere 1999)

This is slightly edited version of a paper originally published in *Canadian Studies in Population* 30 (2003):29–33.

© The Author(s) 2018

T.K. Burch, *Model-Based Demography*, Demographic Research Monographs,
DOI 10.1007/978-3-319-65433-1_9

The same could be said of demography as a science – specifically as a distinct and autonomous science, as opposed to a branch of applied statistics concerned with the collection and descriptive treatment of demographic data. Demography knows more than demographers or others give it credit for. But scientific knowledge is encapsulated in theory. And much of our theory is not recognized as such, buried as it is in 'techniques' or 'methods.'

Whence this faulty self-knowledge of demography? There are many reasons, most of them tied up with the intellectual history of modem demography. There has been the perverse influence of radical positivism (see Ernst Mach or Karl Pearson), intensified in the latter half of the twentieth century by the logical empiricism of Nagel, Hempel, and Popper. There has been the close association of scientific demography with government statistical agencies, an association that had signal advantages for demography, but also disadvantages, notably, a preoccupation with data collection, estimation, and descriptive analysis, at the expense of theory.

9.2   Anatole Romaniuc on Population Projections

Closely related to this neglect of theory, has been a similar neglect of scientific methodology and the logic and epistemology of science as these apply to the study of human population. The demographic literature contains relatively few exceptions to this statement.[1] In this chapter, I focus on one such exception, by Anatole Romaniuc – 'Population projection as prediction, simulation and prospective analysis' (1990). In this paper, Romaniuc transcends the restrictive methodological views of most demographers to highlight the multi-faceted character of population projection, including its role as a substantive model of population dynamics, that is, as theory.

In discussing population projection as *prediction,* Romaniuc is on familiar ground. When one wants to know the future population (size, age and sex structure) of the world, nation, or other well-defined population, one commonly turns to a standard demographic (cohort-component) population projection. We often quibble about the differences among a 'forecast,' a 'prediction' and a 'projection,' but often as not what we're really after is knowledge of the future.

Romaniuc accepts the well-documented fact that population projections viewed as predictions have often turned out to be incorrect, a fact which he attributes to the inherent unpredictability of human behavior. But these limits to the predictive abilities of projections do not disturb him, since he sees two other important roles for population projections.

One is the use of the algorithm for *simulation.* Simulations, in his view, are 'prediction-neutral.' 'No attempt is made to predict the future' (p. 21). Simulations

---

[1]See, for example, Keyfitz (1975), Wunsch (1995), and McNicoll (1992). Keyfitz felt it necessary to apologize in advance to his demographic audience for discussing 'epistemological' questions.

are 'conditional' projections, '... tautological in the sense of one set of numbers (input) being transformed into another set of numbers (output) relevant to the problem at hand' (p. 21). The focus is on using the projection algorithm to investigate interrelationships among demographic and other variables.

This use is less familiar than the predictive use of projection, but has found increasing application since the advent of computers rendered the sheer computational labor of doing a projection almost trivial. Suppose one wants to know in general how immigration can affect the age structure of a population. More specifically, can changes in the number and kind of immigrants slow or even reverse population aging? The question can be answered by computer simulation of several population projections (realistic, but not necessary accurate with respect to any particular population), with varying assumptions about patterns of mortality, fertility, and migration. Using this approach, one can easily demonstrate that for the typical developed nation (e.g., Canada), no imaginable pattern of immigration can have more than a small impact on the age composition of the population, except in the short term, or unless one assumes that immigrants maintain fertility levels well-above prevailing below-replacement fertility.

One could similarly demonstrate the relative influence on age structure of mortality decline versus fertility decline, or the impact of delayed fertility (higher average age at childbearing) on population growth rates. Note that these simulations, if carried out with enough well-chosen assumptions about inputs, yield firm scientific generalizations – knowledge of how specific kinds of populations work in well-defined circumstances. This is the basis of Keyfitz's claim that in demography '... the most important relations cannot be established by direct observation...'; insight and understanding come from models (Keyfitz 1975, p. 267).

The third use of population projection identified by Romaniuc is that of *prospective analysis*. He views it as a middle-ground between prediction and simulation: 'If one pictures the transition from simulation to prediction on a continuum, with predictability ideally increasing in degree along that continuum, the prospective analysis would be found somewhere midway along the axis' (p. 23). The emphasis here is on working out plausible or possible futures for a specific population. 'These projections aim chiefly at unraveling demographic tendencies' (p. 23). Prospective analyses differ from predictions in that they do not seek certainty or even high probability, only plausibility. They differ from simulation in that they are future oriented, and in that they deal with a specific population rather than with general relationships.

The key requirement for a projection as prospective analysis is that it have what Romaniuc terms 'analytic credibility': 'The argument underlying the projection assumptions must be persuasive to both the professional peers of the producers and to the users' (p. 23). In other words, the whole projection process should be based on and should lead to understanding, not just mechanical forecasting or extrapolation. Understanding the processes that lead to the future is important in preparing for it (p. 28).

Finally, Romaniuc argues that being able to predict future population accurately may be less important that getting analytic guidance to change the future: '...the performance [of a projection] is to be gauged not so much by the degree to which the projection predicts the future population...but rather by the extent to which it contributes to the decision-making processes that shape the future' (p. 29).

9.3 Towards Rethinking Demography

Although specifically limited to a discussion of population projections, Romaniuc's paper has much wider relevance, containing as it does powerful ideas that challenge the way we view demography and other empirical social sciences. He does not use the word *theory* in this connection, but many scientists and philosophers of science would say that projection as simulation and projection as prospective analysis are in effect forms of theoretical analysis; the projection model is a theoretical model.

The cohort-component projection algorithm is true in the way that $2 + 2 = 4$ is true, given accepted definitions of numbers and the addition operation. But if I have two apples and you have only one, the $2 + 2 = 4$ model simply does not apply. If you have 200 and I have 199, a $200 + 200 = 400$ model might be close enough for the purpose at hand, with an error of 1/400 or 0.25%. Similarly, the cohort-component projection model is true, based as it is on the basic demographic equation [population change is accounted for by four factors: births, deaths, in-migration and out-migration], and on elementary arithmetic. Given inputs for fertility, mortality and migration, the projected outcome is true. Whether it applies or will apply to the real world is an empirical question. As a prediction, it may or not be realized in the future. It is more apt to be 'true' in this sense over a short period – say, up to 5 years – than over a longer period of a decade or more.

Romaniuc's discussion of projection as prospective analysis and as simulation is a striking illustration of this general principle. In one fell swoop, he shows us that much of formal demography – often belittled as 'mere techniques' or 'human bookkeeping – is in fact theoretical knowledge of population dynamics. It is a reminder that in the hands of a master, methodological reflection – stepping back from everyday work to think deeply about how that everyday work is being done – can yield important insights into what a discipline has achieved and point the way to future progress.

References

Giere, R. N. (1999). *Science without laws*. Chicago: University of Chicago Press.

Keyfitz, N. (1975). How do we know the facts of demography? *Population and Development Review, 1*, 267–288.

McNicoll, G. (1992). The agenda of population studies: A commentary and complaint. *Population and Development Review, 18*, 399–420.

Romaniuc, A. (1990). Population projection as prediction, simulation and prospective analysis. *Population Bulletin of the United Nations, 29*, 16–31.

Romaniuc, A. (2003). Reflections on population forecasting: From predictions to prospective analysis. *Canadian Studies in Population, 30*, 35–50.

Wunsch, G. (1995). 'God has chosen to give the easy problems to the physicists'; Or why demographers need theory (Working Paper No. 179). Institut de Demographie, Université catholique de Louvain.

Chapter 10
The Cohort-Component Population Projection: A Strange Attractor for Demographers

10.1 Introduction

It has been said that all Western philosophy is but a footnote to Plato. I feel as though anything I might say here risks being but a footnote to de Gans, *Population Forecasting, 1895–1945: The Transition to Modernity* (De Gans 1999), to *Frontiers of Population Forecasting*, a supplement to *Population Development Review* edited by Lutz *et al.* (1998), and to Bongaarts and Bulatao [eds.] *Beyond Six Billion: Forecasting the World's Population* (2000). Little in science is ever truly definitive. But taken together these works come close in their treatment of the history and current practice of population forecasting. They will frame discussion of the topic for some time to come, and will have major impact on new developments.[1]

My footnote aims to place the cohort-component population projection algorithm in a broader perspective. I suggest viewing it, not just as a technique for population forecasting, but more fundamentally as a general theoretical model of population dynamics. In this perspective, population forecasting is just one among many analytic uses of the model – an important one, but only one (See Romaniuc 1990, and Chaps. 4 and 9 above).

de Gans chronicles the triumph of the 'demographic' – that is the cohort component – approach to population forecasting in The Netherlands, but also internationally, to the point where it became and has remained to this day the standard method, sanctioned by academic demography, by national governments, and by influential international organizations such as the United Nations and the World Bank. As the title suggests, I sometimes find it strange that its triumph should

---

Based on presentation at a workshop on Population Forecasts in the 1920s and 1930s (17–18 May 1999), at the Max Planck Institute for Demographic Research, Rostock, Germany. Published originally in Fleischhacker, deGans, and Burch 2003:39–57.

[1]See also Cohen's (1995) Part 3 on 'Future Human Population Growth,' especially Chap. 7, 'Projection methods: the hazy crystal ball.'

T.K. Burch, *Model-Based Demography*, Demographic Research Monographs, DOI 10.1007/978-3-319-65433-1_10

have been so complete and so long lasting. I find it easy enough to understand why the cohort-component projection [hereafter CCP] model should have become so popular in the 1920s and 1930s, although even here I have some questions. I find it harder to understand why, with so little change in details of application, it has remained so popular, to the near-exclusion of other methods.

I have sometimes thought that the CCP approach to population forecasting is obsolescent if not obsolete. There is an element of truth in this. But on further reflection, I would put it differently. The CCP method *as currently described and practiced, and as a monopolistic method* is obsolete. But it will continue to be useful in many contexts. In addition, the CCP model contains a kernel of demographic truth that is permanently valid, and therefore will be retained at the core of many future, more elaborate forecasting models. Another, although unconventional, way of saying this is that the CCP is fundamentally a valuable theoretical model of population dynamics, not just a popular technique.

The CCP model remains an excellent tool for many purposes, regardless of its well-publicized failures to predict accurately. With growing sophistication in both scientific and policy analysis, and with the calculating power of the modern computer that makes the CCP projection computationally trivial, there is good reason to keep it our toolbox, along with other, perhaps newer and more powerful analytic tools. But as de Gans reminds us on more than one occasion, demography and statistics are human activities, subject to human foibles. The future of population forecasting will no doubt be influenced by disciplinary and other vested interests, by ego, and by ideology. Our best hope will be to contain these influences in the interests of good science and rational policy analysis.

This chapter touches on three questions, although not separately or systematically:

1. Why did the CCP model become the dominant tool for population forecasting?
2. Why has it remained dominant for so long, to the near exclusion of other methods?
3. What will be its future status?

By way of tentative and partial answer to these questions, I focus on: (a) the inherent strengths of the CCP algorithm, which are many; (b) its mathematical simplicity, involving little more than basic arithmetic; (c) some characteristics of the field of demography, broadly defined, including its relative lack of mathematical sophistication, (d) a general tendency towards parochialism, and (e) what I have come to think of as theoretical and methodological nonchalance. By the latter I mean relative inattention to theory-building and to the philosophy of science in favor of a preoccupation with data and technique.

10.2   The Cohort-Component Population Projection Model: An Overview

It is useful to begin with a reminder of the main features of the CCP algorithm:

1. It is mathematically easy, involving no more than addition, subtraction, multiplication and division, and knowledge of decimal fractions. Most of the individual relationships in the model are obvious after a little thought. It involves some complexity, but little inherent difficulty.

2. It is computationally intensive, especially if the projection is over a long period and uses small (for example, 5-year) age intervals. There are no shortcuts, in the sense that one cannot skip from t_0 to t_{75} without computing results for all the intervening years. Compare the stable population model, which more economically yields some information on long-term dynamics, or the exponential or logistic [or other formulaic] approaches, which easily evaluate the function P [t] at any time. The high calculation costs of CCP projections in the early days, before computers, help explain why most projections were done by government agencies rather than by individual researchers.

3. Model interrelations are necessary relationships. Given a starting population structure and assumptions about fertility, mortality and migration, the outcomes follow with mathematical certainty and considerable precision.[2]

4. Behavioral inputs are strictly exogenous. Nothing in the model impacts on age-specific fertility, survival probabilities, or the amount (number or rates) of migration. More specifically, there are no feedbacks from population size and structure to the basic inputs. Size and structure interact with the rates, of course, to produce births and survivors (and perhaps migrants), but there is nothing in the model to change the rates themselves, even in the face of extreme developments.

5. The model has limited content; socio-economic determinants of population dynamics are excluded. It is thus a demographically self-contained population model. But it is limited even in demographic terms. For example, CCP projections often do not explicitly include marital/quasi-marital status and status-specific fertility as variables. In cases where it is included, it is introduced exogenously; for example, emerging age-sex structures, which might include distorted sex ratios, do not affect marital status. There are no feedbacks from structure to input rates.

6. The exogenous inputs of fertility, mortality and migration typically are not behaviorally modeled. The most common assumption is that they will exhibit continuity with the present or recent past. The continuity assumption is implemented by means of informal judgements: 'The total fertility rate,

---

[2]According to an increasingly influential view of science and scientific theory, this is a characteristic of all good explanatory models. See Giere (1999), Teller (2001), Burch (2003, and Chap. 2 above).

currently 1.6, might rise as high as 1.9 or fall to 1.3 by the year 2020,' or, increasingly, by means of formal methods of extrapolation.

7. Partly because of the computational burden noted above, official population projections became the norm and were considered and used as general-purpose projections. Interestingly, the notion of one set of projections for all purposes runs counter to a cardinal rule of mathematical modeling [found in virtually every book on mathematical modeling or simulation I have encountered], namely, that a good model must be customized for the purpose for which it is being constructed. This issue emerges in de Gans'account of the tension between national and local population forecasters in The Netherlands.

In short, the standard CCP algorithm is limited, linear, and 'open loop,' and assumes continuity in fertility, mortality and migration. Keyfitz (1998) has summarized the matter as follows:

> Demographic models commonly used for analyzing and projecting population are mostly variants of a very simple equation that can be written as y, $= A^t x$, where y the outcome is a vector...say the anticipated future population at time t distributed by five-year age intervals..., x is the corresponding vector for the initial period, the jumping off point in time, A is the square matrix of constants that in practice are usually derived from the fertility and mortality of the jumping-off point..., and depart little from the data of the jumping-off point.... It [the equation] is not only linear, but among linear systems, it is an open loop, i.e., the result in one period does not affect the parameters for the next period; it is assumed applicable unchanged for successive time periods.' (p. 1)

In discussing the CCP model, note the importance of distinguishing the following: the central algorithm, which is formally true and in that sense beyond criticism; assumptions regarding input components, that is, about levels and/or trends in fertility, mortality and migration; and the interpretation and use of results.

10.3   The Many Strengths of the CPP Model

The CCP model is limited, but within those limits it is a powerful and versatile analytic tool. Consider the following advantages:

1. *Accounting for the past*. With respect to the past, assuming historical inputs of fertility, mortality and migration, the CCP algorithm provides a complete account of past population dynamics, including size, growth rates, and changing age-sex composition. The actual historical dynamics, with due allowance for errors in basic data, follow logically from past inputs combined with the algorithm. There are not many social science models that can supply such a sense of closure on historical explanation, at any level of analysis.

2. *Contingent but confident prediction*. Given assumptions about future inputs, future population dynamics follow necessarily and with certainty. Over short prediction horizons, one can be confident of assumptions, so that the results are

nearly inevitable. Again, there is solidity in these predictions seldom encountered elsewhere in social science.

3. *Guide to future intervention.* Besides contingent prediction, the CCP model provides some guidance as to how future population dynamics might be controlled. To a limited degree, it deals with causal mechanisms of future population dynamics, and identifies fertility [and possibly nuptiality], mortality and migration as policy levers that can in principle be used to change those dynamics in a desired direction and to a desired degree. Compare this with the relative lack of any sense of control or policy options when dealing with exponential or logistic models of population growth as these usually are presented.

In what has become one of my favorite books on scientific methodology, Meehan (1968) makes a sharp distinction between prediction and explanation. He points out that the latter is both more demanding intellectually, requiring specification of why something will happen, and more valuable practically, helping us control the future, not just adjust to it. The CCP approach, compared with some other population forecasting models, scores well on these criteria – it can both explain, within its limited compass, and predict.

4. *Details of age-sex composition.* Used for population forecasting, the CCP algorithm can provide meaningful detail on age-sex composition, again in contrast to exponential or logistic forecasts of total population. The feature has made CCP projections particularly useful for sectoral planning, for example, dealing with school-age or labor-force entry sub-populations. The age-sex detail also provides a solid foundation for superimposed age-sex distributions, for example, of marital status or household status (as in the headship rate method of household forecasting).
5. *Continuity as a first approximation.* There is a sense in which an assumption of continuity in levels and trends in fertility, mortality and migration is a natural assumption, in the absence of anything better. Up until World War II, this assumption served demography rather well. It has taken the Baby Boom, the post-1960s rise in divorce rates, the advent of widespread cohabitation, recent mortality increases in some advanced societies (for example, the former Soviet sphere), and other massive demographic discontinuities to accustom us to the view that such discontinuities are not unlikely, even if continuity remains more likely.

It has also taken a gradual weaning from the idea that demography and other human sciences can or must aspire to the discovery of immutable laws of behavior, in the manner of 'celestial mechanics,' an idea that is a *leitmotiv* of de Gans'book.[3]

---

[3]See his valuable discussion of George Herbert Mead's ideas on time, notably, the notion that 'the emergent event is conditioned, but not determined, by the causal chain,' that is, by the past (1999, p. 231).

6. *A powerful and flexible abstract model.* In demographic texts and monographs, the CCP model invariably is presented as a technique for making population forecasts. Other uses certainly have appeared, but they generally have not been emphasized. Romaniuc ([1990](#)) was one of the first to describe systematically some of these other uses, placing them on an equal footing with forecasting. He features three main applications of population projections[4]:

   1. prediction: What will be the future of population growth? This is based on the best possible assumptions of the future course of fertility, mortality and migration.
   2. prospective analysis: What are some realistic scenarios for a given population, assuming, for example, major and successful changes in policy?
   3. simulation: What would happen to population growth if...? This can be based on any assumptions whatever, even unrealistic assumptions.

These are presented as lying on a continuum with respect to the concrete future, from more to less realistic.

Romaniuc thus emphasizes the CCP algorithm as an abstract model of population dynamics. I would take the next step and call it a theoretical model or theory.

Compared with stable theory, for example, the CCP model is more comprehensive, more realistic, and more flexible. It can deal with both sexes, separately but simultaneously; it routinely includes migration flows; it describes 'transient dynamics' as well as the equilibrium situation, a powerful advantage since most of human life is lived amidst such transient dynamics.[5] These virtues were harder to appreciate in the early days of CCP, since computation of projections was no small matter. The stable model, by contrast, provided relatively economical long-term 'projections.' With the advent of computers and spreadsheets, calculating multiple projections for long time horizons is easy and routine. Overall, the CCP algorithm has much to recommend it.

10.4 Easy Mathematics

Not included in the above list of advantages and often overlooked is the fact that the CCP method is mathematically easy. It involves only the arithmetical operations of addition, subtraction, multiplication, and division, and a working knowledge of proportions and decimal fractions – in short, elementary school arithmetic. One

---

[4]See also de Gans's discussion of the different possible roles of the forecaster (De Gans [1999](#), Ch. 8).

[5]The term has its origin in engineering, particularly electronics, where it often is the case that early instabilities disappear rapidly and the system settles into some desirable steady state. The word transient sometimes connotes unimportant. For demographic forecasts, by contrast, early developments are the most important and the most securely known.

does not need to know calculus, differential equations, or linear algebra. de Gans notes 'the relative simplicity of the methods involved' (De Gans 1999, p. 9).

This has appeal both to analysts preparing CCP forecasts, and to non-scientists who use the result. Anyone with ordinary intelligence and a reasonable knowledge of arithmetic can make a projection – given time, patience, or a statistical clerk – or understand one.[6]

Or at least people think they can understand what is involved, although there is a difference between thinking one understands and understanding. de Gans refers to Kuczynski's use of the net reproduction rate, and his conviction that it 'could indicate which populations were to expect an imminent decrease in population' (De Gans 1999, p. 95). We now understand that this is not the case. An NRR of less than one indicates that [neglecting migration] a population *would* begin to decline some time in the future *if* current age-specific fertility and mortality rates were to remain unchanged indefinitely. In some cases, the hypothetical decline may not occur for several decades. But the concept seems simple: above 1.0 means growth; below 1.0 means decline; 0 means replacement. And many people who become acquainted with the concept confused current versus equilibrium conditions, and prediction with abstract modelling. Frank Notestein used to say that the NRR was a troublesome measure precisely because it lent itself to so much confident misunderstanding. In Canada one regularly reads in the popular press that Canada's below-replacement fertility is such that only net immigration is preventing current population decline, whereas in fact current natural increase is still positive.

Similarly, if the core algorithm of a CCP is easy to understand, the subtle questions surrounding its open-loop character, the nature and implications of its assumptions, and its status as a contingent prediction are not. In practice, the meaning of a CCP is often misunderstood by the user.

Many users think they understand the CCP because no unfamiliar mathematics is involved, no calculus or differential equations. Some expositions of the method use matrix algebra, but this can be avoided by using the more common 'book-keeping' approach. Compare this with the mathematics needed to work with the logistic equation or some of its more complex elaborations (Gotelli 2001), or with a dynamic model based on differential equations [note the relative inattention in demography to the Lotka-Volterra predator-prey and similar multi-population models]. It would be interesting to look more closely at the precise way the logistic has been treated since its application to humans early in the twentieth century. Was it routinely viewed as a solution to the corresponding differential equation? Or was it simply a function *ex machina*, which one fitted using some cookbook procedure? Was there concern with the mechanisms that might underlie the curve, for example, falling fertility and rising mortality (see Wilson and Bossert 1971, Ch. 3)? Or, was it just a 'law' that seemed to apply, and to provide a basis for prediction without an understanding of process or of mechanisms?

---

[6]This characteristic of the CCP model was well suited to an era in which calculation was done with mechanical calculators, which could only add, subtract, multiply, and, awkwardly, divide.

In their influential paper on the logistic model, Pearl and Reed (1920), clearly thought they had discovered the true law of human population growth. The word law appears a dozen times in their paper; at one point, they suggest that their fitted curve captures the 'true law of population growth' (p. 84). Their attention to process and behavior is limited – a brief reference to Malthus on checks from the means of subsistence, and a discussion of humans' ability to transcend environmental limits and raise the maximum sustainable population, suggesting a different logistic curve for different demographic eras. Emphasis is on fitting a mathematical function, with its evaluation based on empirical data, with little attention to underlying mechanisms.[7] Current texts and manuals in demography generally introduce the logistic simply as an alternative forecasting tool, often seen as outmoded, rather than as a theoretical model of population dynamics.

The apparent simplicity of the CCP model can also be contrasted with contemporary microsimulation methods. Many non-scientists and not a few social scientists view these procedures with some suspicion, feeling that the results are somehow 'made up' – in contrast with the 'solid' outcomes of a CCP. In fact, both types of procedures make up their outcomes, in the sense that what comes out depends strictly on the assumptions of what goes in. The key difference is that the microsimulation models make the sensible assumption that the inputs involve some stochastic elements. The two approaches do not differ in their fundamental epistemological character. But the CCP approach is more familiar, and is easier in the sense that one does not need even a basic understanding of micro-simulation. Yet one remains accepted, the other held at arm's length.[8]

10.5   Demographers and Mathematics

The fact that the CCP model requires only basic arithmetic may help explain its popularity with demographers. I know of no systematic data on the point but I would hazard the guess that the average practicing demographer in twentieth century has had relatively weak mathematical background – relative to what we have been given credit for, relative to what might have been useful, and relative to the ordinary training in engineering and the natural sciences. From de Gans' accounts of the disagreements between government and mathematical statisticians, I would gather the same could be said of many population scientists from

---

[7]Dorn (1950) gives an interesting quote from Pritchett, who did U.S. population forecasts around 1900 by fitting a third degree polynomial, confidently projecting population for ten centuries into the future: '…it does not in the least diminish the value of such a mathematical formula, for the purpose of prediction, that it is based on no knowledge of the real causes of the phenomena which it connects together' (page 317).

[8]These remarks are less accurate than when first written, given the increasing use of probabilistic population projections. For an early description, see Lee (1998).

other backgrounds. Demographic analysis and projections typically involved extensive analysis of data and much quantification, but not much mathematics.

The validity of this point will obviously differ by time and place. My impressions relate mainly to North America and the international demographic community, and, disproportionately to English-language literature. The case may well be different in other areas – for example, in France, where demography is studied as a separate discipline, often in an engineering context, or in Italy, where it has close ties to mathematics and statistics. But I think the situation I describe has been widespread enough to influence the international practice of demography, including the codification of that practice by international agencies. de Gans mentions the point several times, notably with reference to the Dutch statistician Van Zanten, who was neither a mathematician nor a statistician by training, having studied law (1999, 36–37).

Systematic research on the point is needed, but consider the following:

1. Standard compendia on demography or demographic techniques (for example, Shryock and Siegel 1973; UN Determinants and Consequences 1973) contain little mathematics beyond basic algebra. Shryock and Siegel have only a short section on the use of matrix methods in demography. The sections on stable population theory contain the key integral equations and the ordinary approximations. But for the rest, one can follow the book without any knowledge of calculus, differential equations, linear algebra, or probability theory.

2. The mathematics required for entry into or completion of advanced degree programs in demography frequently has not been very advanced. In my experience at Princeton in the late 1950s, there were no special mathematical requirements for admission to the demography program as a Ph.D. student in sociology. And, one was not required to learn more mathematics to qualify for the degree.[9] I believe the situation was and is similar at many North American university centers for graduate training in demography. The average demography Ph.D. knows less mathematics than the average upper-class undergraduate in engineering, physics, chemistry, and, increasingly, biology and other life sciences.

3. Since demography has not routinely trained demographers in mathematics, it has relied heavily for its development on persons trained outside the discipline – biology and mathematics (Lotka, Cohen), engineering (Henry, Bongaarts, Willekens, Rogers), physics and economics (Coale), mathematics and statistics (Keyfitz, Wachter) – to give a few examples that come readily to mind. The result has been a large intellectual gap between the average demographer and these specialists, whose work often has been viewed as esoteric by non-mathematical demographers.

4. What was viewed as high-level mathematical work in demography has often struck outsiders as less so. Coale used to say that much of early twentieth century

---

[9]The admission requirements and expectations after admission were more stringent for economics. Also, the lack of requirements for further study after admission must be seen in the context of the informality of the Ph.D. program, with no formal course credit requirements.

mathematical demography (notably Lotka's work) could have been done in a few years by a first-rate applied mathematician. When he sent his student, the late Alvaro Lopez, to show his work to Baumol (a mathematical economist) and to Feller (a statistician), neither reacted with great enthusiasm. What seemed like mathematical breakthroughs in demography struck them as routine.

Roger Revell, the oceanographer, soon after being appointed head of the new Harvard population center some years ago, commented undiplomatically that he couldn't see anything in technical demography that a physical scientist couldn't master in a few months. His remark was not well-received by establishment demographers, although it contained a kernel of truth.

Had the average demographer known more mathematics, it seems likely that less time would have been spent on small refinements of the standard CCP algorithm, and more on the exploration of other approaches. Had a working knowledge of differential equations been routine demographic equipment, for example, more dynamic approaches might have been pursued.[10] There might have been a deeper investigation of the logistic model, and of a whole family of differential equations to which it belongs (including some versions of the demographic transition model), with more attention to underlying behavioral mechanisms. Population dynamics might have been viewed earlier in terms of compartment models or dynamical systems, perhaps with less attention to 5-year age detail. This, coupled with a widespread working knowledge of matrix algebra, might have led to an earlier discovery of multistate demography. In fact, the CCP algorithm has close links with differential or difference equations, but given the stylized use of the CCP, these links often go unrecognized.

It is hard, of course, to know what might have been. I do not know, for example, the state of the art in differential equations in the 1920s and 1930s, although much of the basic theory dates to the eighteenth century. And mathematical ability does not always translate into good insight into demographic or behavioral dynamics. I am puzzled by De Gans'account of 't Hooft, identified as an engineer. How could someone presumably familiar with basic concepts of function, first derivative and second derivative [as in position, velocity, acceleration] have confused the demographic implications of *declining* versus *low* mortality, as seems to have happened in his use of the 'conveyor- belt' metaphor?[11] As Cohen rightly comments, in his discussion of the systems dynamics modeling school of population forecasting

---

[10]Abbott (1988) argues that in sociology Coleman's differential equations approach lost out to Blalock's multiple regression approach, and attributes this to the 'commodification' of regression in statistical packages such as SPSS, BMDP and SAS. It also is relevant that, even with the solution of differential equations now similarly 'commodified' in programs like Mathcad, Maple, and Mathematica, the application of differential equations requires a higher level of mathematical sophistication than does the application of multiple regression.

[11]This case particularly interests me because a similar misunderstanding, using a different metaphor [a river dam] recurred in the work of A. Zimmerman (1961), a Catholic theologian. He also argued that rapid population growth would cease naturally, when mortality stopped *declining*, even though fertility rates were to remain high.

(e.g., The Limits to Growth), solving equations numerically is now relatively easy. The hard part in science is finding equations that represent empirical reality well enough for some analytic or practical purpose. What would have been the result if the average demographer had had enough mathematical sophistication to look for those equations in day-to-day work, instead of leaving the job to a small group of mathematical demographers, and instead of assuming that, as Abbott and Keyfitz put it, we live in a linear world adequately represented by the general linear model?

10.6   Some Further Questions

In the periods covered by de Gans'monograph, why was there a felt need to choose among population forecasting techniques, and to elevate one to a position of dominance, to canonize it as the 'standard' technique? Why was population forecasting not seen as a generic problem, serving many different scientific and practical needs, such that a broad repertoire of tools was need rather than just one?

Why did the CCP model become and remain that one technique, despite its many and well-publicized predictive failures, and relatively early criticisms of the continuity assumptions underlying the technique?

Why was there not more emphasis on synthesis and cross-fertilization of technique? Had the logistic model been pursued in depth, it would have led inevitably to questions of mechanism, to the causal dynamics underlying fertility decline or mortality increase (or levelling off) in the face of growing size and density – the same questions that underlie assumptions about future inputs to CCP forecasts.[12] It might have led to greater intellectual connections between human demography and population biology, with earlier appreciation of species similarities and differences, and with greater familiarity with a different but powerful tradition of population mathematics. How many demographers even today are familiar with the Allee effect (Gotelli 2001), whereby for some species an initial increase in population density allows it better to cope, resulting in higher fertility and lower mortality, at least for some period? This is but one modification of the basic logistic model, with plausible applications to human populations. But we continue to think in terms of the stereotypical logistic, involving fruit flies and rats, and often assume it has little relevance to humans.

Granted the importance of internationally comparable data, and the inevitably of conventions (often embodying elements of arbitrariness) in science, why has demography shown a certain narrowness and rigidity in its conventions, and resistance to new or different approaches?

---

[12]Work with standard projections led Whelpton to undertake social surveys of fertility in order to improve assumptions about fertility. But behavioral dynamics continued to be viewed as exogenous to the projection model, which itself remained basically unchanged.

de Gans gives many illustrations of these problems for the past, showing how disciplinary habits pointed in one direction to the exclusion of others, or how personal proprietary interests led to competition among different techniques rather than to synthesis and parallel analysis.

For the post-World War II period, I would again emphasize the limited mathematical sophistication of many demographers. One result has been the development of demographic techniques as a set of distinct procedures applied to different realms of demographic behavior, rather than specific applications of more general concepts. Thus, calculation of a life expectancy, of Hajnal's singulate mean age at marriage, and of the total fertility rate often are presented as three separate procedures, whereas mathematically they all involve the same basic concepts – the area under a curve, or an integral or finite approximation of an integral. Similarly, demographic texts present a vast array of different summary measures, most of which can be viewed as weighted sums or averages, or as vector dot products. But opportunities for this kind of generalization often are overlooked.[13]

Hakkert (1992) has noted demography's relative failure to take advantage of modern statistical and mathematical developments, and its tendency until now to use the computer to implement what he terms 'paper and pencil algorithms.' This relative isolation from mainstream statistics and mathematics has been combined with what I have come to think of as theoretical and methodological nonchalance, that is, a tendency to focus on data and on the elaboration of technique, while paying less attention to the overall structure of the scientific enterprise, including such questions as the logic of science and explanation, and the central role of theory in any discipline.[14]

One might speak of a bureaucratization of demography, with establishment of a canon of 'correct' techniques, some partly arbitrary but valued for their own sake as well as their service of some larger end. Failure to use these specific techniques becomes the basis for a judgement of non-competence.

As an example, the systems dynamics school at MIT [starting with Dynamo and spreading to other software such as Stella, Berkeley Madonna, and Vensim] developed a perfectly usable algorithm for projecting population that is largely ignored by demographers. But the language is 'strange' – the word *rate*, for example, is used in the calculus sense of change per unit of time rather than in the demographic sense of events/exposure. And age categories are not survived to the next highest age, but stand still as it were, with people coming in from the lower category (often called 'aging in') and leaving for the higher category ('aging out'),

---

[13]The search for and presentation of general concepts underlying specific techniques has been more common in the French school of demography than in the North American or English-language school.

[14]Demography is not alone in this respect. In a recent paper on 'modern human origins,' the author comments: 'The disciplines that contribute to the field (archaeology, human paleontology, and molecular biology) tend to be discovery-driven and focused on methodology. Following a strictly empirical approach ('the facts speak for themselves'), they often have little concern for the logic of inference underlying knowledge claims' (Clark 1999, p. 2020).

the proportions determined by the width of the age group (for example, one-fifth of a 5-year age group are assumed to enter the next age group each calendar year). Demographic rates of birth and death are termed 'fractional rates,' with the fractional death rate commonly defined as the reciprocal of life expectancy (which is strictly correct only in the stationary model).

The procedure strikes the average demographer as incorrect, and is likely to be dismissed. But the procedure works: with a few minor modifications, it can yield results that are substantially the same as those from a standard CPP projection using the same inputs. At the same time, it casts population dynamics in a difference equations context, with links to concepts of dynamical systems, using software designed to incorporate feedbacks. The model lends itself to expansion, with the core demographic variables linked to broader environmental, economic, social or cultural variables, as both cause and effect.

The general dismissal of systems dynamics by empirically oriented social scientists, including demographers, deserves further study. Granted a certain naiveté in some early work in this genre (see Berlinski 1976), it included sound elements, including emphasis on dynamics, nonlinearity, and feedback, all ideas that have gained currency, often without credit to early systems theorists.[15]

On a more concrete level, it is interesting to witness such contemporary phenomena as the worldwide depletion of fish stocks in light of analyses and forecasts contained in *The Limits to Growth* (Meadows *et al.* 1972), one of the best known and most maligned of systems dynamics studies. As scientific analysis it certainly had its flaws [which could have been dealt with in replications], but it seems to have been right about some important issues.[16]

In his chapter on population projections, Cohen comments, with perhaps unintended force, that 'demographic projection techniques omit major factors that influence population change' (p. 134), which is a rather heavy indictment of common practice. But he is not willing to opt for a systems approach: 'Predictions based on systems models are too recent to evaluate in terms of their success, but the 20 years of experience with the World3 model gives grounds for serious doubt' (1995, 134). If population projection is put in the broader context suggested above and seen as having many uses in addition to prediction, this judgement seems too harsh. It also seems to overlook the inherent capabilities of the approach – which is nothing more and nothing less than the application of systems of differential equations to specific issues – based on early shortcomings.

The tendency to fall back on the standard CPP approach, essentially unchanged, even when its limitations are recognized – as in Cohen's discussion – is all the more interesting given the fact that predictive failures of the technique have been well publicized, and criticisms more or less continuous from the very beginning. As

---

[15]In his popularizing book on complexity and chaos, for example, Waldrop (1992) does not recognize the anticipation by systems dynamics theorists of many of the ideas he reviews. The word system does not appear in the index.

[16]For a recent, positive evaluation, see Bardi (2011).

early as 1938, just as the CCP approach was achieving its dominant position, Truesdell (1938) commented: 'There still remains a tendency to base forecasts of the future on past rates of increase, though where these rates of increase have been high, the very absurdity of the resulting forecast has brought with it some degree of caution....' (p. 377). He speaks of the 'falsity of the assumption of continued movement in the same direction, even let alone at the same velocity...' (p. 378), and concludes:

> The way out of the difficulty seems to be, therefore, to devote more study to the underlying factors which tend to divert population ...from one area to another, and thus to speed up or retard the velocity of change in the elements for which the forecast is required.... [I]t would seem that large-scale, coordinated study would have more promise of success. (p. 379)

Barlowe (1952), commenting on one of Notestein's early statements of transition theory, notes that

> Our demographers have made numerous predictions as to population trends during the past few decades and a high proportion of these predictions have been wrong. Like the economists and agricultural economists, they are discovering that it is not safe to base future predictions on the simple continuation of present or past trends. (p. 54)

Ascher (1978), assessing population forecasting from the broader perspective of social science forecasting of all types, gives the following summary view:

> Thus, even though the modern methods are more sophisticated in their disaggregation of population growth, the forecaster still faces the dilemma whether current trends represent 'noise' or significant trends. Consequently, the real progress in population forecasting will come not in the further elaboration of technique, which is even now able to accurately and consistently trace out the implications of given fertility and mortality assumptions. It will come via studies of the social, economic, and technological determinants of fertility and mortality. (p. 57)

In the 40 years since Ascher wrote, there have been many studies of the determinants of fertility and mortality. But the results of these studies have not been systematically incorporated into the CCP projection model. They may inform judgements about future levels, but for the most part are still exogenous to the model.

Perhaps the underlying problem has been a failure among demographers and government statisticians to recognize that, when all is said and done, techniques are just tools. Assuming no blatant errors, no one measure or model is inherently better than another, despite much evaluative nomenclature – 'crude' birth rates, the 'true' rate of natural increase, etc. A tool is judged good or bad primarily by reference to the purpose for which it is used. The perfect hammer is no good for driving screws. The 'true' rate of natural increase may be and often is completely false as a description of current natural increase.

de Gans comments with respect to Rooy's 1921 forecast: 'The method is simple but satisfactory, given the task Rooy had set for himself. It is an example of everyday forecasting practice' (p. 128). One can ask why this pragmatic attitude did not become more common in the art and practice of population forecasting. A little later, de Gans continues: 'The incentives for innovation came not from the needs of planning and decision making but from substantial social and scientific interest in the population issues' (p. 130). That which motivated interest – including ideology – also influenced choice of models.

The more pragmatic approach has re-surfaced recently in the new sub-discipline of applied demography. It leads to views somewhat at odds with traditional demographic practice. It leads Swanson and Tayman (1995), for example, to the idea that in some contexts, given time and cost constraints, the best or most practical population forecast may be a 'no cost' forecast, namely, the assumption that population size 3 years from now will be approximately the same as population size today. More generally, Swanson *et al.* (1996) have argued that the prime requirement of applied demographic analysis is that it support sound decision making, including decision making that is timely and within cost constraints. Whether the analysis is 'correct' and whether a prediction comes true are, strictly speaking, considerations of secondary importance. The best scientific analysis is not useful if it comes a year too late or requires resources that are not at hand.

Such an approach would ultimately lead to the heretical view that some good demographic analysis might be qualitative rather than quantitative. Puccia and Levins (1985) have argued that in intervening in complex natural systems, sometimes the most that one can know is that an intervention will push the system in the desired direction. They are speaking in the context of biological ecology, but their comment would seem to apply with even greater force to intervention in human systems, including demographic systems. The idea would be familiar to students of differential equations, who often value qualitative solutions, but foreign to many if not most demographers.

10.7 Conclusion

The fundamental merit of the CCP model is that it embodies sound theory of population dynamics – it is a good theoretical model. The drawbacks to the model relate to the way it was perceived and used, as an exclusively valid approach to population forecasting, often applied and interpreted in a mechanical way. The state of population forecasting in mid-to-late-twentieth century might well have been better had the CCP approach be allowed to take its proper place as one among a variety of approaches to future-oriented analyzes of population dynamics. A more nuanced view of population forecasting could have resulted from the use of a well-rounded collection of forecasting tools instead of the elevation of one tool to canonical status. Recent work referred to in the opening paragraph suggests that demography has turned a corner in this regard.

References

Abbott, A. (1988). Transcending general linear reality. *Sociological Theory, 6,* 169–186.

Ascher, W. (1978). *Forecasting: An appraisal for policy-makers and planners.* Baltimore: Johns Hopkins University Press.

Bardi, U. (2011). *The limits to growth revisited.* New York: Springer.

Barlowe, R. (1952). *Comment on Notestein's paper in Proceedings of the Eighth International Conference of Agricultural Economists.* London: Oxford University Press.

Berlinski, D. (1976). *On systems analysis: An essay concerning the limitations of of some mathematical methods in the social, political, and biological sciences.* Cambridge, MA: MIT Press.

Bongaarts, J., & Bulatao, R.A. (Eds.). (2000). *Beyond Six Billion.* Washington, D.C.: National Academy Press.

Burch, T. K. (2003). Data, models, theory and reality: The structure of demographic knowledge. In F. C. Billari & A. Prskawetz (Eds.), *Agent-based computational demography: Using simulation to improve our understanding of demographic behaviour* (pp. 19–40). Heidelberg: Physica- Verlag. See Ch. 2 above.

Clark, G. A. (1999). Highly visible, curiously intangible. *Science, 283,* 2029–2032.

Cohen, J. E. (1995). *How many people can the earth support?* New York: W.W. Norton.

De Gans, H. A. (1999). *Population forecasting, 1895–1945: The transition to modernity.* Dordrecht: Kluwer Academic Publishers.

Dorn, H. F. (1950). Pitfalls in population forecasts and projections. *Journal of the American Statistical Association, 45,* 311–334.

Fleischhacker, J., de Gans, H. A., & Burch, T. K. (Eds.). (2003). *Populations, projections, and politics: Critical and historical essays on early twentieth century population forecasting.* Amsterdam: Rozenberg Publishers.

Giere, R. N. (1999). *Science without laws.* Chicago: University of Chicago Press.

Gotelli, N. J. (2001). *A primer of ecology* (3rd ed.). Sunderland: Sinauer Associates.

Hakkert, R. (1992). Computing in demographic analysis: Beyond paper and pencil algorithms. Paper at IUSSP/NIDI Expert meeting on demographic software and computing, The Hague, 29 June–3 Jul 1992.

Keyfitz, N. (1998). We live in a nonlinear world. Unpublished ms.

Lee, R.D. (1998). Probabilistic approaches to population forecasting. In Lutz et al. (1998), pp. 156–190.

Lutz, W., Vaupel, J.W., Ahlburg, D.A.. (1998). Frontiers of population forecasting. *Supplement to Population and Development Review, 24.*

Meadows, D. H., Meadows, D. L., Randers, J., & Behrens, W. W., III. (1972). *The limits to growth.* New York: Universe Books.

Meehan, E. J. (1968). *Explanation in social science: A systems paradigm.* Homewood: The Dorsey Press.

Pearl, R., & Reed, L. J. (1920). On the rate of growth of the population of the United States since 1790 and its mathematical representation. *Proceedings of the National Academy of Sciences, 6,* 275–288.

Puccia, C. J., & Levins, R. (1985). *Qualitative modeling of complex systems: An introduction to loop analysis and time averaging.* Cambridge, MA: Harvard University Press.

Romaniuc, A. (1990). Population projection as prediction, simulation and prospective analysis. *Population Bulletin of the United Nations, 29,* 16–31. New York: United Nations.

Shryock, H., & Siegel, J. (1973). *The methods and materials of demography.* Washington, DC: U.S. Government Printing Office.

Swanson, D. A., Burch, T. K., & Tedrow, L. M. (1996). What is applied demography? *Population Research and Policy Review, 15,* 403–418.

Swanson, D. A., & Tayman, J. (1995). Between and rock and a hard place: The evaluation of demographic forecasts. *Population Research and Policy Review, 14,* 233–249.

Teller, P. (2001). The twilight of the perfect model model. *Erkenntnis, 55*, 393–415.

Truesdell, L. E. (1938). Residual relationships and velocity of change as pitfalls in the field of statistical forecasting. *Journal of the American Statistical Association, 33*, 373–379.

U.N. Department of Economic and Social Affairs. (1973). *The determinants and consequences of population trends*. New York: United Nations.

Waldrop, M. M. (1992). *Complexity: The emerging science at the edge of order and chaos*. New York: Simon and Schuster.

Wilson, E. O., & Bossert, W. H. (1971). *A primer of population biology*. Sunderland: Sinauer Associates.

Zimmerman, A. F. (1961). *Catholic viewpoint on population*. Garden City: Hannover House [Doubleday].

Part III
Teaching Demography

Chapter 11
Teaching Demography: Ten Principles and Two Rationales

11.1 Introduction

Livi-Bacci once spoke of the danger of demography becoming 'more a technique than a science...' (1984). Caselli has noted that 'Demographers over the last decades...have largely focused on measures, on how to adapt ever more sophisticated methodologies to the issues at hand' (memo to IUSSP Working Group on Teaching Demography 2000). A call for papers from another IUSSP working group underlines a preoccupation with data and technique, speaking of '...papers that present innovative work based on macro- or micro-level data...' and '...a preference for work using new or recent data sets, or new methods of analysis.' Nothing is said about new ideas, or the development or testing of older theoretical ideas, except insofar as this might be implicit in the word *innovative*.

Demographers, individually and collectively, have a choice. We can rest content with being and being seen as technicians, doing 'demographic accounting.' We can leave many of the most important population problems of the day to others, accepting demography as a small sub-discipline of statistics, economics, sociology, or environmental science. Or we can develop and promote demography as a distinct and autonomous science – an extensive, coherent, and empirically grounded body of knowledge about how populations work, and how demographic dynamics are related to society, the economy and the environment. To do this, we must give more weight to theory – as opposed to techniques and empirical data – since theory, properly considered, is nothing less than a summary of what is known. It codifies our understanding of how populations work in a way that data, technique, and description cannot. Nowhere is this more important than in the teaching of demography, where students and other non-specialists are first exposed to the discipline.

This chapter is based on a contribution to the session on teaching demography, organized by Graziella Caselli at the Brazil meetings of the International Union for the Scientific Study of Population, 2001. Originally published in *Genus* 58(2002):21–34.

T.K. Burch, *Model-Based Demography*, Demographic Research Monographs,
DOI 10.1007/978-3-319-65433-1_11

How then should demography be taught if it is to realize its full potential as a science? I offer ten principles for teaching demography – and by implication, for the design of texts. These are stated briefly and dogmatically, with only a few illustrations and little or no systematic attempt at justification. I then consider two sources of support for the approach suggested – two rationales. The first is found in current pedagogy in other fields, particularly the physical sciences. These are disciplines of unquestioned scientific stature and effectiveness, with longer and broader experience in teaching courses on basic principles, and more highly evolved textbooks. But the approach in these disciplines is not accidental or arbitrary – it is founded on sound principles of scientific methodology, based in turn on a sound understanding of the nature of science.

I develop briefly the view that demography, like much of contemporary empirical social science, is burdened with a faulty understanding of the nature of science. This is the view of logical empiricism, popularized in social science by such philosophers as Reichenbach (1968), Nagel (1961), and Hempel (1965) following World War II. I sketch an alternative and potentially more fruitful approach, found in the writings of several social scientists and contemporary philosophers of science.

Three qualifications:

1. Clearly the application of the principles must be modified depending on the character of the course and students – undergraduate or graduate, developed country or developing, specialist or generalist. But in some sense, they should apply to any demography course.
2. How demography is taught differs considerably within and across nations. But there is no adequate body of information on the details of actual practice. My impression is that European demography (especially the French school – including Quebec – but also the Italian, and, increasingly, the German) comes closer to the ten principles in their teaching than do the British or North American schools. But this is a matter for further empirical study. Clearly, what follows assumes that demography generally is not taught as well as it might be.
3. My characterization of demographic methodology is meant to apply to mainstream demography and social demography. It is less relevant to economic demography, whose scientific methodology and pedagogical practice come closer to the ideal sketched below, given an emphasis on mathematical theory and modelling. Economics has been hampered by other problems, however, notably its penchant for axiomatic theory based on what many see as a restrictive set of axioms.

11.2   Ten Principles for Teaching Demography

1. *Put more emphasis on theory, that is, abstract models of population dynamics and demographic behavior.* Teach demography as a body of theoretical knowledge, as well as a body of data, techniques, and descriptive findings. This assumes that one wants to present demography as a science.

2. *Hold onto older and simpler – even 'oversimplified' – models insofar as they contain valuable insights and can help students begin to understand.* Judith Blake once dismissed microeconomic models of fertility with the question 'Are babies consumer durables?' We might as well dismiss Newton and classical mechanics with the question 'Do falling bodies fall in a vacuum, without air resistance?'

3. *Put more emphasis on student activity in which they use theoretical models to analyze real-world – or at least realistic – problems and exercises.* The problems will be of increasing orders of difficulty. The analytic tools used will be of increasing orders of complexity. The aim will be development of students' ability to reason demographically, to explain, predict, or suggest policy interventions.

4. *Set problems and exercises that will lead students to face the limitations of the analytic tools they have learned and encourage them to try to think of improvements.* Some problems should suggest the need to add other variables to their models, or to relax one or more simplifying assumptions. Theory and theoretical models are presented as potential tools for understanding the real world, not as some sort of absolute truth.

5. *Teach or require the tools students need to work rigorously with the theoretical models.* The classic tool in physical science has been mathematics. A more flexible and accessible tool for many demography students (certainly in sociology departments) will be some form of computer modelling. The emphasis here is not so much on the rigor that comes with quantification as on the ability to perform complex logical inferences correctly.

6. *Integrate formal demography ('techniques') and population studies ('substance') rather than teaching so-called 'technical demography' in completely separate courses or relegating it to an appendix, as is typical in many English-language demographic texts.* The time-honored distinction between formal demography and population studies, based on a sharp distinction between necessary and contingent relationships, is called into question by recent work in the philosophy of science. In a 'model-based' view of science, to be described later, a good theoretical model is based on relationships *assumed* as necessary. This is true of a 'formal' model such as the stable population model, but also of a 'behavioral' model such as the microeconomic theory of fertility. As theoretical models, they share the same epistemological status. The relevant empirical question is not whether they are true or false, but whether they adequately represent some portion of the real-world, adequacy judged with reference to a specific analytic purpose.

7. *Teach the basic principles of formal demography in every demography course, unless it can be assumed that students already know them. Otherwise, it is not a demography course.* It may be a good course, but it is not demography. These principles represent a solid core on which behavioral demography must build. In North America especially, one sees many courses on the 'sociology of population,' courses taught by persons with little or no demographic training, and making little use of the central concepts of demography.

8. *Emphasize the general principles underlying many apparently disparate measures and models to make the teaching of formal demography more efficient.* A large collection of demographic measures can be grasped quickly, for example, if students have a firm understanding of the notion of weighted sums and averages. These sums and averages in turn can be represented as functions of some area under the relevant curves. How often do we teach students that the life expectancy at birth, the total fertility rate, and Hajnal's singulate mean age at marriage are based on the same underlying measurement concept, differing only in detail?

9. *For beginning students of demography especially, put less emphasis on data collection, errors in data, and precision in techniques.* This is not a counsel of sloppiness, but rather a recognition that it is not sound pedagogy to immerse beginning students in data-collection techniques and rather discouraging claims about errors. Similarly, it is inappropriate to introduce all the measurement refinements that have been developed over the years. Students first need to grasp the basic concepts. In any event, there is some unresolved inconsistency in demography in the fact that, although we know errors in our data tend to be large, we often do not restrict ourselves to two or three significant digits, and generally avoid use of scientific notation. A mature science is comfortable with the use of approximations adequate to the task at hand. Precision is sought not for its own sake but only when it really is necessary.

10. *Rely more heavily on visual representation of theoretical ideas and processes.* Many of the relatively simple theoretical models emphasized in the above approach can be expressed, in lectures and texts, by means of diagrams. These will be visual representations of ideas, in contrast to graphic representations of data, which predominates in demographic writing. The basic demographic equation typically is presented as an equation, and often in the form of an accounting sheet giving a numerical example. But many students, especially beginners, do not think easily in terms of equations or balance sheets. Why not give them the added help of a picture?[1]

---

[1]Recent texts are instructive in this regard. Preston *et al.* (2001) discuss the basic demographic equation at several points, but give no diagram. Hinde (1998) gives the equation and then immediately introduces a corresponding multistate diagram. In her classic paper on 'Graphics in Demography' (1985), Watkins discusses the basic equation in the first two paragraphs, but ironically nowhere presents a graphic representation.

11.2.1 Teaching and Texts in Other Disciplines

One source of ideas for the teaching of demography is to look at teaching and textbooks in other disciplines, especially those that are older and better known, and respected for their scientific maturity and achievements. This approach was used by Stephan and Massey (1982) with respect to the teaching of introductory sociology.[2] Their ideas also are relevant to demography.

Stephan and Massey start from the assumption that '...the public's generally unfavorable perception of sociology is due in large part to the way in which sociology is presented in introductory courses.' They argue that the introductory course does not attract the right people into the field, and that it 'ill-prepares those who go on professionally.' The remedy they propose is to develop the introductory sociology course '...along the lines followed by more established scientific disciplines' (423).

They ask what introductory courses in other fields have in common, and how these common characteristics distinguish these courses from introductory sociology. Stephan and Massey list five common characteristics (424–425):

1. The subject matter is *primary*, that is, the *earliest* material to become an established part of the field, and *basic* to the discipline.
2. Much of the material is relatively *simple*: 'Though there may be much of it, it is for the most part uncomplicated.' They add: 'Much of the subject matter can be pictured in one way or another, a particular help when learning about unfamiliar material.'
3. The subject matter is *consensual*, material on which most people in the field can agree.
4. Much of the material is *quantitative*, since the 'precision and non-ambiguity characteristic of quantitative statements seems to lend itself to introductory presentations.'[3]
5. Much of what is learned is *do-able* by the student, who becomes an active participant: 'There is something for the student to perform as well as learn.' Thus most courses involve laboratory work.

The authors comment that the typical introductory sociology course manifests characteristics almost the exact opposite of the five listed.

A recent examination of some popular North American introductory physics texts leads to a similar list of characteristics. There are two different types of physics text, one designed for science majors with substantial mathematics

---

[2]I am grateful to Frank Trovato for bringing this paper to my attention.

[3]But non-quantitative statements also can be precise and unambiguous, and physical science often deals in qualitative principles as well. Electromagnetic charges, for example, are positive or negative; and opposite charges attract, while like charges repel. Quantification comes only later. It is often pointed out by physical and biological scientists that much of the scientific value of mathematics lies not in quantification, but in its use as a tool of rigorous reasoning.

background, and one designed for students in the arts and humanities and the social sciences. An important point is that the subject matter is much the same in both kinds of text. The differences relate primarily to matters of detail and of level, especially with respect to mathematics required. But the underlying assumption is that teaching physics is teaching physics: one doesn't present one set of topics to one type of student and a different set to the other. Both present material that Stephan and Massey label as *primary*.

The text chosen is *Fundamentals of Physics* by Halliday *et al.* (1997). Now in its 5th edition, the work is available in several different formats, the largest, the so-called 'extended' edition running to 45 chapters. The version considered here contains 38 chapters, covering approximately 1000 pages.

One expects the general pedagogical quality of physics texts to be high, partly because it is such a well-developed science, and partly because it has been so widely taught for so long. The modern text is the result of a strong evolutionary process. In demography, as we well know, the number of students taught and the level at which they are taught (seldom in first year of university) are such that textbooks are not economically attractive to publishers, and there have been correspondingly few.

Some noteworthy features of the above text include the following:

1. Emphasis on fundamental principles, including classical mechanics (Newtonian) and simple abstract models. Despite a common impression to the contrary, physicists do not reject the older ideas as outmoded by relativity and quantum theory. The unreal models of classical mechanics (straight-line motion, no friction or air-resistance, constant acceleration, etc.) are presented as valid knowledge when applied to appropriate parts of the real world.

2. Emphasis on developing the student's ability to reason; an active approach to the subject matter. '...[W]e have enhanced the applications that help students forge a bridge between concepts and reasoning. We not only tell students how physics works, we show them, and we give them the opportunity to show us what they have learned by testing their understanding of the concepts and applying them to real-world scenarios' (p. vii). The aim is '...to establish a connection between conceptual theories and applications,' and to 'force a bridge between concepts and reasoning and to marry theory with practice' (p. vii). To this end, the text contains 1000 'checkpoints' and questions, and approximately 3400 exercises. The checkpoint questions '...require decision making and reasoning on the part of the student; they ask the student to organize the physics concepts rather than just plug numbers into equations' (p. viii). One is reminded of the adage: 'I hear and I forget; I see and I remember; I do and I understand.'[4]

3. Frequent use of illustrations. The authors write: 'Because the illustrations in a physics textbook are so important to an understanding of the concepts, we have

---

[4]This quote is from the first edition of *An Introduction to Computer Simulation Methods* by H. Gould and J. Tobochnik. I no longer have the exact reference, and it is not repeated in the second edition (1996).

altered nearly 30 percent of the illustrations to improve their clarity' (p. viii). The number of illustrations is large, both in expository text and in problems and exercises. Chapter 2, for example, on straight-line motion, contains 31 illustrations in 25 pages, more than one per page. A few are photographs or graphs of functions, but many are visual representations of objects or processes. Compare this with the infrequent use of visual representation and diagrams in demography, other than those used to graph data.

4. Relatively brief expository text. In many chapters, the expository text occupies only a fraction of the overall space. In the chapter on motion mentioned above, problems and exercises occupy 9 of the 25 pages; in the remaining 16 or so, the basic text occupies at most 2/3 of the space, with the rest devoted to checkpoints, sample problems, illustrations, and problem-solving suggestions.

One way to summarize the above is that in each chapter a few basic concepts and principles are clearly stated and then applied to a wide variety of topics or problems. In one sense, the amount of subject matter introduced is small. Emphasis is on the power of its application. By contrast, many 'population texts' (notably in North America) cover an enormous range of topics but in less depth and with less rigor. And challenges to apply the basic ideas, in the form of student exercises and problems, are less common.

11.3 A Philosophical Rationale

The shape of introductory courses in other disciplines is not accidental or arbitrary. It is the product of a long and strong evolutionary process. Introductory courses in physics, biology and chemistry are taught to thousands of students in virtually every university or in the world, as well as in secondary school science courses. The number of students has made it economical to write and publish many texts over the years. Demography, by contrast, is text-poor, if for no other reason than that it seldom is taught to first-year university students.

But the kinds of courses described above also embody a particular view of science and of scientific procedure. It is a view in which theory – understood as over-arching general systems but also as simple theoretical models – occupies central place.[5] Theory, thus broadly conceived, is the codification of what is known in a field. And it provides the tools with which scientists explain and predict,

---

[5]Many social scientists would be surprised to learn that a book such as Baylis's *Theoretical Methods in the Physical Sciences* (1994) has as its subtitle '*...an introduction to problem solving using Maple V.*' That is, doing elementary physics using a computer mathematical package is seen as theoretical work.

which are the ultimate aims of science of science. Everything else is instrumental and secondary to the development of theory.[6]

This approach to theory is at odds with the doctrine that has permeated empirical social science since the mid-twentieth century, logical empiricism. According to this view, the aim of science is to discover 'scientific laws,' universal empirical generalizations arrived at through empirical research. When sufficient laws have been 'discovered,' they can serve as a foundation for theory, through a process of further generalization. Several empirical regularities, for example, might be subsumed under a theoretical generalization. Several theoretical generalizations might be subsumed under still more general propositions, in a hierarchical fashion. The criterion for the validity or truth of a theoretical proposition is its logical consistency with empirical data. A theory which is inconsistent with some substantial body of data is 'falsified,' to use Popper's term.

Explanation of a specific phenomenon, in this view, consists in showing that it follows logically from some theoretical generalization, 'a covering law,' plus some relevant concrete facts. In Reichenbach's words, 'What we mean by explaining an observed fact is incorporating that fact into a general law' (p. 6). The central element in science, in the logical empiricist view, is the scientific law, induced from empirical regularities.

Contemporary philosophers of science have increasingly questioned the logical empiricist approach, whether applied to physics or more generally. An early work by Nancy Cartwright (1983) is entitled *How the Laws of Physics Lie*, the point being that many so-called laws are not literally true representations of reality, but abstract and oversimplified representations that fit the real world in some cases but not others. In a later work (1999), she speaks of theories and theoretical models as 'nomological machines,' the idea being that laws come from theoretical models, not the other way around.

In a similar vein, Ronald Giere (a philosopher with physics background) writes in *Science Without Laws* (1999) that most scientific laws are not universal, and that they are in fact not even true: '...understood as general claims about the world, most purported laws of nature are in fact false. So we need a portrait of science that captures our everyday understanding of success without invoking laws of nature understood as true, universal generalizations' (p. 24). The reason is that any law of nature contains '...only a few physical quantities, whereas nature contains many quantities which often interact one with another, and there are few if any isolated systems. So there cannot be many systems in the real world that exactly satisfy any purported law of nature' (p. 24).

For Giere, the primary representational device in science is not the law but the *model*, of which there are three main types: physical models; visual models; and theoretical models. Models are inherently abstract constructions that attempt to

---

[6]An exception relates to the earliest years of a new scientific field, in which empirical description of subject matter is primary. An explanatory science must have well-documented empirical phenomena to explain. I would argue that demography now has a sufficient empirical base on which to build more and better theory than we currently have.

represent only certain features of the real world. They are true only in the sense that definitions are true. The question of whether they are empirically true is irrelevant, since they cannot be. The relevant question is whether they correspond to some part of the real world (a) in some respects, (b) to a sufficient degree of accuracy, (c) for some well-defined purposes. Giere gives the example of the model for the earth-moon system, which is adequate to describe and account for the moon's orbit and perhaps for putting a rocket on the moon, but is inadequate to describe the Venus-earth system. For Giere, the prototype of scientific knowledge is not the empirical law, but a model plus a list of real-world systems to which it applies.

A model explains some real-world phenomenon (a) if the model fits the real-world system in the three respects noted above, and (b) if the model logically implies the phenomenon, in other words, if the phenomenon follows logically from the model as specified to fit part of the real world. It would never occur to most physical scientists to add the second condition. But in social science, including demography, we are so accustomed to loose inference that its explicit statement is necessary.

Note that in this account of science, all models are *formally* true (assuming, of course, no logical errors or internal contradictions), that is, true by definition. The empirical question then becomes one not of empirical truth or validity, but whether a valid model applies to a particular empirical case.

Of course, some models are more widely applicable than others, and, other things equal, science will focus on models with the widest applicability, but without necessarily discarding others. In demography, for example, the fundamental demographic equation is true by definition and applicable to every well-defined real population (neglecting error in data). The exponential growth formula is true by definition, and, for the purpose of calculating the average annual growth rate over a period is also applicable to every real-world population. For the purpose of describing a population's actual growth trajectory, however, the exponential growth formula applies more or less to some populations, but not at all to others.

A behavioral model such as the theory of demographic transition can be stated in such a way that it is formally true. Its applicability to the real world has been a matter of debate for over 50 years. But it is worth noting, in terms of Giere's criteria, that it correctly represents many actual cases of mortality/fertility decline, at least in qualitative terms.[7]

In my reading of Giere's and Cartwright's accounts of science, they come close to the what has long been the standard approach in the literature on mathematical modelling, and more recently of computer modelling. A model is an abstract construct that may or may not be useful for a certain purpose. In science, that purpose often will be explanation or prediction as opposed to practice. And in some

---

[7]An interesting point about transition theory is that there has been a tendency to dismiss it as not fitting all cases or as not providing details of timing, pace, etc. There seems to have been relatively little effort to accept it as a valid model and work towards a more precise specification by defining functional forms for fertility or mortality decline as functions of 'development,' and parameters representing size of lags, slopes, etc., with different model specifications appropriate to different historical cases.

schools of computer modeling, the emphasis is on less abstract models, trying to capture more of the complexity of the real world. But the central ideas are the same.

The model-based approach to science described above does not make a sharp distinction between a model and a theory. Some authors distinguish the two on a general/specific axis; but then differences are in degree only not in kind. Giere speaks of 'theoretical models,' and sometimes describes a 'theory' as a collection of such models.

Note that this position does not agree with the view of post-modernists and others that science is totally a social construction. A model is the creation of a scientific mind, but it is not just a fantasy. A good model is good precisely because it captures some important aspects of the real world. In Giere's words, there is 'realism without truth.'

Similar ideas have occasionally been anticipated by social scientists, but they do not seem to have been taken seriously by empirically oriented researchers. Eugene Meehan, a political scientist, set forth a 'system paradigm' for explanation in social science that comes close to Giere's ideas in many respects (Meehan 1968). Explicitly rejecting logical empiricism, he advocates the construction of formal 'systems' (Giere would call them 'models'), logically consistent systems of relationships. Explanation consists in applying this 'formal calculus' to some empirical phenomenon. The phenomenon is explained if (a) it follows logically from the assumptions of the system, and (b) if the formal system is 'isomorphic' with respect to the real-world system in which the phenomenon occurs, that is, if the system fits the real world. Fit clearly is a matter of degree, and whether a fit is a good one depends very much on the purpose for which the analysis has been undertaken. An explanation or prediction based on a 'system' may be good enough for some purposes, but not others. Meehan considers the logical empiricists' failure to include purpose in its criteria for judging scientific theories a fundamental flaw.

In a 1975 paper, Nathan Keyfitz introduced such thinking into demography, but there is little evidence that we took it to heart. Asking 'How do we know the facts of demography?' Keyfitz replies: 'Many readers will be surprised to learn that in a science thought of as empirical, often criticized for its lack of theory, the most important relations cannot be established by direct observation, which tends to provide enigmatic and inconsistent reports' (267). He illustrates his point with several examples, some from 'formal demography,' some from 'behavioral demography.' Methodologically, he does not draw a sharp line between the two.

In his conclusion, he writes:

> The model is much more than a mnemonic device, however; it is a machine with causal linkages. Insofar as it reflects the real world, it suggests how levers can be moved to alter direction in accord with policy requirements. The question is always how closely this constructed machine resembles the one operated by nature. As the investigator concentrates on its degree of realism, he more and more persuades himself that his model is a theory of the real world (285).

Note the equation of model and theory in the final sentence. The general sense of the quote is such that it would be right at home in the works of Giere or Cartwright.

11.4 Concluding Comments

The ideas sketched above suggest a view of demography somewhat different from that to which we are accustomed. Theory and theoretical models are center-stage, rather than subordinated to data, technique and descriptive findings. But the notion of theory is broadened such that a simple equation like the exponential or a complex algorithm like the cohort-component projection model can be viewed as theoretical models, realistic substantive representations of how populations work. By the same token, behavioral models such as the microeconomic theory of fertility or transition theory can be seen as useful models and therefore good scientific knowledge, even if they admit of exceptions or do not agree with all the facts.

Older models need not be discarded because they are old or simple, even over-simplified and 'unrealistic.' Most models contain some kernel of truth. Rather than discarded, they should be 'polished,' refined and stated in rigorous terms, and added to the demographer's toolkit of potentially useful models. If physicists rejected older, simpler, and 'unrealistic' models, a large portion of the standard introductory text would disappear.

Rather than putting so much emphasis on testing our theoretical models against specific data sets (statistical modelling), there could be more emphasis on using models to analyze and explain important demographic events, and to predict demographic futures. Often as not, our models will prove useful even if they are not true in any absolute sense.

Arraying demographic knowledge in the manner suggested would yield a large and rich body of substantive ideas about how populations work, suggesting more and deeper understanding than demographers typically are given credit for – or than is apparent in many of our routine multivariate analyses, technical manuals, or highly discursive undergraduate texts.

For students at all levels, especially for beginning students, such an approach to demography might be more demanding, both intellectually and psychologically.[8] But in the long run, it could attract more and better students, and better prepare them for future work involving demographic analysis. What is more satisfying to a student than to know that the concepts they are learning are useful? What is more satisfying than to know that these ideas enable the student to do something – namely to think in an organized way about important demographic developments, and to arrive at coherent explanations, grounded predictions, or well-reasoned policy advice? What is more reassuring than the feeling that one is learning a discipline, rather than a jumble of vague and often competing, if not contradictory ideas, or a set of measurement tools? What would be healthier than to learn in a demography course that science is a balanced process of continual exchange between empirical

---

[8]The emphasis here is on beginning or survey courses in demography. Clearly there will be specialized courses at more advanced levels of instruction, including seminars or courses specifically on techniques, data-collection, estimation, etc.

observation and theoretical reflection, and that theorizing and model building are creative acts?

References

Baylis, W. E. (1994). *Theoretical methods in the physical sciences: An introduction to problem solving using Maple V*. Boston: Birkhauser.

Cartwright, N. D. (1983). *How the laws of physics lie*. Oxford: Clarendon Press.

Cartwright, N. D. (1999). *The dappled world: A study of the boundaries of science*. New York: Cambridge University Press.

Caselli, G. (2000). Call for papers from IUSSP Working Group on the Teaching of Demography.

Giere, R. N. (1999). *Science without laws*. Chicago: The University of Chicago Press.

Gould, H., & Tobochnik, J. (1996). *An introduction to computer simulation methods* (2nd ed.). Reading: Addison-Wesley Publishing Co.

Halliday, D., Resnick, R., & Walker, J. (1997). *Fundamentals of physics* (5th ed.). New York: Wiley.

Hempel, C. G. (1965). *Aspects of scientific explanation*. New York: The Free Press.

Hinde, A. (1998). *Demographic methods*. London: Arnold.

Keyfitz, N. (1975). How do we know the facts of demography? *Population and Development Review, 1*, 267–288.

Livi-Bacci, M. (1984). Foreword to Nathan Keyfitz (ed.). In *Population and biology*. Liege: Ordina Editions.

Meehen, E. J. (1968). *Explanation in social science: A system paradigm*. Homewood: Illinois, The Dorsey Press.

Nagel, E. (1961). *The structure of science*. New York: Harcourt, Brace and World.

Preston, S. H., Heuveline, P., & Guillot, M. (2001). *Demography: Measuring and modeling population processes*. Oxford: Blackwell Publishers Ltd.

Reichenbach, H. (1968). *The rise of scientific philosophy*. Berkeley: University of California Press.

Stephan, G. E., & Massey, D. S. (1982). The undergraduate curriculum in sociology: An immodest proposal. *Teaching Sociology, 9*, 423–434.

Watkins, S. C. (1985). Graphics in demography. *Studies in Visual Communication, 11*, 2–21.

Chapter 12
Teaching the Fundamentals of Demography: A Model-Based Approach to Fertility

12.1 Introduction

This chapter sketches some guidelines for teaching the fundamentals of demography, and gives concrete illustrations of their application to the demography of and fertility. The principles are based on: (a) over 40 years of experience in teaching demography; (b) some characteristics of a leading introductory physics text (Halliday, Resnick, and Walker 1997); and (c) recent work in the philosophy of science, notably by two representatives of the so-called *semantic* or *model-based* school, Ronald Giere (1988, 1999) and Nancy Cartwright (1983, 1999).[1]

The focus is on demography viewed as a science, a body of valid scientific knowledge, and on providing students of all kinds with an understanding of and ability to use this knowledge for a variety of purposes. From this perspective, the collection of demographic data by means of censuses, registers, and sample surveys, although clearly important, is seen as an ancillary activity, not part of the unique core of demographic knowledge and more a matter of applied general statistics. It is what we know about how human populations work that makes demography distinctive.

Much of our best knowledge of how populations work is to be found in the sub-area of formal demography, often labeled with the partly misleading term *techniques*. The argument here is that much of formal demography, while technical in some respects, can also be viewed as substantive (theoretical) knowledge. By the same token, in a *model-based* view of science, behavioral demography can be seen to contain, among other things, formal models whose structure is not fundamentally different from that of formal demographic models. The distinctions between

---

This is a slightly edited version of a paper originally published in *Genus* 58(2002)73–90.

[1]See also the stimulating suggestions for teaching introductory sociology by Stephan and Massey (1982). See Chap. 11 above.

© The Author(s) 2018

T.K. Burch, *Model-Based Demography*, Demographic Research Monographs,
DOI 10.1007/978-3-319-65433-1_12

technical and substantive demography, and between formal and behavioral demography are blurred. In the model-based view of science, all models or theories are formal.[2]

The guidelines for demographic teaching are meant to apply to almost any context. Fundamental principles of a science do not change depending on who is learning them. There will be differences in depth and detail, but not in the core knowledge.

I do not know whether or to what extent contemporary practice in the teaching of demography exemplifies these guidelines or the view of science on which they are based. My impression is that demographic instruction in North America does not closely correspond, and could be greatly improved. Teaching in Italy or in the French school probably comes closer to what I view as ideal.[3]

Support for these guidelines can be found in the practice of other, more established scientific disciplines, especially introductory courses and texts, and in the semantic or model-based school of the philosophy of science. Earlier chapters [especially Chapter 11] have discussed these rationales in some detail, so there is no need to repeat those discussions here.

12.2   Some Concrete Examples of Abstract Fertility Models

How might these guidelines be implemented in introducing students to the study of fertility? As a first example, let's consider the *total fertility rate*. This concept typically is introduced as a summary measure of age-specific fertility rates, most commonly period rates, calculated as a weighted sum (weighted by widths of age intervals) of the rates. The student may or may not have been introduced to the concept of *exposure* at this point. A synthetic cohort interpretation will often be used to introduce the statistical calculation, or added afterwards to give more meaning to the result – 'How many children would a woman have on average if she experienced these fertility rates?' Depending on level and context of teaching, it may be noted that the same procedure can be applied to a set of age-specific rates for a real cohort, observed over time.

This approach does not begin at the beginning. The most fundamental concept is that of a cohort of women surviving over their lifetimes and producing children. Even the distinction between real and synthetic cohort is less fundamental. And treatment of fertility behavior of a real cohort immediately raises issues such as data

---

[2]This is an unconventional view in demography, but see Keyfitz (1975).

[3]Book titles over the years suggest an underlying difference in attitude and approach. Lotka, writing in French, included in the title of his masterwork the phrase *theorie analytique*. Pressat's well-known text is called *Analyse Demographique*. English-language works on 'formal' demography characteristically use the words *techniques* or *methods*. The latter set of words connotes an instrumental approach, the former, notions of substantive insight.

availability, incomplete experience and differential survival. The fundamental concept is that of *any* cohort.

An alternative approach would start with an abstract model of the lifetime fertility behavior of a cohort, and, in the manner of physics, spend a long section setting forth the basic concepts. The concepts would be represented visually to the extent possible, and used to solve several problems or carry out several 'experiments.' Initially, the only reference to data would be to a set of age-specific rates (plausible but not necessarily real) without reference to a temporal dimension other than age.

Thus:

1. Let's look at the births of a well-defined group of women (say, 1000 women at age 15) during their reproductive period, roughly ages 15 through 49. We assume for the sake of simplicity that none dies during this period, and that they do not lack sexual partners or other means of conceiving. These are unreal assumptions, but then so is the assumption of no air-resistance or friction in beginning classical mechanics. Later we will make them more realistic. It might be worthwhile to show a graph of the number of women alive at each age, admittedly only a horizontal line. But then so is the position/time graph in a physics text showing a stationary object (zero straight-line velocity).

2. At each age, the women bear children at a given rate – births per woman in each year of age. We start with individual years of age – 15, 16, etc. Later we'll deal with 5-year age intervals. Note that for this model, the student needs only to grasp the notion of a rate as a relative number; the distinction between probability and central rate is not yet relevant since all 1000 women survive throughout. But the student is presumed to know one of the fundamental principles of demography: *events=rate[s] × structure* (exposure, population at risk). For example: births in a given year = total population times the crude birth rate, since the crude birth rate is defined as births in a given year/total population. The analogy with *distance = rate × time* or *rate = distance/time* is often helpful at this point.

3. The calculation of births during a given year of age is now straightforward, as is the calculation of total births over the reproductive period, and the calculation of average births per woman over the reproductive period.

4. The rates can be graphed and total births over the reproductive period viewed as the area under the curve. The typical shape of the age-specific fertility curve can be noted. It would be useful at this point, even for students without much calculus, to associate total fertility with the definite integral of the fertility-age function over all ages (or over 15–49), and to contrast this with the finite sum typically used in practice. A diagram would make the distinction clear. It also can be noted that there is no 'law of fertility,' represented by one generally accepted mathematical function (contrast Newton's law of falling bodies), although total fertility can be calculated by integration of an approximating function fit to a particular set of data (see above, Chap.7).

5. After introducing [or assuming] the notions of weighted sum and weighted average, one can define the mean age of fertility and indicate it on the graph. The same could be done for the median age, although this measure is seldom used.
6. The basic concepts can then be modified to deal with data in 5-year intervals.
7. The notion of sex-ratio at birth can be introduced, and a calculation made of the number of daughters born as opposed to total births. This can be done overall, or, age-by-age, introducing the notion that the sex ratio at birth differs slightly (but only slightly) by age or birth order. The student is thus introduced to the idea of a one-sex population model.

At this point, the student will have learned (or reviewed) several primitive concepts in demography: relative rate; exposure; events as the product of rate [s] times population at risk; weighted sums as summary measures of rates; sums as area under an age-curve of demographic rates; areas as integrals or finite sums; 'laws' of demographic behavior and approximating functions; the sex ratio at birth; one-sex population model; 5-year versus single-year data. Note there has been no mention of period versus real cohort data, with all the complications involved.

Still, the student can do many things with the basic concepts.[4] They can reverse the order of some or all the rates to convince themselves that order does not matter for total fertility, but does matter for average age. They can calculate how much difference it would make to total fertility if there were no births before age 20 or after age 35 or both. This exercise could be introduced as relevant to the frequent policy aim of eliminating teen-age fertility.[5] They can calculate incomplete fertility, e.g., up to age 30, and compare it with total fertility. These numerical exercises can be done using finite sums and, in classroom demonstrations at least, by integration of an approximating function (see Chap. 7). They can experiment with radical changes in the sex ratio at birth, such as might accompany social fads relating to gender preferences, or the consequences of China's one-child policy. In short, they can use the simple tools provided to gain greater understanding of how human reproduction works or might work.

This is demography in slow-motion and by experiment. An extremely simple abstract concept has been developed at length and in detail, and is then used to answer several substantive questions about human fertility, and provide important insights into how population reproduction works. The virtue lies not in the slowness as such, but in the fact that the student has been given a rigorous introduction to

---

[4]This assumes knowledge of how to do such calculations efficiently. Spreadsheets are useful and universally available. Mathematics programs are more powerful in the long run. Most statistical packages are not well-suited to demographic calculation unless they support programming (R, for example).

[5]Recent news stories from the United States report an increase in the average age at childbearing, partly due to a substantial reduction in teen-age fertility.

basic concepts on which new and more complicated ideas can be built later in the course.

Some next steps are obvious, but note they are next steps, not first steps. The basic notions presented above can be applied to two radically different temporal contexts: the lifetime fertility experience of a real birth cohort; the cross-sectional experience in a calendar year of many different birth cohorts at different ages – the experience of a synthetic or fictitious cohort. Each would be treated in a separate section. The basic concept developed above would be seen as leading to the ordinary total fertility rate as a measure of current fertility. But it is now placed in a proper context.

This approach – developing a general concept and then applying it to two different temporal contexts (observation plans) – would by its explicitness help avoid the frequent confusion of cohort versus period data and measures. And it would be repeated, with appropriate changes, in dealing with mortality, marriage, divorce, migration, and other demographic behaviors.

The first example takes what is usually presented as a demographic measure or technique and treats it like a substantive model of demographic behavior, a summary of important knowledge of population dynamics. It is a simple model, involving unreal assumptions. But it is a good starting point.

The second example is Easterlin's *socio-economic model of marital fertility*, a behavioral model. It is here treated as a formally valid abstract model of fertility and fertility control. It is taken to be true 'by definition,' valuable for giving students insight into fertility decision processes, and for clarifying important behavioral issues relating to fertility. Whether or how it applies to the real world is another question. Why does fertility remain high in some developing nations? Why is it so low in Europe and North America? How might policy interventions raise or lower it? Can family planning programs help to lower fertility?

For these purposes the early, simple statement of the model (Easterlin 1975) will suffice, using equations only, or, depending on the economics background of the students, some of the indifference curves found in the original article. And again, to develop the model and present it to students, one need not have real data for all the variables. Plausible data will do. One can admit that some of the concepts and variables are difficult or even impossible to measure (for example, *psychic costs of fertility control*, or *lifetime utility*). But this does not prevent the student from gaining insight from learning and applying the model. One of the main barriers to theory development in demography has been the requirement of a one-to-one correspondence between theoretical ideas and successful, or even easy, measurement.

The Easterlin model can be summarized as follows:

Definitions:

F = marital fertility [the total marital fertility rate]
N = natural marital fertility, the number of births that a couple wouldhave if they
   did nothing to limit births

S = the probability of surviving from birth to adulthood (age 20)

C_n = the number of surviving children a couple would have if they did nothing to limit births

C_d = demand for children, the number of surviving children a couple wants; the number they would have if fertility control were costless

M = motivation to control fertility

RC = the costs of fertility control, both economic and 'psychic' costs

Propositions:

1. The level of marital fertility F relative to natural marital fertility N is a function of the extent of effective fertility control.
2. Motivation to control fertility M is a function of a comparison of potential surviving children C_n and demand for children C_d. The simplest functional specification is C_n-C_d but others are possible (for example, addition of a parameter, use of ratio rather than a difference).
3. The extent of effective fertility control is a function of motivation and of costs of control RC. Limitation will occur when motivation>costs. A simple functional specification would be:

   fertility control $= k \ [M - RC]$ if $M - RC > 0$, else no fertility control; that is, fertility control is proportional to the difference between motivation and costs.
4. C_n is a function of natural fertility N and S, the probability of surviving from birth to adulthood, age 20: $C_n = N \ x \ S$.
5. C_d is function of income, prices of children and other goods, and tastes or preferences for children – taken directly from elementary microeconomics.
6. Natural fertility N is a function of coital frequency, fecundity, and fetal mortality (excluding induced abortion, which is considered a form of fertility control).
7. Fecundity is a function of many variables, notably lactation.
8. Costs of fertility control RC include money costs, time and effort, and psychic costs (guilt, annoyance, fear of side effects).

As stated above, this is a relatively simple behavioral model which can be written, with suitable shorthand, on half a sheet of paper or on one panel of a classroom chalkboard. It is easily grasped by most students. A full quantitative specification is much more difficult, but again, that can come later. Even this simple model provides students with a powerful tool to help them begin thinking analytically about complex real-world problems. In my undergraduate classes, after presenting the model, I typically ask students (in discussion or exams) to use it to deal with the following questions[6]: (a) Why is Canadian fertility so low? (causal analysis); (b) Do you expect it to rise appreciably over the next 10–20 years? (prediction).

---

[6]By this point, the notion of overall fertility as a function of marital fertility and marriage patterns would have been presented, and the Easterlin model is presented in this context.

Later, I ask them to use the same model to deal with the policy question: If the Canadian government were to decide to try to raise fertility levels, what specific measures would you advise? (policy analysis). This leads to some interesting dead-ends, e.g., lower motivation for fertility control by reducing natural marital fertility, or substantially increasing the costs of fertility control (this leads to a brief discussion of the infamous Rumanian case). After considering all the possibilities, students tend to focus on the notion of raising the number of children wanted $- C_d -$ by reducing the costs of children (notably through subsidized daycare).

The important point about the exercise is not that they reach the correct answer, if there is one, but that they have had the experience of analytic thinking about important demographic problems, using as an analytic tool a logically (if not yet quantitatively) rigorous model. There is active discussion, but it is disciplined active discussion, with the discipline supplied by the model.

12.3   Towards More Complex Models

The models discussed above are abstract and simple – some would say oversimplified. But so is the introductory physics of straight-line motion, or of a body falling in a vacuum under the influence of gravity. But these simple models provide an introduction to analytic thinking, as opposed to passive learning, and are the foundations of more complex models to come. A recent review of a book on migration and microevolution (Lahr 2000) includes the following as one of the book's three major conclusions: 'The frequent violation of the assumptions underlying classic population genetic models call for the development of more complex models, for which computer simulations are the main tool' (p. 2057).

Of course, more complex models will have to be developed in demography as well (Burch 1996). The assumption of no mortality in the model underlying the total fertility rate clearly is unrealistic, more so for some populations than others. Easterlin's assumption of a onetime fertility decision to maximize lifetime utility, is unrealistic in many, perhaps most, contexts. But that does not mean that one should start with these more complex models in the teaching of demography. This would be justified only if the simpler, often older, models were judged to be worthless. But they are not if they are viewed from an appropriate methodological perspective.

The simple Easterlin model can serve as a starting point for greater complexity in different ways. It can be elaborated on as a microeconomic model of fertility decision making, and there is a vast economic literature doing just that. Or it can be placed in a broader context. With the assumption that mortality or desired number of children or costs of fertility control – or any combinations of these, or other variables in the Easterlin model – are inversely related to 'development,' it can provide a behavioral underpinning to a model of demographic transition (cf. the biologists' development of the logistic model).

If development leads to lower mortality, given constant fertility, the number of children surviving to adulthood $[C_n]$ will rise, perhaps exceeding the number wanted $[C_d]$. By definition, this creates motivation for fertility control. Assuming C_d also declines with development, motivation will increase even more. Unless fertility control is very costly in the broad sense defined by Easterlin, deliberate fertility control will begin and fertility will decline.

Note again that this scenario is 'true' by definition – it follows inevitably from the Easterlin model and the assumptions about relationships between development and key model variables, and it is logically coherent. Cartwright might say that it is 'true' in that it correctly captures the 'nature' of aggregate human behavior over time: we do not generally persist in accepting what we clearly do not want unless the costs of avoidance are too high. The Easterlin model, thus expanded, can be seen as a 'nomological machine,' generating the 'law' of the classic demographic transition.

Even in its simplified form – or perhaps especially in its simplified form – the Easterlin model provides students with a tool for analytic thinking about complex behavioral issues. As students work with the model to deal with various problems and exercises, it will not take long before they begin to raise questions about timing. Does the inevitable fertility decline occur immediately, in concert with mortality decline, or is there some delay or lag? Students will have no difficulty in introducing the notion of reaction time. And, depending on the level of instruction, this notion can be introduced explicitly into the model in the form of a delay.

The empirical question, as always, is whether the model can be usefully applied to one or more observed fertility transitions, whether, in Giere's words, it fits sufficiently closely in certain respects to provide an explanation, or perhaps a prediction. There is ample evidence that it does: strong empirical associations between development, mortality, and fertility; observation of the mortality/fertility lead/lag pattern in most historical transitions.

But is it the best model, in general or to explain a particular case (for example, early fertility decline in France)? Of course not, nor is it the only good model. In due time the student can be introduced to other, more complex models that emphasize culture, social interaction, wealth transfers, and other classes of variables not included or highlighted in the Easterlin model or in classic transition theory.

In short, the Easterlin model and classic transition theory are not taught as the truth about fertility decision-making and long-term transitions, but as sensible models that can serve as useful tools for the analysis of some but not all cases. Given their simplicity, they are particularly appropriate for students in the early stages of learning demography. Our physics text spends the best part of one chapter dealing with the case of motion in a straight line in the case of constant acceleration. This material is simplified, and unrealistic for almost all but laboratory settings –

but appropriate for students to learn to understand simple systems before moving on more complex systems.

It is not that much teaching in current demography doesn't present the full panoply of models found in the literature. But it is my impression that they are often presented in fairly broad conceptual terms and passed over quickly. Older models are often presented as outmoded and of historical interest only. My suggestion is that all sensible models be taken more seriously, presented in greater detail and rigor, and then used to deal with important real-world problems.

12.4   Concluding Comments

There is little under the sun that is brand new. Most of the ideas outlined above can be found somewhere in the literature and practice of social science and demography. Mathematical demographers will be comfortable with the application of these ideas to formal demography. Economists will respond with a 'ho-hum' to the emphasis on teaching students to think analytically using oversimplified models, as will some sociologists who remember discussions of 'abstract analytic theory' or Lave and March's (1975) *An Introduction to Models in the Social Sciences*. Many social demographers will feel comfortable with the emphasis on a multiplicity of theories, with no one singled out as best.

But other ideas are apt to evoke puzzlement or resistance. One is the notion that the models of formal and behavioral demography have the same fundamental epistemological status, as abstract models of some part of the real world, 'true' by definition (assuming they are clearly and logically structured). Another, closely related, is the abandonment of logical empiricist notions of proving or disproving scientific laws. In this view, the 'underdetermination of theory by empirical data' (Turner 1987) is not some passing flaw in our science, but a central feature of all scientific knowledge, one we simply have to learn to live with and to help our students live with.

Some will wonder where this approach leaves our disciplinary penchant for multivariate analyses of census or survey data. This issue needs further study, and cannot be dealt with here. It is likely, however, that in the approach sketched above, descriptive studies using the general linear model may indeed play a smaller role, notably in teaching, giving way to more emphasis on theoretical thinking, often involving non-linear models. But statistics clearly is needed to test how closely a theoretical model fits some particular empirical case, which in any event will be described using statistics.

Historical demographers may rally against such total reliance on abstract models, preferring a more personal notion of knowledge, an 'understanding' of or 'feeling for' concrete historical cases, acquired by immersion in historical detail. Each of these and other possible objections has its merits. And not all are diametrically opposed to the ideas sketched above; some are complementary. But there are strong arguments for the suggested reorientation of demographic teaching. The thinking of a growing number of philosophers of science points in that direction, providing an alternative to the frustrating dead-ends of logical empiricism and its search for universal laws. Pointing in the same direction is the pedagogy of some of the strongest sciences, tried and proven in the teaching of multitudes of students that we demographers could only dream of. I have focused on physics, but other disciplines provide similar examples, notably in biology (see, for example, Gotelli 1998; for a similar approach to teaching introductory sociology, see Stephan and Massey 1982).

My suggestions are made in the context of a growing concern that demography risks losing its status as a distinct scientific field unless it pulls up its scientific – specifically theoretical – socks. In many quarters, demography is seen as a purely descriptive field, the sort of descriptive work done by government statistical agencies; one often hears the terms *human bookkeeping or demographic accounting*. Demography is often seen as narrowly technical, concerned only with 'data grubbing.' Economists often find little in demography that they think cannot be subsumed under their discipline. In some sociological circles, demography is being surreptitiously replaced by the *sociology of population,* the notion being that a social gerontologist, for example, can teach demography while being innocent of the details of cohort analysis, life-table construction, or the stable population model.

My suggestions point toward a stronger demography, a discipline or sub-discipline that is unique, based on a distinctive blending of formal and behavioral models, and an unusual wealth of descriptive data. It is this discipline that we should present to our students.

References

Burch, T. K. (1996). Icons, strawmen, and precision: Reflections on demographic theories of fertility decline. *The Sociological Quarterly, 37*, 59–81.

Cartwright, N. D. (1983). *How the laws of physics lie*. Oxford: Clarendon Press.

Cartwright, N. D. (1999). *The dappled world: A study of the boundaries of science*. New York: Cambridge University Press.

Easterlin, R. A. (1975). An economic framework for fertility analysis. *Studies in Family Planning, 6*, 54–63.

Giere, R. N. (1988). *Explaining science: A cognitive approach*. Chicago: The University of Chicago Press.

Giere, R. N. (1999). *Science without laws*. Chicago: The University of Chicago Press.

Gotelli, N. J. (1998). *A primer of ecology* (2nd ed.). Sunderland: Sinauer Associates.

Halliday, D., Resnick, R., & Walker, J. (1997). *Fundamentals of physics* (5th ed.). New York: Wiley.

Keyfitz, N. (1975). How do we know the facts of demography? *Population and Development Review, 1*, 267–288.

Lahr, M.M. (2000). Wandering genes. In: *Review of M. Fix, migration and colonization in human microevolution*. New York: Cambridge University Press, 1999. In *Science, 289*, 2057.

Lave, C. A., & March, J. G. (1975). *An introduction to models in the social sciences*. New York: Harper and Row.

Stephan, G. E., & Massey, D. (1982). The undergraduate curriculum in sociology: An immodest proposal. *Teaching Sociology, 9*, 423–434.

Turner, S. P. (1987). Underdetermination and the promise of statistical sociology. *Sociological Theory, 5*, 172–184.

Chapter 13
On Teaching Demography: Some Non-traditional Guidelines

13.1   Introduction

I am grateful to Frank Trovato for the opportunity to discuss some of my recent writings on scientific methodology – on the relations among theory, models, and data – and on their implications for the teaching of demography. I am particularly pleased to get the reactions of such distinguished panelists. I am confident that by the end of the session, my thinking will have been clarified and, where necessary, corrected, and that I shall go away with new insights. These are difficult issues on which there seldom is consensus. Only occasionally do I have a sense that I have got it just right.

I have always felt that demography needed more and better theory. Until just a few years ago, I attributed the status of theory to simple neglect and to lack of sufficient interest – an opportunity cost, one might say, of demography's heavy emphasis on data, techniques, and empirical description (Burch 1996). I now believe that the problem goes deeper, and is due to the influence of a misleading philosophy of science that has dominated twentieth century empirical social science in general and demography in particular. This view is the logical empiricism of Ernest Nagel and Carl Hempel, combined with the ideas of Karl Popper on falsification, and with deeper roots among scientists of the nineteenth (for example, Ernst Mach) and early twentieth centuries (for example, Karl Pearson).

13.2   Logical Empiricism

The central difficulty lies in logical empiricism's view of the nature of theory and its relations to empirical data. In the logical empiricist program, it is empirical generalizations or 'laws' that provide the foundation for theoretical propositions, arrived at by a process of induction – from particular cases to more general theory.

© The Author(s) 2018

T.K. Burch, *Model-Based Demography*, Demographic Research Monographs,
DOI 10.1007/978-3-319-65433-1_13

The process can go through several levels, from empirical generalizations to so-called 'middle-range' theory, up to the most general and abstract theory. The relations between empirical data on the one hand and theoretical propositions on the other are purely logical. A valid proposition is one that is consistent with the data.

In this system, explanation of a phenomenon is achieved by subsuming it under some general law – thus the term the 'covering law' approach to explanation.

In many versions of logical empiricism and frequently in research practice, an empirical generalization or a theoretical proposition will be rejected ('falsified') by the discovery of empirical data that do not support the generalization – exceptions, 'counter-examples,' negative findings, etc. A classic case in demography is the frequent rejection of demographic transition theory due to exceptions discovered in detailed historical research.

A central feature of the logical empiricist approach is that theory is a super-structure derived from and therefore limited by empirical findings. In demography, this feature finds expression in the heavy reliance on statistical models, which have no place for unmeasured (directly or indirectly) variables.

Among the many difficulties with this approach identified by scientists and by philosophers of science, two stand out:

1. There are few broad empirical generalizations (without exceptions) and hardly any universal generalization in social science, so that the foundations on which to build theory in this way are sparse and weak.
2. The acceptance or rejection of a theoretical idea is unrelated to the specific purpose or purposes for which it is to be used. A theory is or is not logically consistent with the data; such logical consistency is the sole criterion for acceptance.

Some social scientists have come to see logical empiricism as a frustrating and self-defeating approach. Not a few philosophers of science have argued, and some physical scientists have testified on their own behalf, that logical empiricism does not describe how they actually work. Roger Newton, writing about Isaac Newton's laws, comments '...Newton's laws of motion are not simply inductive consequences of observations but are products of a very fertile imagination' (Newton 1997, p.15).

13.3   An Alternative to Logical Empiricism

An alternative view is found in many quarters but is not the mainstream view in contemporary demography. Theoretical economics provides a partial departure from the above characterization of logical empiricism. Its central theory is derived from axioms, but its development and range have been cramped by rigid adherence to a limited axiom set. The political scientist Eugene Meehan outlined an alternative approach as early as 1968 (*Explanation in Social Science: A System Paradigm*). Nathan Keyfitz did much the same in his 1975 paper 'How do we know the facts of demography?' Hedstrom and Swedberg (1998) have advocated a return to 'middle-range' analytic theory, again in an approach that departs sharply from logical empiricism.

An influential school of contemporary philosophy of science (the 'semantic' school) has elaborated ideas similar to those of the authors just mentioned. An accessible and authoritative work is by Ronald Giere (1999). Giere call this alternative view a 'model-based' view of science. For Giere, the prototype of scientific knowledge is not the scientific law, but the theoretical model plus a list of cases to which it applies. In this approach, a theory or theoretical model – the distinction is seen largely as one of scope – is constructed in such a way that it is formally true, in Giere's words 'true in the same way that a definition is true.' The model consists of clear concepts with well-specified relations among them, forming a logically consistent and coherent system. It is this clarity and coherence that yields a model's analytic power. The empirical question, then, is not whether a model is true or false, valid or invalid – it is true by definition. The relevant empirical question is whether it fits some empirical phenomenon, some well-described part of the real world (a) closely enough (b) in certain respects (c) to be useful for some well-defined purpose – prediction, explanation, intervention and control, and – especially relevant to today's topic – teaching. If a model does not meet all three of these criteria, then it is not used, but it also is not rejected as a theoretical model that may well prove useful for other purposes in other contexts. If it fits well enough, then it is considered acceptable for the purpose at hand.

Theory is viewed not as Truth, but as an analytical tool. Taken as a whole it constitutes a toolbox of many theoretical models, some simple, some complex, some useful for one purpose, another for other purposes. It is these tools, so long as they are fashioned with clarity, rigor and logical consistency, that give theory its analytical, predictive, and explanatory power.

Where do data and empirical research fit in? Empirical work is needed first of all the to give an accurate description of some phenomenon or some portion of the real world. Secondly, it is needed to test how well one or more of the seemingly relevant theoretical models fits that portion of reality – goodness of fit, but in a much broader sense than in statistical modelling. Finally, if empirical generalizations on the topic at hand exist, there is nothing to prevent their incorporation into the model itself.

In this model-based approach, theory is a response to empirical data, but is not derived from and therefore limited by data. The construction of theoretical models is an act of creative imagination.

In this view, demographic transition theory, especially if it were stated more rigorously, would be seen as a perfectly good and useful theoretical model, even though it does not fit some cases (e.g., France) very well, in respect to the relative timing of fertility and mortality decline. But it fits a large number of historical cases well enough for us to assert with confidence, for example, that any highly developed human society (by the conventional definitions of development) will have low fertility.

13.4   Questioning the Formal/Behavioral Distinction

This view of scientific theory has many implications for how we view and teach demography. One of the most important is that it erases the traditional sharp distinction between formal demography and population studies, based on the distinction between necessary and contingent relationships. With respect to theory, in the model-based view, all theoretical models and theories are formal, that is, true by definition.

It is customary in demography to consider formal demographic models as expressions of necessary relationships, for example, the fundamental demographic equation, or the stable model. Behavioral models such as transition theory or microeconomic models of demographic behavior are seen as involving contingent relationships, which must therefore be tested against data.

In the model-based view, however, a behavioral model can and must be stated in such a way that it is formally and necessarily true. The logistic model of population growth, for example, assumes linear relationships between population density and both mortality and fertility. The classic transition model assumes strong relationships between development and both mortality and fertility. These relationships can be precisely specified, even if they seldom are. Are the relations between density and birth and death rates, or between development and birth and death rates necessary or contingent? The answer is that they are contingent in the real world, but necessary in the model – assumed, given, defined – true in the way that definitions are true.

Thus, the exponential equation $P[t] = P[0]e^{rt}$ is a theoretical model, a formal representation of the inherent nature of the growth of a biological population. No one would question the validity of this functional definition. Empirically it may or may not provide an accurate account of real world populations; over some specified period, some populations may grow approximately exponentially. But for many populations the model will not be even close. By this same reasoning, the life-table or the cohort-component projection models can be seen as theoretical models of population dynamics, as well as a measure of mortality and a forecasting tool respectively.

On the other hand, a simplified version of the Easterlin economic model of fertility and fertility control can be stated in such a way that it is true by definition:

Definitions:

    -> Motivation = expected minus desired surviving children
    -> Costs = money, time, effort, and 'psychic' costs

Propositions:

    {-> IF motivation > costs of control, THEN fertility control will occur}
    {-> IF motivation < costs of control, THEN fertility control will not occur}

The brackets suggest that this is a definition of a function, although not yet a mathematical function (although it could be developed into one). The model is true by definition and therefore completely general. Whether it applies to any particular real-world system is an empirical question.

By this same reasoning, many other behavioral models in demography can be stated in such a way that they are formally true – transition theory, Lee's model of migration, Hernes' model of first marriage, and Coale- and Hoover's model of population and development, to give only a few familiar examples.

One of the advantages of this perspective is that many older, simpler models – often discarded or neglected – are retained as useful tools.

13.5   Concluding Comment

There is a paradox in all of this. Many of our demographic techniques are elevated to the status of theory, while theory is downgraded to an analytic tool, a thinking technique. But the model-based approach may offer a better way to advance demography as a science. To be faithful to the spirit of the model-based view, of course, we must not advance it as the only useful model of how science works or should work. There may be scientific laws (universal or nearly universal empirical generalizations) even in the social and behavioral sciences, so that there may be topics for which the logical-positivist approach to theory and explanation will work. But for demography now, I suggest that a model-based view will provide a liberating and more fruitful approach to theory, modelling, and demographic explanation. It also has many implications for the teaching of demography, some of them at odds with current practice. I have discussed these at length elsewhere (Burch 2001a, b and Chaps. 11 and 12 above), and shall only summarize them here by appending a statement of ten principles for teaching basic demography. These principles or guidelines are suggested by the approach to scientific methodology sketched above. They also are consistent with pedagogical practice in well- developed physical sciences, notably physics. Several of them correspond closely to the characteristics of teaching in the physical sciences outlined by Stephan and Massey (1982) in their thought-provoking paper on teaching undergraduate sociology.

13.6   Ten Principles for Teaching Basic Demography

1. Put more emphasis on theory, that is, abstract models of population dynamics and demographic behavior. Teach demography as a body of theoretical knowledge, as well as a body of data, techniques, and descriptive findings.
2. Retain and develop older and simpler – even 'oversimplified' – models insofar as they contain valuable insights that can help students begin to understand how populations work.

3. Put more emphasis on student activity – getting them to use the theoretical models that have been learned to solve real-world (or at least realistic) problems and exercises. The goal is the development of the student's ability to reason demographically, to explain, predict, or suggest policy interventions.

4. Set problems and exercises that lead students to face the limitations of available models, and to try to construct better ones. Allow students – even encourage them – to be theorists.

5. Require students to have or to learn the tools needed for rigorous reasoning in the use of analytic models. The classic tool is mathematics. A more flexible and accessible tool for many demography students (notably in sociology departments) is some form of computer modelling, notably systems dynamics.

6. Integrate 'formal demography' or 'techniques' with 'substantive' or 'behavioral demography' in the same course, rather than in distinct courses.

7. The basic principles of demography (technical and behavioral) must be taught or assumed in every demography course. Otherwise, it is not a demography course.

8. For efficiency and understanding, teach the most basic and general principles first. For example, subsume many of the standard demographic measures under the concepts of weighted sums or averages. For another example, present e_0, TFR and the singulate mean age at marriage as measures of the area under some curve, not as three totally disparate measures.

9. For beginning students, put less emphasis on data collection, errors in data, and the most precise techniques. This is not a counsel of sloppiness. It is not sound pedagogy to immerse students in data-collection techniques and discouraging claims about errors, at the expense of substantive ideas.

10. Since many demographic models lend themselves to visual representation, use more diagrams in texts and lectures. Use visual representation for ideas, not just for graphing data.

References

Burch, T. K. (1996). Icons, strawmen and precision: Reflections on demographic theories of fertility decline. *The Sociological Quarterly, 37*, 59–81.

Burch, T. K. (2001a). Teaching the fundamentals of demography: A model- based approach to family and fertility. *Genus, 58*, 73–90. See Ch.12 above.

Burch, T. K. (2001b). Teaching demography: ten principles and two rationales. *Genus, 58*, 21–34. See Ch.11 above.

Giere, R. N. (1999). *Science without laws*. Chicago: University of Chicago Press.

Hedstrom, P., & Swedberg, R. (1998). *Social mechanisms: An analytic approach to social theory*. Cambridge: Cambridge University Press.

Keyfitz, N. (1975). How do we know the facts of demography? *Population and Development Review, 1*, 267–288.

Meehan, E. J. (1968). *Explanation in social science: A system paradigm.* Homewood: The Dorsey Press.

Newton, R. (1997). *The truth of science: Physical theories and reality.* Cambridge, MA: Harvard University Press.

Stephan, G. E., & Massey, D. (1982). The undergraduate curriculum in sociology: An immodest proposal. *Teaching Sociology, 9,* 423–434.

Part IV
Conclusion

Chapter 14
Concluding Thoughts

Models can be of many types – verbal, mathematical, visual – and there can be many models dealing with the same topic or subject area, some large and complex, some relatively simple. A collection of related models may be termed a *theory* (Giere 1999). Commenting on the many migration models in the literature, Le Bras (2008) evokes an architectural metaphor: '. . .models are viewpoints on migration. They are not mutually exclusive but combine to form a whole, in the way that architectural drawings made to show plan, section, and elevation complement each other' (p. 316). This accords with Giere's notion of *perspectival realism* (1999, 2006): all models are incomplete, but good models are realistic representations of a limited portion of the real world. There is 'realism without truth.'

From the model-based perspective, demography has always had an abundance of theoretical models, ranging from simple mathematical models – the basic demographic equation, the exponential growth function – to broad verbal models dealing with large-scale population dynamics over long periods and in many areas – demographic transition theory. But these often were not recognized as theoretical models, or were questioned because they did not agree with empirical observations of one or more concrete cases.

As early as 1958, Coale and Hoover studied the interrelations of population growth and economic development by linking the cohort-component projection model to a standard economic growth model, in an exercise we would now call macrosimulation. But it was not viewed as theory; Notestein in his forward would refer to it as 'a careful factual analysis' (1958, pp. v–vi).[1] Nor did it inspire replications or similar modeling exercises by other demographers. Other economists, however, used time-series and international regression analyses of data on population growth and economic development to question the view that slowing

---

[1] Of course, he wrote without benefit of hindsight based on over 50 years of experience with computers.

T.K. Burch, *Model-Based Demography*, Demographic Research Monographs,
DOI 10.1007/978-3-319-65433-1_14

population growth could enhance economic growth. The model was dismissed because some data were found which did not support its conclusions.

In the 1980s, Wachter and Hammel developed Socsim, a powerful microsimulation model of population, household, and kinship dynamics (Hammel et al. 1990), which they used to great effect to study a variety of issues, from future kin relations of the elderly to the demography of incest. Socsim was not widely adopted by other demographers to become part of their workaday toolkit (but see Murphy 2003).

In the 1990s, the economist/demographer Warren Sanderson and his colleagues constructed a substantial systems dynamics model of population, economic and environmental interrelations, using a kind of software[2] that for many demographers had been discredited by its use in *The Limits to Growth* studies beginning in the 1970s (see Sanderson 1994; Milik *et al.* 1996). The model was described as '…allowing economists, policy analysts and environmentalist to study the interactions between the economic, demographic and anthropogenic sectors of an idealized world, thereby enabling them to obtain insights transferable to the real world,' a perfect statement of the spirit and purpose of abstract modeling. But again, not many other demographers adopted their approach or worked to replicate or refine it. And systems dynamics software remains outside the ken of the mainstream demographer.

One could find many more examples of early efforts at modeling human populations -mathematical models, microsimulation, macrosimulation – that never became mainstream. Traditional demographic analysis and multivariate statistics have continued to dominate research and training.

Demography has been ambivalent about computer modeling and about its theoretical heritage, preferring the imagined safety of detailed empirical analyses of data. I can think of no major effort to collect and systematize the vast array of demographic models and theories, and few if any books or monographs with titles such as *Theories of Human Population Dynamics* or *Demographic Theory: An Overview.* Coleman and Schofield's edited volume *The State of Population Theory: Forward from Malthus* (1986), is now over 30 years old.

But it is theory that summarizes knowledge in a field, and provides a reasoned approach to further research, explanation, prediction and policy guidance. Without well-organized theory, demography is not a full-fledged scientific discipline. And computer modeling is an essential tool of theoretical work in the twenty-first century.

Recent developments give reasons for hope. LeBras' *The Nature of Demography* (2008), for example, argues for a new approach to demography very much in keeping with the model-based view. A focus on *process* is central, the processes of individual behavior that give rise to observed macro-demographic period observations. Demographic measurement is important ('a sort of land surveying applied to populations'), but secondary to the development of demography as an

---

[2]The model was implemented using Vensim systems dynamics software.

independent scientific discipline. Macro-demographic observations are often unreliable guides to the actual process, because of censoring. LeBras works primarily with mathematical models, which are solved analytically if possible, otherwise by micro-simulation. A model is considered interesting or useful if provides insight into the workings of the demographic system.

Another example is the increasing use of agent-based modeling to study demographic processes. A pioneering work, which documented early work and encouraged more to follow, is *Agent-Based Computational Demography: Using Simulation to Improve our Understanding of Demographic Behaviour* (Billari and Prskawetz 2003). But agent-based modeling and other forms of micro-simulation are still used by a small minority of demographers.[3]

A major impetus to new approaches in demography has come from the Methodos Project, led by Daniel Courgeau and Robert Franck, and an associated series of monographs. The first of these, *The Explanatory Power of Models* (edited by Franck 2002), explored the role of modeling in a variety of disciplines, including demography. As context, Franck develops at length the idea of *classical induction*, which was replaced in twentieth century social science by Hume's idea of induction and by *logical empiricism,* to the detriment of social science.

> The covering law approach hinders social science research and leads to a pessimistic view of the explanatory capacities of the social sciences… To hold law-like generalizations necessary for true scientific explanation is to sacrifice any possibility of the social sciences deserving such scientific status. … [It] deprives the social sciences of the advantages which the natural sciences enjoy, since they never stopped using the method of classical induction (Franck 2002, p. 4).[4]

Courgeau edited the second Methodos volume (2003a), entitled *Methodology and Epistemology of Multilevel Analysis*. This was followed in 2004 by his own monograph, *Du Group À L'Individu: Synthèse Multiniveau*. In both publications, multilevel analysis is considered as it applies to traditional statistical analysis and to more recent techniques of computer modeling.

Courgeau and colleagues outline an historical progression of 'paradigms' in demography, from period analysis, to multilevel analysis, to agent-based models. As a next step, they see the use of ABMs as leading to '…a broader model-based research program, which would rely more on computer simulation as a tool of analysis' (Courgeau *et al.* 2017). Computer simulation provides powerful tools for the integration of micro- and macro-demographic phenomena.[5]

So, there are many signs of methodological progress in contemporary demography. But looking to the future, what else is needed? A few concrete suggestions:

---

[3]Wider use of ABM may be encouraged by the development of user-friendly software, some of it free (for example, NetLogo, Insight Maker).

[4]Meehan (1968, pp. 5–6) makes a similar comparison of methodology in the social and the physical sciences.

[5]For example, agent-based modeling supports the bottom-up or micro approach; systems dynamics supports a top-down or macro approach. This leads to opportunities for triangulation, and ultimately to integrated models.

1. Every working demographer might commit to adding a computer modeling tool to her or his everyday toolkit, to supplement traditional demographic methods and multivariate statistics. For the mathematically proficient, the focus might remain on mathematical modeling and analytic solutions. Those with more programming skills will build models from scratch using powerful and versatile software such as Mathematica or R (see, for example, Willekens 2011). Many will adopt less demanding tools, software for systems dynamics, or microsimulation and agent-based modeling.
2. Similarly, students of demography should be introduced to these tools, even if at an elementary level. In addition to teaching the more traditional skills in statistics and demographic techniques – the modeling of data – demographic training will require students to acquire some facility at modeling ideas and theories.
3. Existing demographic theories and models need to be systematically collected and codified. This is especially the case for behavioral and substantive models not generally covered in monographs on techniques or methods. Given the scope of the task, this would better be done as a collaborative project. It would lead to a compendium or handbook of demographic models, a reference work for everyday use.
4. Rather than dismissing otherwise promising models that don't agree with some data, there should be more emphasis on refinement and replication. This will result in collections of several good models of a phenomenon, each giving a different perspective.
5. Demographic models need to used routinely in scientific research, analysis of population problems, and policy formation – really used, not just mentioned in opening and closing sections of publications. Purely descriptive research will not be abandoned, especially in government statistical agencies. Academic/scientific research will be more theory-driven – testing the adequacy of theoretical models and using them for rigorous explanation.

These and other concrete steps to implement the model-based view of science could lead to a more complete and mature discipline of demography, an autonomous discipline with strong theory as well as strong data and technique.

References

Billari, F. C., & Prskawetz, A. (Eds.). (2003). *Agent-based computational demography: Using simulation to improve our understanding of demographic behaviour*. Heidelberg: Physica-Verlag.

Coale, A. J., & Hoover, E. M. (1958). *Population growth and economic development in low-income countries*. Princeton: Princeton University Press.

Coleman, D., & Schofield, R. (1986). *The state of population theory: Forward from Malthus*. Oxford: Basil Blackwell.

Courgeau, D. (Ed.). (2003a). *Methodology and epistemology of multilevel analysis*. Dordrecht: Springer Netherlands.

Courgeau, D. (2003b). From the macro-micro opposition to multilevel analysis in demography. In D. Courgeau (Ed.)., 2003 *Methodology and epistemology of multilevel analysis* (pp. 43–91). Dordrecht: Springer Netherlands.

Courgeau, D. (2004). *Du groupe à L'individu: Synthèse multiniveau*. Paris: L'Institut National D'Ètude Démographiques.

Courgeau, D., Bijak, J., Franck, R., & Silverman, E. 2017. Model-based demography: Towards a research agenda. In A. Grow, & J. van Bavel (Eds.), *Agent-based modeling in population studies: Concepts, methods and applications* (pp. 29–51). Springer International.

Franck, R. (Ed.). (2002). *The explanatory power of models*. Dordrecht: Kluwer Academic.

Giere, R. N. (1999). *Science without laws*. Chicago: University of Chicago Press.

Giere, R. N. (2006). *Scientific perspectivism*. Chicago: University of Chicago Press.

Hammel, E., Mason, C., & Wachter, K.W. (1990). *Socsim II: A sociodemographic microsimulation program. Rev.1.0 Operating Manual*. Regents of the University of California.

Le Bras, H. (2008). *The nature of demography. Translated from the French*. Princeton: Princeton University Press.

Meehan, E. (1968). *Explanation in social science: A system paradigm*. Homewood 1968.

Milik, A., Prskawetz, A., Feichtinger, G., & Sanderson, W. (1996). Slow-fast dynamics in wonderland. *Environmental Modeling and Assessment, 1*, 3–17.

Murphy, M. (2003). Bringing behavior back into mico-simulation: Feedback mechanisms in demographic models. In F. Billari & A. Prskawetz (Eds.), *Agent-based computational demography: Using simulation to improve our understanding of demographic behaviour* (pp. 159–174). Heidelberg: Physica-Verlag.

Sanderson, W. (1994). Simulation models of demographic, economic and environmental interrelations. In W. Lutz (Ed.), *Population, development and environment: Understanding their interactions in Mauritius* (pp. 33–71). Berlin: Springer.

Willekens, F. J. C. (2011). A comment to Thomas K. Burch's paper 'Does demography need differential equations?'. *Canadian Studies in Population, 38*, 169–178.

Index

© The Author(s) 2018

T.K. Burch, *Model-Based Demography*, Demographic Research Monographs,
DOI 10.1007/978-3-319-65433-1